THE AMG

CONCISE

BIBLE SURVEY

DR. HARRY ADAMS

THE AMG CONCISE BIBLE SURVEY

published by

✳AMG *Publishers*

The AMG Concise Bible Survey

Copyright © 2003 by Harry Adams
Published by AMG Publishers
6815 Shallowford Rd.
Chattanooga, Tennessee 37421

ISBN 0-89957-414-9

First printing—January 2003

Cover designed by ImageWright, Inc., Chattanooga, Tennessee
Interior design and typesetting by Reider Publishing Services, West Hollywood, California
Edited and Proofread by Agnes Lawless, Dan Penwell, Warren Baker, and Jody El-Assadi

Printed in Canada
09 08 07 06 05 04 03 –T– 8 7 6 5 4 3 2

To Susan,
my helpmeet of thirty years, I lovingly dedicate this work.
"For her worth is far above rubies."

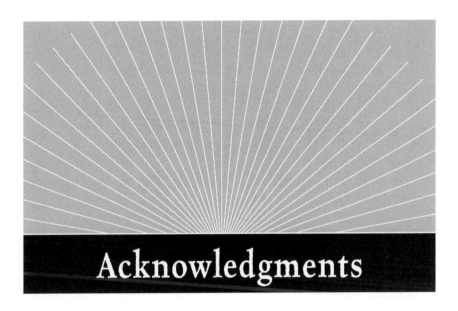

Acknowledgments

To the faculty of Dallas Theological Seminary, under whom it was my great privilege to study;

And to Dr. Ralph Richardson, Dr. Donald Wire, and Dr. Boyd Ayers who entrusted me to teach Bible at their colleges;

And to the students both in schools and churches that gave me the high honor of opening the Word of God to them;

And to Annette Dammer for starting me on the path to publication;

And to Bruce Barbour for believing the *Concise Bible Survey* was worthwhile;

And to the good people at AMG Publishers, especially Dan Penwell, for giving birth to this work;

And to Andrea Reider for taking my work, designing and typesetting it, and making it look beautiful on paper;

And to Agnes Lawless, Jody El-Assadi, and Warren Baker for doing a wonderful job of editing and proofreading my manuscript;

I say from the depths of my heart, thank you! "*They are the excellent ones, in whom is all my delight.*" (Psalm 16:2)

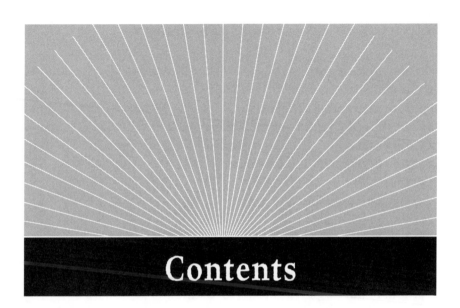

Contents

Maps

Charts and Diagrams

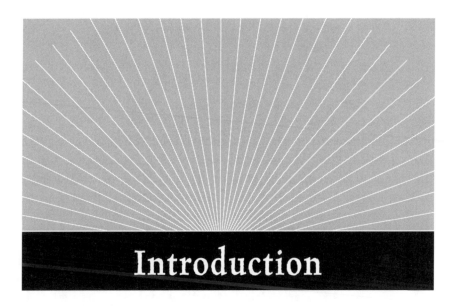

Introduction

"No man is uneducated who knows the Bible, and no man is wise who is ignorant of its teaching." [1]

Embark on a tour, not of a country but of a book, the most fascinating and powerful book ever written. Since the Bible is the Book of books, stops are made in each of the sixty-six books of the Bible.

Features of each tour include:

- Authorship of the book
- Time of writing
- The theme and purpose (To help retention, the themes are given in three or four words, the first of which begins with the same letter as the book's title.)
- History and archaeology
- Geography (including easy-to-read maps that may be reproduced for instructional purposes)
- An outline of the book
- An overview of the contents
- Theological highlights

- Where to find Christ in that book (Old Testament only)
- Key verses and chapters
- The enduring message of each book

Before embarking on our tour, three orientation lessons are given that set the tone for the journey. These stress that to benefit most from the Bible, we must approach it as uniquely God's Book, trustworthy because it is true (absolutely), and revealing Jesus Christ in all its parts.

Like any tour, this one can only give you the highlights of the places we visit. But once completed, you will be in a better position to visit the books of the Bible in more depth. Bon voyage.

The Bible Is God's Word

The Bible's claim to be the Word of God

In many places, the Bible claims to be given by God to people. As such, it is a message or "word" from God. Paul wrote, "All Scripture is given by inspiration of God, and is profitable for doctrine, for reproof, for correction, for instruction in righteousness" (2 Tim. 3:16). Peter expressed a similar thought, saying, "For prophecy never came by the will of man, but holy men of God spoke as they were moved by the Holy Spirit" (2 Pet. 1:21). In addition to such direct claims, the Bible makes many indirect claims that it is the Word of God, with expressions such as "thus says the Lord" and "the word of the Lord that came to so-and-so." We must decide whether or not to believe such claims. So let's take a look at the evidence that the Bible is what it claims to be, the Word of God to man.

Three reasons to believe the Bible is God's Word

1. *Logic.* Experience teaches us that nothing can come into existence by itself. So there must be a Creator. Furthermore, if God created us with the desire and ability to communicate, he must also possess to a greater degree the same desire and ability. This being so, we should expect God would communicate with us. Therefore, it is reasonable that God would give mankind the Bible.

2. *Prophecy.* Fulfilled prophecy provides supernatural evidence that the Bible has its origin in God. Consider the following prophecies and their fulfillment:

When Jeroboam led the revolt of the ten northern tribes against Rehoboam, the son of Solomon, he instituted idolatry. Immediately, a prophet predicted the destruction of the idolatrous shrine by a descendant of David named Josiah:

> And behold, a man of God went from Judah to Bethel by the word of the LORD, and Jeroboam stood by the altar to burn incense. Then he cried out against the altar by the word of the LORD, and said, "O altar, altar! Thus says the LORD: "Behold, a child, Josiah by name, shall be born to the house of David; and on you he shall sacrifice the priests of the high places who burn incense on you, and men's bones shall be burned on you." And he gave a sign the same day, saying, "This is the sign which the LORD has spoken: Surely, the altar shall split apart, and the ashes on it shall be poured out." (1 Kings 13:1–3).

Three hundred years later, the prophecy was fulfilled:

> Moreover the altar that was at Bethel, and the high place which Jeroboam the son of Nebat, who made Israel sin, had made, both that altar and the high place he broke down; and he burned the high place and crushed it to powder, and burned the wooden image. As Josiah turned, he saw the tombs that were there on the mountain. And he sent and took the bones out of the tombs, and burned them on the altar, and defiled it according to the word of the LORD which the man of God proclaimed, who proclaimed these words. (2 Kings 23:15–16)

Isaiah predicted the captivity of Judah by Babylon and then predicted that Cyrus the Persian would allow the captives to return. "Who says of Cyrus, 'He is My shepherd, and he shall perform all My pleasure,' saying to Jerusalem, 'You shall be built,' and to the temple, 'Your foundation shall be laid.'" (Isa. 44:28). Approximately two hundred years later, Cyrus issued such a decree, as recorded in Ezra 1:1–3:

Now in the first year of Cyrus king of Persia, that the word of the LORD by the mouth of Jeremiah might be fulfilled, the LORD stirred up the spirit of Cyrus king of Persia, so that he made a proclamation throughout all his kingdom, and also put it in writing, saying, Thus says Cyrus king of Persia: All the kingdoms of the earth the LORD God of heaven has given me. And He has commanded me to build Him a house at Jerusalem which is in Judah. Who is among you of all His people? May his God be with him, and let him go up to Jerusalem which is in Judah, and build the house of the LORD God of Israel (He is God,) which is in Jerusalem.

Micah, a contemporary of Isaiah, predicted the birthplace of Christ: "But you, Bethlehem Ephrathah, though you are little among the thousands of Judah, yet out of you shall come forth to Me the One to be Ruler in Israel, whose goings forth are from of old, from everlasting." (Mic. 5:2) Seven hundred years later, it came to pass:

Now after Jesus was born in Bethlehem of Judea in the days of Herod the king, behold, wise men from the East came to Jerusalem, saying, "Where is He who has been born King of the Jews? For we have seen His star in the East and have come to worship Him." When Herod the king heard this, he was troubled, and all Jerusalem with him. And when he had gathered all the chief priests and scribes of the people together, he inquired of them where the Christ was to be born. So they said to him, "In Bethlehem of Judea, for thus it is written by the prophet: 'But you, Bethlehem, in the land of Judah, are not the least among the rulers of Judah; for out of you shall come a Ruler who will shepherd My people Israel.' (Matt. 2:1–6)

The most significant thing about these prophecies is that they give specific names of people, places, and the events connected to them hundreds of years in advance. Clearly, only God could see so far into the future.

3. *The teaching of Christ.* Never was there a man like Jesus, performing miracles, predicting his own death and resurrection, and then showing

himself alive to many witnesses just as he said he would do. Rightly do we call him "Lord." Yet if he is Lord of our lives, he should also be Lord of our view of the Bible. Note that Christ considered Scripture to be the unbreakable Word of God: "If He called them gods, to whom the word of God came and the (Scripture cannot be broken)" (John 10:35; see also Matt. 19:4–5; Matt. 22:31–32).

Thus, we see that we can approach the Bible with the confidence that it is a God-inspired book that can guide us through this life and into the next.

The Bible Gives Us Truth

The testimony of Jesus

In his prayer at the Last Supper, Jesus said to the Father, "Sanctify them by Your truth. Your word is truth" (John 17:17). God's Word is truth. This was the consistent testimony of our Lord.

In the following passages, Jesus taught that the Scriptures came from God. A few examples follow:

- Matthew 4:4, "But He answered and said, 'It is written, Man shall not live by bread alone, but by every word that proceeds from the mouth of God.'" Here, he asserts that Scripture is as important as nutrition since it came from God.
- Luke 11:28, "But He said, 'More than that, blessed are those who hear the word of God and keep it!'" In other words, those who hear the Scriptures read are hearing not the words of man but God's.
- John 10:34–36, "Jesus answered them, 'Is it not written in your law, "I said, You are gods?" If He called them gods, to whom the word of God came (and the Scripture cannot be broken) do you say of Him whom the Father sanctified and sent into the world, 'You are blaspheming,' because I said, 'I am the Son of God?'" Notice that he explicitly attributes the origin of the Scriptures to the word of God coming to those who wrote the Bible.

To be truthful, God's Word must be *entirely* free of falsehood, not just in general but even down to the details. Again, consider what Jesus had to say about this in the following passages:

- Matthew 5:18, "For assuredly, I say to you, till heaven and earth pass away, one jot or one tittle will by no means pass from the law till all is fulfilled." The *jot* refers to the smallest letter in the Hebrew alphabet. The *tittle* is a small dot or stroke used to distinguish one letter from another, like an F is distinguished from an E by one little line. So, he was saying that even the smallest parts of God's Word are trustworthy.
- Matthew 22:31–32, "But concerning the resurrection of the dead, have you not read what was spoken to you by God, saying, 'I am the God of Abraham, the God of Isaac, and the God of Jacob'? God is not the God of the dead, but of the living." Jesus wins a dispute with the Sadducees (who denied the resurrection of the dead) by appealing to the present tense of the verb. That, too, was inspired and trustworthy.

Thus, we see that our Savior held the Scriptures in highest esteem. They were unchangeable, absolutely reliable, and authoritative. In holding such a view, Jesus was merely standing in the tradition of the writers of Scripture who preceded him. For example,

- Psalm 12:6: "The words of the LORD are pure words, like silver tried in a furnace of earth, purified seven times."
- Psalm 18:30, "As for God, His way is perfect; the word of the LORD is proven; He is a shield to all who trust in Him."
- Psalm 119:89, "Forever, O LORD, Your word is settled in heaven."
- Proverbs 30:5, "Every word of God is pure; He is a shield to those who put their trust in Him."

The Bible is true in all its parts

Jesus' above comments about the truthfulness of Scripture pertain to the Old Testament Scriptures. Since the New Testament was not yet written in his day, can we be equally confident that it, too, is true? For an answer, consider the following verses, bearing in mind that they were spoken to his apostles.

- John 14:26, "But the Helper, the Holy Spirit, whom the Father will send in My name, He will teach you all things, and bring to your remembrance all things that I said to you."
- John 16:13, "However, when He, the Spirit of truth, has come, He will guide you into all truth; for He will not speak on His own authority, but whatever He hears He will speak; and He will tell you things to come."

No doubt, these promises by Christ were intended to reassure the apostles that their teaching would come from God, even as the teachings of the Old Testament had come from God.

Paul wrote much of the New Testament (thirteen letters in all). Because he was not among the twelve original apostles to whom Jesus made the above promises, we must ask if his writings are to be considered as Scripture as well. The best testimony concerning this comes from Peter, the leader among the early apostles. His closeness to Jesus gives his testimony credibility. Notably, he classified Paul's letters as Scripture in 2 Peter 3:15–16: "And consider that the longsuffering of our Lord is salvation—as also our beloved brother Paul, according to the wisdom given to him, has written to you, as also in all his epistles, speaking in them of these things, in which are some things hard to understand, which untaught and unstable people twist to their own destruction, as they do also the rest of the Scriptures."

Since Jesus held such a high view of Scripture we can be confident that the Bible is true in both the Old and New Testaments, from Genesis to Revelation.

Questions raised by the idea of Scripture as truth without error

Some people find it difficult to accept the truthfulness of the Bible without question. To be better witnesses, we should anticipate some questions they might have and how we would reply. The exercise below may help.

- Question: Is it possible to have absolutely truthful Scripture since it was written by sinful and fallible men? Answer: God's guidance kept them from error.
- Statement: The Bible may be true for you but not for me. Everyone has to find his or her own truth. Answer: God's Word to humanity is true for everyone, like the laws of physics.
- Question: Could the Bible contain factual and historical errors and still be spiritually true? Answer: If the Bible could be shown to be factually and historically wrong in some instances, we would have no reason to think it was spiritually true in every case, thus casting doubt on all its spiritual teaching.

A final thought

God wants his Word to be more than an interesting or informative book. He means for it to be a source of transforming power. Five ways in which it can do this are mentioned in 2 Timothy 3:15–16: "And that from childhood you have known the Holy Scriptures, which are able to make you wise for salvation through faith which is in Christ Jesus. All Scripture is given by inspiration of God, and is profitable for doctrine, for reproof, for correction, for instruction in righteousness." The Scriptures 1) make us wise for salvation, and 2) are profitable for doctrine, 3) for reproof, 4) for correction, and 5) for instruction in righteousness.

Yet while the entire Bible is inspired, some parts are more easily applied than others. Portions of the Bible that were applicable to Israel, such as the food laws in Leviticus, might seem to have no value for Christians. Yet even those portions that are no longer strictly applicable reveal principles that can be applied to our lives, such as, "Therefore, whether you eat or drink, or whatever you do, do all to the glory of God" (1 Cor. 10:31). So let us study the Bible diligently and with complete confidence that all of it is the Word of God, free from error.

The Bible Is About Jesus

How the Bible is arranged

The Bible has two major portions, the Old Testament and the New Testament. The Old Testament has thirty-nine books whereas the New Testament has twenty-seven books. Here is an easy way to remember this.

- If you count the number of letters in Old and in Testament, you find three and nine letters respectively and likewise for New and Testament.
- Put these numbers together, and you have three and nine, which make thirty-nine, the number of Old Testament books.
- Multiply three times nine, and you have twenty-seven, the number of New Testament books.

Testament is another word for covenant, an agreement between two parties—two people, two nations, or between God and man. We call our two parts of the Bible the Old and New Testaments because each revolves around a major covenant made between God and man.

The term Old Testament has reference to the covenant made between God and Israel at Mt. Sinai through Moses (Exod. 19ff.). This covenant provided the basis of Israel's legal system and worship. Paul calls the Law a tutor designed to bring people to Christ (Gal. 3:24). The chart below explains the organization of the Old Testament.

Organization of the Old Testament

17 History Books	5 Poetry Books	17 Prophecy Books
5 written by Moses	5 books of Poetry	5 Major Prophets
Genesis–Deuteronomy	Job–Song of Solomon	Isaiah–Daniel
12 other writers of history		12 Minor Prophets
Joshua–Esther		Hosea–Malachi

The New Testament focuses on the New Covenant or agreement between God and man that was predicted by Jeremiah (31:31) and put in effect by Christ Jesus. At the Last Supper, Jesus said, "This cup is the new covenant in My blood, which is shed for you" (Luke 22:20). By these words, he taught us that his death would put into effect a new relationship between God and humanity, that which provides the forgiveness of sins through faith in him. The chart below describes the organization of the New Testament.

Organization of the New Testament

The Life of Christ	The Early Church	Paul's Letters	Other Letters	Final Prophecy
The Four Gospels Matthew– John	The Book of Acts	The first 13 Letters Romans– Philemon	The other 8 letters Hebrews– Jude	The Book of Revelation

Christ is in both the Old and New Testaments

Often Christians feel much more at home in the New Testament than the Old. Perhaps this is because the New Testament presents us with Jesus and teaching meant directly for Christians, whereas much of the Old Testament seems concerned with the ancient nation of Israel and its myriad laws and rituals that we no longer observe. Yet Jesus is also found in the Old Testament.

The Lord often spoke about himself as the subject of some of the Old Testament as the following verses show:

- Luke 24:27, "And beginning at Moses and all the Prophets, He expounded to them in all the Scriptures the things concerning Himself."
- Luke 24:44, "Then He said to them, 'These are the words which I spoke to you while I was still with you, that all things must be fulfilled which were written in the Law of Moses and the Prophets and the Psalms concerning Me.'"

- John 5:39, "You search the Scriptures, for in them you think you have eternal life; and these are they which testify of Me."

So, where do we find the Lord Jesus in the Old Testament? To begin with, he is found in the great promises of the Old Testament. These promises were made to Abraham, David, and Jeremiah. Sometimes these are called the Abrahamic covenant, the Davidic covenant, and the new covenant because God entered into agreements whereby he promised to do certain things. All these promises concern Christ. To learn what these promises are, study the chart below:

Old Testament Covenant Promises Fulfilled in Jesus

Old Testament Passage	What God Promised	New Testament Fulfillment in Jesus
Genesis 12:3; 22:18; 26:4; 28:14	To bless all the families of the earth through the seed of Abraham	Galatians 3:8,14
2 Samuel 7:16; Psalm 89:35–37	The seed of David would occupy the throne forever	Matthew 1:1; Luke 1:30–33
Jeremiah 31:33–34	Forgiveness of sin through the new covenant	Matthew 26:28; Luke 22:20

Jesus is also found in pictures, either people or objects that somehow portrayed him. Theologians call these pictures *types*. For instance, in Romans 5:14 it is said that Adam was a type of Christ. The points of comparison between them are below:

- Both entered the world through a special act of God.
- Both entered the world without sin.
- Both represented groups: Adam represented fallen humanity and Christ represented the redeemed.
- Each did something decisive for the human race.

Other types of Christ in the Old Testament include the sacrificial lamb (see John 1:36), the high priest (see Heb. 4:14–15), the tabernacle (see John 1:14, where *dwelt* is literally "tabernacled") to mention but a few.

Finally, Christ is found in prophecies of the Old Testament. Perhaps the most famous of these is Isaiah 53. Take a moment to read this passage, then review the chart below:

Isaiah 53 Fulfilled in Christ

Prediction in Isaiah 53	Fulfillment in Christ
53:3, He was to be despised, rejected, and acquainted with grief.	Luke 18:31–33, "Then He took the twelve aside and said to them, 'Behold, we are going up to Jerusalem, and all things that are written by the prophets concerning the Son of Man will be accomplished. For He will be delivered to the Gentiles and will be mocked and insulted and spit upon. They will scourge Him, and kill Him. And the third day He will rise again.'"
53:4, To bear our griefs and carry our sorrows	Matt. 8:17, "That it might be fulfilled which was spoken by Isaiah the prophet, saying:'He Himself took our infirmities and bore our sicknesses.'"
53:5, To be wounded for our transgressions	1 Cor. 15:3, "For I delivered to you first of all that which I also received: that Christ died for our sins according to the Scriptures."
53:7, To maintain silence in judgment	Matt. 27:13–14, "Then Pilate said to Him, 'Do You not hear how many things they testify against You?' But He answered him not one word, so that the governor marveled greatly."
53:9, He would be buried with the rich.	Matt. 27:57, 59, 60, "Now when evening had come, there came a rich man from Arimathea, named Joseph, who himself had also become a disciple of Jesus. . . . When Joseph had taken the body, he wrapped it in a clean linen cloth, and laid it in his new tomb which he had hewn out of the rock; and he rolled a large stone against the door of the tomb, and departed."

From these few examples, it is clear that Christ is present in the Old Testament. As we continue our study of Old Testament books, we will see this repeatedly.

Christ is the central figure of the New Testament

Continuing the themes of the Old Testament, the New Testament presents Jesus as the Davidic King, the initiator of the new covenant, and the means of blessing the nations as promised to Abraham.

- The Gospels tell the story of his life, death, and resurrection.
- Acts tells of the early preaching of Christ by the apostles.
- The New Testament letters explain how faith in Christ should be lived out in this world.
- Finally, Revelation ends the New Testament by describing the return of Christ in glory and triumph.

So it is no exaggeration to say that the Lord Jesus Christ is the central theme of the Bible from Genesis to Revelation. Our studies in each book will help this become clearer to us.

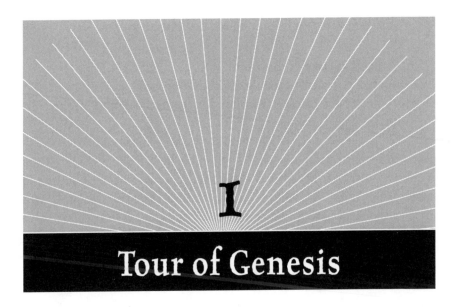

Tour of Genesis

"The major themes of Scripture may be compared to great rivers, ever deepening and broadening as they flow; and it is true to say that all these rivers have their rise in the watershed of Genesis." [2]

Preview of Genesis

Genesis means *"beginning"* or *"origin."* It tells of the beginning of the world and of God's redemptive work. Virtually every major Bible doctrine begins in Genesis. Herbert Lockyer said, "The roots of all subsequent revelation are planted deep in Genesis and whoever would truly comprehend that revelation must begin here." [3]

As a book of beginnings, Genesis includes a number of firsts, such as the first days of creation, the first people, the first sin, and the first death. Most importantly, Genesis records the beginnings of the nation of Israel. It tells of God's dealings with Abraham, Isaac, and Jacob, the patriarchs of the nation.

Three things God promised to Abraham in Genesis 12:1–3 were

- A land God would show him (v. 1)
- A great nation God would make of him (v. 2)
- A blessing to him and through him to all the nations of the earth (v. 3)

Abraham was a hundred years old when his heir, Isaac, was born (Gen. 21:5). In turn, Isaac became the father of Jacob whom later God would name Israel, meaning, "he strives against God" (since he struggled with God's angel, Gen. 32:28). According to Genesis 35:22, Jacob had twelve sons, destined to become the heads of the twelve tribes of Israel.

Introduction to Genesis

Author. From ancient times, Moses has been recognized as the author of Genesis and the four following books. Together, these five books are sometimes called the Pentateuch (meaning "five scrolls"). Among the Jews, they are called the Torah (meaning "the Law," since they contain the laws given to Israel at Sinai). While some critics deny that he wrote these books, biblical writers recognized Moses as the author, including Joshua (Josh. 1:7), Jesus (John 7:19), and Paul (Rom. 10:19). In addition to the Bible's own teaching, ancient Jewish and Christian sources also attribute the Torah to Moses.

Date of writing. Solomon began building the temple 480 years after the Exodus from Egypt (see 1 Kings 6:1). It is fairly certain that Solomon's work on the temple began in 966 B.C. Therefore, the Exodus would have occurred in 1446 B.C. Assuming Genesis was written a year or two later, a date of composition around 1445 B.C. seems likely.

Theme. The Book of Genesis begins by describing the creation of the world. While the creation itself is "very good" (1:31), it is marred by the entrance of sin (chap. 3). Thereafter, humanity grows progressively worse spiritually (6:5). Even the flood does not stop the downward slide (chaps. 6—11). When humanity seems beyond remedy, God implements his plan to bless all the families of the earth. This plan involves the call of Abraham who would become the father of the nation of Israel. God makes a covenant with Abraham in which he promises him a land, a great nation, and blessing. The importance of the call of Abraham is seen in the proportion of the book devoted to the story of Abraham and his descendants. Thirty-nine chapters, from chapter 12 to the end of the book, are about Abraham and his descendants, whereas only eleven chapters are given to the time preceding him. Given this emphasis on Abraham, the theme of Genesis might be stated as *God calls Abraham.*

Purpose. Genesis was written to explain the role of the nation of Israel in the plan of God. It gives the historical and theological basis for God's covenant with the nation.

History and archaeology. Archaeological investigation into the times and customs of the second millennium before Christ has demonstrated that the stories of the patriarchs fit what is known of the period. Even beyond that, numerous flood legends from around the world bear testimony to the Genesis account of the flood of Noah. Howard F. Vos writes:

> Flood stories have been discovered among nearly all nations and tribes. Though most common on the Asian mainland and the islands immediately south of it and on the North American continent, they have been found on all the continents. Totals of the number of stories known run as high as about 270, of which more than 220 are definitely know to the writer of this article. [4]

Geography. The geographical span of Genesis reaches from Mesopotamia to Egypt. It traces the journey of Abraham to Canaan and the later move of the family from Canaan to Egypt and back.

The arch of land from Ur up to Haran and down to Canaan is called the "Fertile Crescent" due to its agricultural fertility. Abraham followed the this rich land area on his migration. The land directly between Canaan and Mesopotamia is arid.

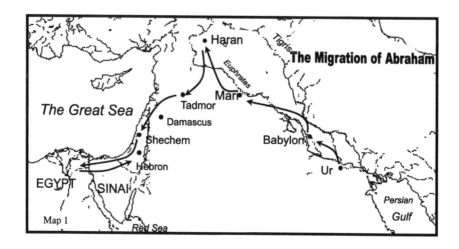

Map 1

Outline of Genesis

  I. The creation of the world by God (chaps. 1—11)
     A. Creation in the beginning (chaps. 1—2)
     B. The fall of man (chaps. 3—5)
     C. The flood and recreation (chaps. 6—9)
     D. The origin of nations after the flood (chaps. 10—11)
 II. The creation of Israel by God (chaps. 12—50)
     A. The call of Abraham (12:1—25:11)
     B. Continuation of the call with Isaac (25:12—26:35)
     C. The continuation of the call with Jacob, also known as Israel (chaps. 27—36)
     D. The preservation of the clan through Joseph (chaps. 37—50)

Overview of Genesis

The creation of the world by God (chaps. 1—11). Four major *events* take place in these chapters.

- The creation of all things (chaps. 1—2)
- The fall of man (chaps. 3—5)
- The flood of Noah (chaps. 6—9)
- The origin of nations (chaps. 10—11)

After describing the creation of the world in six successive days, the creation of man is given special attention (chap. 2). Placed into an ideal environment, the man and woman fail to obey God and come under his curse (chap. 3). Sin and death spread (chaps. 4—5). To temporarily halt the spread of sin, God sends the flood (chaps. 6—9). He graciously spares one man, Noah, who, along with his family, builds an ark to escape the flood and brings some of every kind of animal aboard. Following the flood, people again fail to obey God's command to fill the earth; instead they cluster around an idolatrous tower. As a result, God confuses their languages and disperses them across the earth (chaps. 10—11).

The creation of Israel by God (chaps. 12—50). Four major characters dominate chapters 12—50. They are

- Abraham
- Isaac
- Jacob
- Joseph

When it seems that humanity is incorrigible and beyond saving, God calls Abraham. Three promises are made to him, the promise of a land, a nation, and blessing (12:1–3). These promises are repeated several times (13:15–16; 15:12–21; 17:1–8; 22:16–18), and they provide the basis for the development of the rest of the Bible. The Old Testament tells about the acquisition of the Promised Land and the growth of the nation. The New Testament tells how the promised blessing comes to all nations of the earth. Galatians 3:8 says this about the blessing: "And the Scripture, foreseeing that God would justify the Gentiles by faith, preached the gospel to Abraham beforehand, saying, 'In you all the nations shall be blessed.'"

The promises to Abraham are reiterated to his son Isaac (26:1–5). The faith of Abraham is tested when he is told to offer Isaac as a sacrifice. Once Abraham demonstrates his great faith, God tells him to spare Isaac (22:1–19). The promises are then given to his son Jacob (chaps. 27—36), whom God renames Israel (32:28). Jacob has twelve sons who become the heads of the tribes of Israel. Prominent among them is Joseph who is hated by his brothers but is favored by God. This man, rejected by his kinsmen, becomes their deliverer, making him a type of Christ (chaps. 37—50). With his help, the family escapes a famine in Canaan and moves to Egypt.

Theological Highlights

Genesis makes many contributions to biblical theology. Certainly, the creation account provides the basis for belief in one God, which is called monotheism. In addition, the call of Abraham sets in motion the theme of redemption.

Christ in Genesis

Christians find both prophecies and pictures of Christ in Genesis. Three notable prophecies and their New Testament fulfillment include the following:

- The seed of the woman would bruise the head of the serpent (Satan) (3:15, cf. Gal. 4:4–5).
- All families of the earth would be blessed (12:3, cf. Gal. 3:8, 14).
- The coming king from Judah (49:10). The title of *king* is given to Jesus in the New Testament (e.g., Rev. 12:5; 19:16).

Pictures of Christ include Adam (Rom. 5:12–14); Melchizedek (Gen. 14:18–20; Heb. 6:20—7:25); Isaac, the son who nearly was a sacrifice (Gen. 22:1–14; Heb. 11:17–19); and Joseph, the man rejected by his brothers who became their deliverer (Gen. 37—45; Rom. 9:1—11:26).

Key Verses

Genesis12:1–3: "Now the LORD had said to Abram: Get out of your country, from your family and from your father's house, to a land that I will show you. I will make you a great nation; I will bless you and make your name great; and you shall be a blessing. I will bless those who bless you, and I will curse him who curses you; and in you all the families of the earth shall be blessed."

Key Chapters

Chapter 1: Creation

Chapter 12: Abraham's call

Message of Genesis

The most personal lesson to emerge from Genesis is that God plans to bless fallen man. The creation gave a pattern of this blessing. Just as God brought order out of chaos, light out of darkness, and life out of lifelessness, so he will step into people's personal chaos, darkness, and death to bring sanctification, illumination, and eternal life.

The Old Testament World Compared to the United States

If imposed on the U.S., the Old Testament lands would extend from the Great Lakes almost to the Gulf of Mexico and from Virginia to Texas.

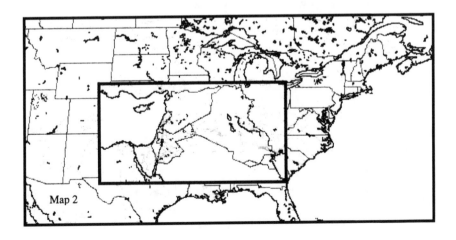

Map 2

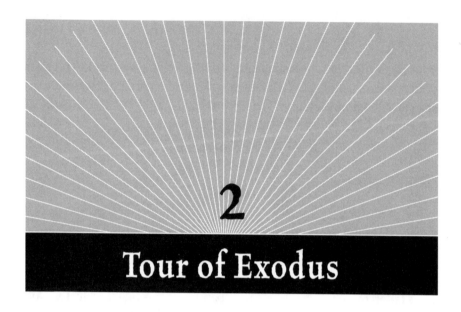

Tour of Exodus

Is there in all history a more amazing spectacle than the Exodus? — a more august and solemn revelation of God than at Sinai? — a more significant piece of architecture than the Israelite Tabernacle? — a greater human figure than the man Moses? — a more influential national epoch than the founding of the Israel theocracy? All these are found in this second book of Scripture. It is the very fount and origin of the national life, law, and organized religion of Israel.

— J. Sidlow Baxter, *Explore the Book*[5]

Preview of Exodus

The relationship of Exodus to Genesis has been compared to the relationship between the New Testament and the Old Testament. The Old Testament tells about humanity's entrance into sin; the New Testament presents redemption from sin. Similarly, Genesis tells about Israel's entrance into Egypt; Exodus tells about Israel's redemption from Egypt. The title *Exodus* means "departure" or "exit," and it has reference to this redemptive act whereby Israel left Egypt.

The redemption of Israel from Egypt occurs because of the promise God made to Abraham (Gen. 15:12–16). This promise is referred to in Exodus 2:24, "So God heard their groaning, and God remembered His covenant with Abraham, with Isaac, and with Jacob." Again in 6:5, "And I have also heard the groaning of the children of Israel whom the Egyptians keep in bondage, and I have remembered My covenant."

Introduction to Exodus

Author. Moses (see introductory notes to Genesis)

Date of writing. 1445 B.C. or soon after.

Theme. Emancipation from slavery. This book describes a work of salvation. God sets his people free from their enslavement to Pharaoh.

Purpose. Exodus was written to describe how Israel progressed from being a clan to a nation. At Mount Sinai Israel received its "constitution" in the form of the Law. Moreover, the book makes clear that Israel was God's nation. By virtue of his redemptive work on her behalf, Israel belonged to him.

History and archaeology. The question is often asked, when did the Exodus occur? The Bible gives an answer in 1 Kings 6:1, "And it came to pass in the four hundred and eightieth year after the children of Israel had come out of the land of Egypt, in the fourth year of Solomon's reign over Israel, in the month of Ziv, which is the second month, that he began to build the house of the LORD." Since the fourth year of Solomon's reign was 966 B.C., the Exodus would have occurred in 1446 B.C. during the reign of Amenhotep II. History and archaeology offer evidence that supports this Bible date.

- There is archaeological evidence that Amenhotep II of Egypt (1447–1421 B.C.) was not succeeded by his firstborn son, just as the pharaoh of the Exodus was not.

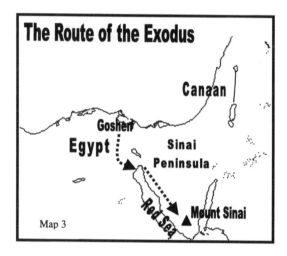

The Route of the Exodus

Canaan

Goshen

Egypt

Sinai
Peninsula

Red Sea

Mount Sinai

Map 3

- Moreover, Amenhotep II is known to have resided in the Egyptian Delta, near the land of Goshen where Israel was quartered.
- Further, Amenhotep was a relatively weak pharaoh. His father, Thutmose III, was a great conqueror. In contrast, Amenhotep was unable to launch any major campaigns, perhaps due to the destruction by the plagues and the loss of his chariots and soldiers in the Red Sea.

Geography. The Book of Exodus begins in Egypt and ends at Mount Sinai. On the map below, the approximate route of the Exodus is shown. (The exact route of the Exodus is unknown, as is the exact location of Mount Sinai. The traditional site of Mount Sinai is Jebul Musa, a peak in the southern part of the peninsula.)

Outline of Exodus

I. Redemption from slavery (chaps. 1—18)
   A. Oppression of Israel (chaps. 1—2)
   B. Call of Moses (chaps. 3—4)
   C. Miracles of deliverance (chaps. 5—13)
   D. Refinement in the wilderness (chaps. 14—18)

Overview of Exodus

Redemption from slavery (chaps. 1—18). This section tells how Egypt enslaves Israel, and God raises up a deliverer in Moses. Ten plagues strike Egypt with increasing devastation (6:28—12:29). The final plague—distinctly set apart from the other nine—is on the first-born of Egypt. In anticipation of Israel's deliverance, the memorial feasts of Passover and Unleavened Bread are instituted (12:1–30).[6]

After leaving Goshen, God guides the Hebrews with a pillar of fire by night and a cloud by day (13:21–22). Shortly, the Israelites come to the Sea of Reeds. Pharaoh experiences a change of heart and pursues the fleeing tribes with his chariots. God miraculously parts the sea. Israel goes through upon dry ground, but when the army of Pharaoh attempts to follow, the sea returns and they are drowned (chaps. 14—15).

Evidencing no faith in God, the Israelites complain about their lack of food (16:2–3), so God sends them quail and manna.[7] Soon after, they complain of the lack of water. To satisfy their thirst, God provides water from a rock (17:1–7; cf. 1 Cor. 10:4).

As they continue their journey, the Amalekites, a warlike tribe attack but are defeated by the power of God (17:8–13). Later, Moses institutes Israel's first judicial system (chap. 18).

Receiving the Law (19:1—24:8). Three months after leaving Egypt, Israel arrives at Mount Sinai (chap. 19). Here God makes a covenant with them so they might become "a kingdom of priests and a holy nation" (19:6).[8] The obligations of this covenant are stipulated in the Law, the Ten Commandments being the core (20:1–17). Other laws dealing with civil affairs and sacred observances are given (chaps. 21—23), and then the covenant is ratified with blood (24:1–8).

The Ten Commandments

1. "You shall have no other gods before Me."
2. "You shall not make for yourself a carved image, or any likeness of any thing that is in heaven above, or that is in the earth beneath, or that is in the water under the earth."
3. "You shall not take the name of the LORD your God in vain."
4. "Remember the Sabbath day, to keep it holy."
5. "Honor your father and your mother."
6. "You shall not murder."
7. "You shall not commit adultery."
8. "You shall not steal."
9. "You shall not bear false witness against your neighbor."
10. "You shall not covet your neighbor's house, you shall not covet your neighbor's wife, nor his male servant, nor his female servant, nor his ox, nor his donkey, nor anything that is your neighbor's."

Constucting the tabernacle (24:9—40:38). Moses then returns to the top of the mountain where God gives him detailed instructions concerning the tabernacle, a portable shrine where sacrificial worship was carried out (24:9—31:18). Essentially a tent, it consisted of two parts. The inner room of the tabernacle, called the Holy of Holies, contained the ark of the covenant. In the course of worship, only the high priest could enter this room, and then only once a year. The outer part of the tabernacle was called the Holy Place and contained the altar of incense, the table with "the bread of the Presence," and the lamp. Surrounding the tabernacle was a courtyard defined by a long rectangular curtain. The sacrificial altar and the laver were located there.

Due to the lengthy time Moses is upon the mountain, the people decide that he is dead and fashion a golden calf to worship. God directs Moses to return to the camp where he punishes their idolatry (chap. 32). Following their repentance (chap. 33), the covenant is renewed (chap. 34),

Plan of the Tabernacle

(Objects are not to scale.)

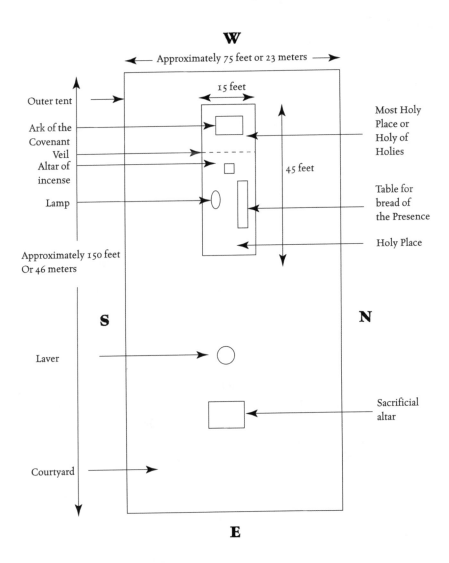

and the construction of the tabernacle begins (chap. 35). A year after the Exodus from Egypt, the tabernacle is completed (40:17) and filled with the glory of God (40:34).

Theological Highlights

Concerning salvation. The Exodus was an act of salvation. As such, it set forth in typical fashion the later salvation by Christ.

- As God broke the power of Pharaoh through Moses, so he breaks the power of Satan through Christ.
- Just as the salvation described in Exodus brought redemption from slavery, the salvation of Christ brings redemption from sin.
- Both were affected with a sacrifice—the Passover lamb and the Lamb of God (John 1:36).

Christ in Exodus

Multiple pictures of Christ are found in the Book of Exodus.

- The Passover lamb; see 1 Corinthians 5:7
- The manna in the wilderness; see John 6:32–35
- The rock of Horeb; see 1 Corinthians 10:4
- Aaron the high priest; see Hebrews 5:4–5
- The tabernacle; the tabernacle was the place of God's dwelling. It localized his presence (functionally). The Gospel of John draws upon the symbolism of the tabernacle when it says, "And the Word [i.e., Christ] became flesh and dwelt among us" (John 1:14). John uses a term that means "tabernacled among us." Thus, John says that just as the presence of God was localized in the tabernacle, so it was later localized in Christ.

Concerning Sanctification

Israel's special relationship with God called for special behavior (Exod. 19:3–8). As God's people, they were set apart from the Gentile nations, just as priests are set apart from people. Their behavior was to be holy, for God is holy (Lev. 19:2). The same can be said for Christians (1 Pet. 2:9).

Key Verses

Exodus 19:5–6: "'Now therefore, if you will indeed obey My voice and keep My covenant, then you shall be a special treasure to Me above all people; for all the earth is Mine. And you shall be to Me a kingdom of priests and a holy nation.' These are the words which you shall speak to the children of Israel."

Key Chapter

Chapter 20: the Ten Commandments.

Message of Exodus

Exodus reveals God as a promise-keeping God. He acts on the previously made covenant with Abraham. Furthermore, Exodus reveals God as Savior. What he did for Israel illustrates our salvation today.

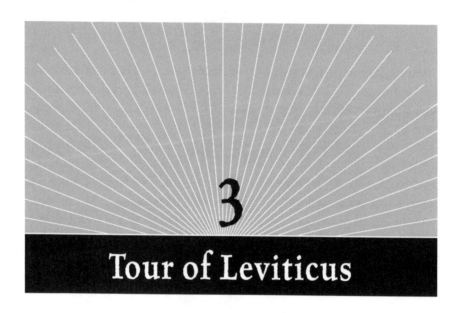

Tour of Leviticus

Preview of Leviticus

Exodus describes the construction of the place of worship, the tabernacle; Leviticus then describes the way of worship, the regulations for worshipers. Acceptable sacrifices, properly prepared priests, holy living, and holy days form the focus of the book. Leviticus does not advance the chronological story of the Bible. All these regulations were given while Israel was camped at Mount Sinai.

Introduction to Leviticus

Title. The name *Leviticus* comes from "Levi," the priestly tribe prominent in the book.

Author. Moses. For arguments in support, see Genesis.

Date of writing. Around 1445 B.C.

Theme. Laws of holiness. The Hebrew word for *holy* is qadosh, meaning "set apart." God is holy in that he is distinct and apart from all creation. His people are to be set apart both in their separation from sin and their separation unto the service of God. Everything in Leviticus can be understood as defining interaction between a holy God and his people. Thus, they are given sacrifices and priests by which they may approach this holy God, ritual regulations designed to promote holy living, and sacred occasions by which they further sanctify the Lord.

Purpose. The Book of Leviticus was written to give Israel a sanctified manner of life and worship.

History and archaeology. The practice of laying on hands (Lev. 8:14; 16:21, and elsewhere) was known among the Hittites where it symbolized the substitution of the sacrificial victim for the worshiper.

Outline of Leviticus

I. Holy worship
   A. In practice; laws of sacrifice (chaps. 1—7)
   B. In priesthood; laws of priests (chaps. 8—10)
   C. In people; laws of cleanliness (chaps. 11—15)
   D. In proxy; Day of Atonement (chap. 16)
II. Holy living
   A. Practices; code of holiness (chaps. 17—26)
   B. Promises; laws of vows (chap. 27)

Overview of Leviticus

In practice; laws of sacrifice (chaps. 1—7). Leviticus begins with the description of five types of sacrifices to be offered by the people of Israel. Merrill F. Unger explains the origin of sacrifice:

> Archaeology and history have demonstrated the universality of sacrifice in human religions from earliest times. Hebrew sacrifices showed both likeness and significant differences to the sacrificial

ritual of the Canaanites, Babylonians, Egyptians, Greeks, and Arabs. Sufficient similarity existed to demonstrate a common *origin* in a God-given revelation to the human race just after the Fall.[9]

The fundamental idea of sacrifice is that of a means of approach to God. The broadest term for sacrifice, *qorban*, means "to draw near."

In priesthood; laws of priests (chaps. 8—10). Priests offered sacrifices on behalf of Israel. The consecration and inauguration of Aaron as high priest and his sons as priests of Israel is described in chapters 8 and 9. God put two of his sons, Nadab and Abihu, to death shortly after their inauguration for attempting to approach God "with strange fire," incense fire that came from a place other than the altar of sacrifice (16:12). By this severe discipline, God emphasized the necessity of approaching him through the altar where atonement was made.

In people; laws of cleanliness (chaps. 11—15). Laws for ceremonial cleanliness are explained in these chapters. Contact with things that were "unclean" rendered a person unfit for worship in the sanctuary (15:31).[10] These regulations served to set Israel apart from other nations while giving them a heightened awareness that the pursuit of God required separation from all things profane. Being "set apart" or "separated" is the basic idea of holiness.

Yom Kippur (chap. 16). The Hebrew holy day known as Yom Kippur or the Day of Atonement is described here. Central to the observances of that day were the offering of two goats, one as a sin offering and the other as a scapegoat. The latter was sent into the wilderness after the High Priest laid his hands on its head, symbolically transferring the sins of the nation to it, which it then bore away (16:21–22). The term translated *atonement* means "covering." By these ceremonial provisions, the sins of the people were "covered" or removed from God's sight.

Practices; code of holiness (chaps. 17—26). Known as "the holiness code," these chapters list practices common among the Canaanites but not to be found in Israel. The section also includes instructions for holy participation in the sacrifices, the major festivals of Israel,[11] and the tabernacle activities.

Promises; laws of vows (chap. 27). Leviticus concludes with a chapter on vows. A vow was a promise to give oneself or one's possessions to God. While it may seem strange to end the book this way, we must remember that the root idea of holiness is being set apart for God. Thus, a vow represents the pinnacle of holiness.

Theological Highlights

Concerning God. In its regulations, Leviticus stresses the absolute holiness of God. Because he is holy, he must be treated with reverence and approached through a priest and a sacrifice. The New Testament continues this theme by presenting Jesus as the great High Priest and sole sacrifice for the believer (Heb. 8—10).

Concerning salvation. Leviticus 17:11 states, "For the life of the flesh is in the blood, and I have given it to you upon the altar to make atonement for your souls; for it is the blood that makes atonement for the soul." The Book of Leviticus contains over eighty references to the blood of the sacrifices. The New Testament points to the shed blood of Christ as making atonement for our sins in a way far more efficacious than the blood of bulls and goats (Heb. 10:4–19).

Concerning sanctification. Because God is himself holy, his people must also be holy. This does not mean they will be perfect, but they must confess their sins and offer appropriate sacrifices (Lev. 1—7). The New Testament applies this principle by saying that Christians are to confess their sins so that the blood of Christ can cover them (1 John 1:7—2:2).

Christ in Leviticus

- The burnt offering. Totally consumed, it pictures Christ in total submission to the Father.

- The grain offering. Made of the finest flour without yeast but anointed with oil, it pictures Christ as without sin and anointed by the Holy Spirit.
- The peace offering. This pictures Christ as our peacemaker (Rom. 5:1).
- The sin offering. This pictures Christ as the one who justifies us by his blood (Rom. 5:9).
- The guilt offering pictures Christ as the one who secures our forgiveness, thus reconciling us to God (Rom. 5:10).
- The two birds in Leviticus 14:49–53 picture the death and resurrection of Christ.
- The two goats in Leviticus 16 reflect the substitutionary death of Christ and his ability to bear our sins away.
- The Passover Feast (Leviticus 23), which commemorated the redemption from Egypt, anticipates the greater redemption of Christ (1 Cor. 5:7).
- The Feast of Firstfruits (Leviticus 23) typifies the resurrection of Christ (1 Cor. 15:20–23).
- The Day of Atonement pictures the cleansing work of Christ (Heb. 10:1–10).
- The high priest, Aaron, pictures Christ our great High Priest (Heb. 5:4–10).

Key Verses

Leviticus 17:11: "For the life of the flesh is in the blood, and I have given it to you upon the altar to make atonement for your souls; for it is the blood that makes atonement for the soul."

Leviticus 19:2: "Speak to all the congregation of the children of Israel, and say to them: 'You shall be holy; for I the LORD your God am holy.'"

Key Chapters

Leviticus 18—20: moral and spiritual standards.

Message of Leviticus

Leviticus, with all of its confusing ritual, makes a clear point: His people were to treat God with reverence and worship through his prescribed sacrifices. Today we are often cavalier towards God. Many church services are lacking in reverence. Some believers feel that one way of approaching God is as good as any other. However, the lessons of Leviticus as seen through the lens of the New Testament teach us that we should worship God in spirit and truth (John 4:23) and through his sacrifice, the Lord Jesus Christ.

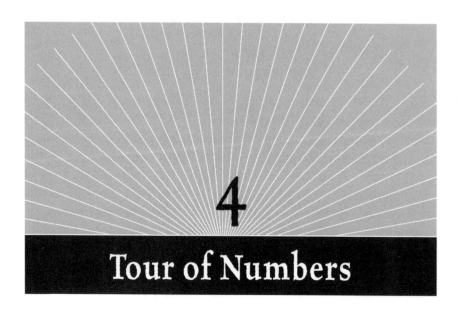

4

Tour of Numbers

Preview of Numbers

When the Book of Numbers opens, the nation is in the wilderness of Sinai. Forty years and a generation later, they have moved to the Plains of Moab just east of the Jordan River. Another name for this book might be the "Long Detour." After doubting God in chapter 14, the nation is sentenced to wander in the wilderness for forty years until everyone twenty-years old and upward who doubted God passes away. Favorite stories in the book include the sending of the twelve spies into Canaan, the disbelief of the people, their frequent complaints against the Lord, and the attempt by Balak, king of Moab, to enlist the services of the prophet Balaam to curse Israel.

Introduction to Numbers

Title. The Book of Numbers is so named because twice in the book, the people are numbered or counted. These censuses are found in chapters 1 and 26 during different generations.

Author. Moses. See the discussion of authorship under Genesis.

Date of writing. Around 1445–1440 B.C.

Theme. Nomadic wilderness wanderings. Numbers describes the forty years Israel spent wandering in the wilderness of Sinai (Deut. 1:3). A quick entrance into the Promised Land was denied the generation that left Egypt due to their unbelief (Num. 14:23). They did not conquer until a new generation arose.

Purpose. The Book of Numbers was written to show the absolute necessity of following God's directions. Failure to trust and obey him resulted in the loss of blessing.

History and archaeology. In 1967 at Deir Alla, Jordan, an ancient text was found that mentions Balaam the son of Beor three times, using the identical name given to him in Numbers 22:5. The text dates from 760 B.C., but seems to have a much older source referred to as "the Book of Balaam." This strongly supports the biblical account.

Geography. The Book of Numbers traces the movements of Israel from Mount Sinai to the Plains of Moab as shown on the map below.

Outline of Numbers

   I. Marching from Mount Sinai (1:1—10:10)
  II. Mutiny at Kadesh (10:11—21:35)
 III. Mustering on the Plains of Moab (22:1—36:13)

Overview of Numbers

Marching from Mount Sinai (1:1—10:10). Before leaving Mount Sinai, the first census is taken (chap. 1). God gives directions to Moses as the how the tribes are to be organized for their march (chap. 2). This illustrates the maxim that "order is heaven's first law." Various duties are assigned to the Levites who had the responsibility of transporting the

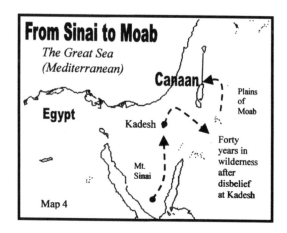

From Sinai to Moab
The Great Sea
(Mediterranean)
Canaan
Egypt
Kadesh
Mt. Sinai
Plains of Moab
Forty years in wilderness after disbelief at Kadesh
Map 4

Tabernacle during the march (chaps. 2—4). However, not only are the people to be organized, but they are to be sanctified. The camp was to be kept free of three types of defilement: unclean people, hurtful behavior, and marital strife (chap. 5). A special type of sanctification, the Nazirite vow, is described in chapter 6. It epitomized the dedication God sought from his people.

The famous Aaronic benediction (6:24–26) is also given. Perhaps it is placed here to show that when sanctified, God's people may expect his blessing. Chapter 7 records the offerings made by the leaders of the tribes. Chapter 8 records the consecration of the Levites. Chapter 9 recalls the observance of Passover.

The ending of chapter 9 (9:15–23) is curious. It describes how God guided his people by means of a cloud. This section goes to some length to stress that God was providentially leading his people.

The final chapter in this section begins with the description of two silver trumpets. They told the people when it was time to march, time to assemble, or as a call to arms. They were also sounded on feast days (10:1–10).

Mutiny at Kadesh (10:11—21:35). The march begins, and the tribes move northward towards Canaan. Before long, the people complain and weep about having nothing to eat but manna (11:1–9). Moses complains to God that the burden of the people is too great. So God places his Spirit on seventy elders who will share the burden of leadership with Moses (11:16–30). Then he sends quail into the camp (11:31–32). However, the greediest of the people die of a plague (11:33–35). Even Moses' family does not support him fully. His sister, Miriam, and his brother, Aaron, criticize Moses for marrying a Cushite and suggest that he is not the only person through whom God speaks. In response, God strikes Miriam with leprosy for seven days, moving her and Aaron to repent (12:1–16).

The complaints and disbelief reach a new level when the tribes arrive at Kadesh-Barnea. Twelve spies enter the land of Canaan (13:1–26). When they return, ten of the spies convince the people that conquest is impossible. Only Caleb and Joshua believe that with God's help they can conquer. The nation sides with the ten unbelieving spies; with the result that God sentences them to wander and die in the wilderness over the next forty years (14:34). The ten spies die by the plague. Belatedly, the people decide that they will invade the land after all, but the Lord does not go with them, and they are driven back (14:40–45).

To encourage the future generation, God immediately gives various laws and regulations that will apply when the nation eventually enters the land (chap. 15). Amazingly, rebellion against Moses continues at the instigation of Korah, Dathan, and Abiram, and 250 men join in their rebellion. In a mighty display of God's power, the ground opens beneath these three and their families, then closes over them. Fire comes out from God and consumes the men who joined the rebellion. In their horror at what has happened, the people blame Moses, with the result that plague takes another 14,700 people (16:1–50). As this rebellion was partly an attempt to usurp the priesthood from Aaron, God confirms him by causing his staff to bud and bear almonds (chap. 17).

After giving instructions for the Levites (chap. 18) and describing a means of purification (the red heifer sacrifice, chap. 19), Moses himself sins. When commanded by God to speak to a rock from which water will come, Moses strikes the rock in a public display of temper that reveals a lack of reverence for God's holiness. As a result, God forbids him to enter the land of Canaan (20:1–13).

Telescoping through many years, the nation arrives in Moab. Aaron dies, and his son, Eleazar, succeeds him as high priest. The Israelites encounter much opposition from the inhabitants of the land, but the Lord enables them to overcome it (20:14—21:35).

Mustering on the Plains of Moab (22:1—36:13). By now a new generation has grown up, and the conquest is about to begin in earnest. Balak, the king of Moab, hires the prophet Balaam to curse Israel (22:1–41). Much to Balak's consternation, God turns the cursing into blessing (23:1—24:25).[12] Balaam was unable to curse Israel, so their enemies then try to seduce them, resulting in many being unfaithful to the Lord. (Idolatrous practices in the ancient world involved immorality and drunkenness.) Again, God sends a plague on the transgressors (25:1–18).

Final preparations begin with the new generation. A second census is taken and further instructions given (chaps. 26—30); Joshua is commissioned to lead the nation after Moses (27:12–24); and revenge is taken on the Midianites who had previously corrupted Israel (chap. 31). The tribes of Reuben and Gad are granted permission to settle east of the Jordan River on the condition that they assist the other tribes in the conquest of the land west of the river (chap. 32). Moses then reviews their long journey (chap. 33). The borders of the land are given, and Moses commands the tribes to divide it by lot (chap. 34). Because of their religious service, the Levites are not to receive a share of the territory. Instead, they are given forty-eight cities. Six of them are cities of refuge where those who accidentally kill people may flee for safety (chap. 35). Finally, the right of women to inherit land when their fathers have no sons is established (chap. 36).

Theological Highlights

Concerning God. Numbers shows what happened to those who did not sanctify him. This book reveals that sanctification is a life of complete trust in God. Nothing displeases him more than complaining and disregarding his commands.

Christ in Numbers

- Christ is identified with the rock (20:11; 1 Cor. 10:4).
- The bronze serpent (21:1–9) is a picture of Christ crucified (John 3:14–18).
- The predicted Star (24:17) refers to Christ (Rev. 22:16).

Key Verses

Numbers 14:22–23: "Because all these men who have seen My glory and the signs, which I did in Egypt and in the wilderness, and have put Me to the test now these ten times, and have not heeded My voice, they certainly shall not see the land of which I swore to their fathers, nor shall any of those who rejected Me see it."

Key Chapters

Numbers 13—14: disbelief at Kadesh.

Message of Numbers

Speaking of the events in Numbers, 1 Corinthians 10:11 says, "Now all these things happened to them as examples, and they were written for our admonition, upon whom the ends of the ages have come." Just as they were on a journey to the Promised Land, so we Christians are on a heavenward journey. Both walks require faith and obedience in order to be blessed.

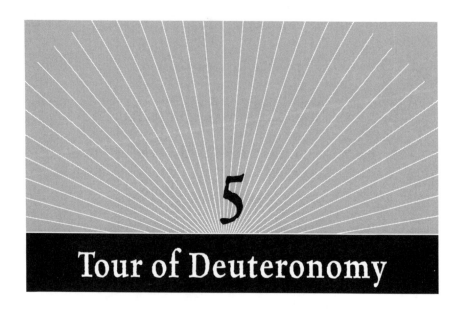

5

Tour of Deuteronomy

Deuteronomy is a book of remembrance. The name Deuteronomy means "second law" which indicates that the law is repeated. This Moses did to remind the people what God had done for them and what they were to do to serve Him when they reached the promised land. It omits the things that relate to the priests and Levites and includes the things that the people should know.[13]

— Henrietta C. Mears, *What the Bible Is All About*

Preview of Deuteronomy

Deuteronomy is Moses' farewell address to the nation. The book concludes with Joshua's formal consecration as his successor and Moses' death. The bulk of the material consists of historical review, a reiteration of the Law, and a prophetic look at the future.

Introduction to Deuteronomy

Title. Deuteronomy means "second law," derived from the Greek, *deutero* ("second") *nomos* ("law"). It is a retelling of the Law for the generation that grew up in the wilderness.

Author. Moses. Note the first verse and the firsthand experiences referred to in 5:4–5; 9:25—10:11. While it is obvious that Moses could not have written the account of his own death in chapter 34, there is sufficient evidence to support the traditional view that he wrote the remainder of the book. Perhaps the high priest, Eleazar, or Joshua added the epilogue.

Date of writing. About 1405 B.C., with the bulk written just prior to the death of Moses and the invasion of Canaan and the account of his death added shortly after.

Theme. Duplication of Law. The Law of God is repeated for the new generation. The people are admonished to remember the Lord over a dozen times. Moreover, they are told to hear, do, keep, and obey his Word over two hundred times.

Purpose. Deuteronomy was written to renew the covenant made at Mount Sinai with a new generation.

History and archaeology. Scholars have discovered treaty-covenants made at the time of Moses between kings and vassals. Known as "suzerainty" treaties, these follow a set pattern that bears a notable similarity to Deuteronomy. This lends weight to the argument that the work is by Moses, who, having been schooled in the court of Pharaoh, would have been familiar with this type of document. Also, the Code of Hammurabi (c. 1725 B.C.) has many parallels to the laws of Deuteronomy. Texts from Mesopotamia have been found that guide people in the casting of spells and omens, shedding light on the prohibitions in 18:9–20.

Geography. Chapter 1, verse 5 tells us that the message of Deuteronomy was given "on this side of the Jordan in the land of Moab." See map 4, page 24.

Outline of Deuteronomy

   I. The historical message (1:1—4:43)

  II. The legal message (4:44—26:19)

III. The prophetic message (chaps. 27—30)
IV. The final words and deeds of Moses (chaps. 31—34)

Overview of Deuteronomy

The historical message (1:1—4:43). After giving the setting of the book (1:1–5), Moses reviews the previous forty years. He traces the events that led from Mount Sinai to Moab (1:6—3:29). Based on that long experience, he then calls them to obey the commandments given by the Lord their God (4:1–43).

The legal message (4:44—26:19). This exposition of the Law falls into two parts. The first begins with a repetition of the Ten Commandments (5:1–21) and continues by stressing the importance of obeying these to show love and devotion to God (5:22—11:32). The second part elaborates on the general laws that deal with ceremonial and civil duties (12:1—26:19).

The prophetic message (chaps. 27—30). This message concerns Israel's future relationship to the land. Moses tells the people to set up memorial stones covered with lime on which they are to write the Law (27:1–8). Then they are to go to Mount Gerizim and Mount Ebal and recite the blessings and curses that will follow either obedience or disobedience to the Law (27:11–28:68; see Joshua 8:30–35 for the actual enactment of this ceremony). As 2 Kings and 2 Chronicles show, the curses of 28:15–68 accurately came to pass, including their being torn from the land (28:63).

The final words and deeds of Moses (chaps. 31—34). Having finished his prophetic discourse, Moses gives his final charge to Israel and then commissions Joshua to assume leadership (chap. 31). To fix his prophetic teaching in the minds of people, he incorporates it into a song that he teaches them to sing (32:1–43). The Lord then commands Moses to climb Mount Nebo to survey the land across the river before he dies. Prior to ascending the mountain, Moses gives his final blessing to the people (chap. 33). Then Moses goes up the mountain and dies at the age of 120 (chap. 34).

Theological Highlights

Concerning God. For the first time in the Bible, the love of God is mentioned (4:37; 7:7–8; 10:15). His love is presented as his gracious choice rather than man's dessert. Another key teaching concerning God is his oneness. In what is known as the Shema (Hebrew for "hear"), Israel was taught, "The LORD our God, the LORD is one!" (6:4). The people were to love God with all their hearts, souls, and might (6:5).

Concerning the future

Deuteronomy 28 accurately predicts the calamities that would befall Israel in the course of her history. However, chapter 30 predicts a future return of Israel to the land, along with a change of their hearts—a theme taken up by later prophets in connection with the new covenant (Jer. 31:31–33; Ezek. 36:26). Jesus put the new covenant into effect by his death (Luke 22:20), and Paul wrote that all Israel will finally turn to the Lord Jesus (Rom. 11:25–32). So Moses' prediction awaits further fulfillment.

Christ in Deuteronomy

Moses predicted the coming of a Prophet like him (18:15). See Acts 3:22 and 7:37 for early Christian identification of this Prophet with Jesus. Note the following points of comparison between Moses and Jesus:

- Both were in danger of death during infancy.
- Both experienced rejection by those they tried to deliver.
- Both functioned as saviors.
- Both led the way to better places.
- Both are intercessors.

Key Verses

Deuteronomy 10:12–13: "And now, Israel, what does the LORD your God require of you, but to fear the LORD your God, to walk in all His ways and to love Him, to serve the LORD your God with all your heart and with all your soul, and to keep the commandments of the LORD and His statutes which I command you today for your good?"

Key Chapters

Chapter 5: Ten Commandments.

Chapters 27—28: blessings and curses.

Message of Deuteronomy

Deuteronomy stresses the importance of living by God's Word, being careful to do all that he says. It especially urges us to avoid idolatry. Idolatry is more than the worship of gods made of wood and stone. It is giving something other than the Lord the primary place in our hearts. Thus, Paul writes that greed is idolatry (Col. 3:5), and 1 John warns us not to love the world (2:15) and to keep away from idols (5:21). Judging from the number of times it is quoted in the New Testament, Deuteronomy must be considered one of the most important books of the Old Testament.

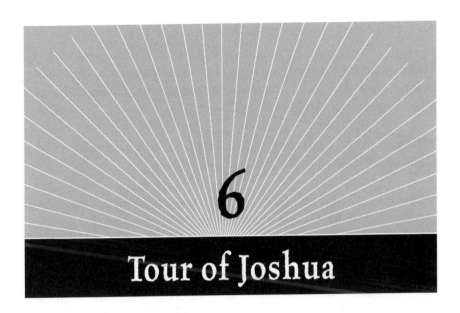

6

Tour of Joshua

Preview of Joshua

Joshua is a transitional book, bridging the Pentateuch and the remaining historical books. In three military campaigns, Israel defeats more than thirty enemies, while learning that victory does not depend on military prowess but on faith in God and obedience to his commands.

Introduction to Joshua

Title. Named after the leading figure of the book, the name Joshua is the Hebrew equivalent of Jesus. Pronounced Y'shua, the name means "The Lord saves."

Author. According to the tradition, Joshua wrote the book. Obviously, he could not have written certain sections (15:13–17 that Judges 1:9–13 places after his death, see Joshua as well as Joshua 24:29–31 which tells about his death). So perhaps Joshua provided the information that forms the bulk of the book, and a younger contemporary put it in its final form.

Date of writing. Judging from the comment in 6:25 about Rahab being alive at the time of writing, composition must have been soon after the conquest, c. 1380 B.C.

Theme. Joshua leads conquest. This book describes the conquest and allotment of Canaan under Joshua's leadership.

Purpose. The purpose of the book is to show how God fulfilled his promise to Abraham (Gen. 15:18–21) to give Israel the land.

History and archaeology. 1 Kings 6:1 states that Solomon began to build the Temple in Jerusalem 480 years after the Exodus. Since Solomon's construction began around 966 B.C., the Exodus must have occurred around 1446 B.C. The conquest would have begun near the end of that century, c. 1405 B.C. The archive of Pharaoh Akhnaton at Tell el-Amarna has what seems to be a Canaanite version of the invasion.

Geography. See map below.

Canaan at the Time of Conquest

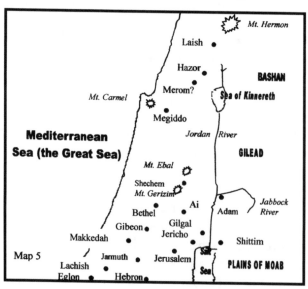

Outline of Joshua

I. The defeat of the Canaanites (chaps. 1—12)
    A. Preparation for warfare (chaps. 1—5)
    B. Battles and campaigns (chaps. 6—12)
II. The distribution of Canaan (chaps. 13—24)
    A. Assessment of the land yet to be taken (13:1–7)
    B. Division of the land among the tribes (13:8—22:34)
    C. Joshua's charge and covenant renewal (23:1—24:28)
    D. The deaths of Joshua and Eleazar the priest (24:29–33)

Overview of Joshua

The defeat of the Canaanites (chaps. 1—12). The Lord commissions Joshua to cross the Jordan and take the land, promising to give him victory (chap. 1). The conquest begins with spies being sent into Jericho. The harlot Rahab protects them because she recognizes the Lord as God (chap. 2). Then, in a miracle similar to that at the Red Sea (Exod. 14), God parts the waters of the Jordan, allowing the tribes to cross (chaps. 3—4). In an act of faith, the men are circumcised as the sign of the covenant, and the manna stops (5:1–12; see Gen. 17). The Angel of the Lord appears to Joshua and gives him instructions as to how to take Jericho (5:13—6:5). Israel is to march around the city once a day for six days, then seven times on the seventh day. They do so, and the walls fall (6:6–27). In the aftermath of this great victory, sin in the camp causes a temporary defeat to occur at Ai (chap. 7). Once the sin is removed, victory follows (chap. 8). The people of Gibeon, fearing Israel, deceive them into making a treaty of peace (chap. 9). The deception succeeds because Israel makes the treaty without first seeking the Lord (9:14). Next, a coalition of Canaanite kings from the south attacks Israel and is defeated (chap. 10). A similar coalition from the north likewise fails (chap. 11). Chapter 12 summarizes the battles fought by Israel, the warfare stretching over some seven years.

The distribution of Canaan (chaps. 13—24). The tribes of Reuben and Gad and half the tribe of Manasseh receive land to the east of the Jordan River (chap. 13). Other tribes are given portions of Canaan (chaps. 14—21). Joshua then gives three farewell messages (22:1—24:28). The book closes with the account of the deaths of Joshua and Eleazar, the high priest who followed Aaron (24:29–33).

Theological Highlights

Concerning God. Joshua shows how God faithfully keeps his promises. The land promised to Abraham and the victory promised to Joshua both came to pass. In the same way, not one of God's promises to us today will fail.

Christ in Joshua

Christians have long seen a type of Christ in the person of Joshua. (A type is someone or something in the Old Testament that prefigures someone or something in the New Testament.) Christ and Joshua are similar in at least three ways.

1. They had the same name.
2. Both led God's people to victory.
3. Both completed something that Moses began.

Another type of Christ has been seen in the Angel of the Lord (Josh. 5:13–15). The following points of comparison can be made:

1. Both commanded God's host (5:14; Rev. 19:14).
2. Both were shown reverence (5:14; John 9:38).
3. Both were equated with the Lord (Josh. 6:2; John 10:33).

Interestingly enough, the Angel of the Lord disappears in the New Testament, although other angels appear there.

Key Verses

Joshua 1:8: "This Book of the Law shall not depart from your mouth, but you shall meditate in it day and night, that you may observe to do according to all that is written in it. For then you will make your way prosperous, and then you will have good success."

Joshua 24:15: "And if it seems evil to you to serve the LORD, choose for yourselves this day whom you will serve, whether the gods which your fathers served that were on the other side of the River, or the gods of the Amorites, in whose land you dwell. But as for me and my house, we will serve the LORD."

Key Chapter

Chapter 6: the fall of Jericho

Message of Joshua

Joshua teaches us that victory comes through faith in God and obedience to his Word (cf. 1 John 5:4). It goes without saying that victory follows warfare. God is himself at war with evil. In Genesis 1, he is at war with the primeval chaos. In Genesis 6—8, he is at war with the preflood world. In Genesis 19, he bombards Sodom and Gomorrah. In Exodus, he defeats Pharaoh and the gods of Egypt. This warfare continues to the second coming of Christ that climaxes in the Battle of Armageddon (Rev. 19). Accordingly, the Christian life will not be without struggle as we war against sin (Heb. 12:4).

Review - Genesis Through Joshua

	Genesis	Exodus	Leviticus	Numbers	Deut.	Joshua
Person	Abraham	Moses	Aaron	Caleb	Moses	Joshua
Event	Promises	Law	Sacrifices	Unbelief	Farewell	Conquest
Time	2000 B.C.	1447 B.C.	1445 B.C.	1439 B.C.	1405 B.C.	1405 B.C.
Theme	Origins	Exit	Holiness	Wandering	Recalling	Conquest

7

Tour of Judges

Few periods in Israel's eventful history are as important as the period of the judges. During these centuries the nation took the wrong turning that led to her downfall and near-destruction. The apostasy of the later generations has its origin in the early years of the settlement, and there is a clear line between the time when the nation first went after Baal and the dark age when the Jerusalem Temple itself was defiled with all the trappings of the Baal worship, not excluding cultic prostitutes (2 Kings 23:4–7). There is much in Judges to sadden the heart of the reader; perhaps no book in the Bible witnesses so clearly to our human frailty. But there are also unmistakable signs of the divine compassion and long-suffering. It may be that the modern reader of Judges will hear the warning voice of the Spirit, "This is not the way, walk ye not in it." Or, as the lives of these lesser-saviours are considered, there may be a realization of the need in modern times of a greater Savior, of unblemished life, who is able to effect a perfect deliverance, not only in time but for eternity.[14]

Preview of Judges

Beginning where Joshua leaves off, Judges tells the story of how spiritual compromise turned victory into defeat. "Another generation arose after them who did not know the LORD" (2:10). This new generation adopted the idolatrous ways of the Canaanites. As a result, God sent a succession of oppressors to chasten them. Yet he did not abandon them but sent deliverers to set them free when they turned back to him.

Introduction to Judges

Title. The word *Judges* refers to the charismatic saviors God raised up to deliver the people from their enemies and then to administer justice. No single word in English expresses fully the Hebrew word for judges, *shophetim*. The English title is misleading, since in our culture judges have no military function. *Chieftains* would be more accurate.

Author. Exact certainty is impossible, but an old belief is that the prophet Samuel wrote this book.

Date of writing. Judging from the internal evidence within the book (Judg. 17:6, etc.), it was written by the time of David. So a tentative date of c. 1050 B.C. can be assigned it.

Theme. Judges is the journal of decline. The book traces the worsening fortunes of Israel as they turned from the Lord and worshipped Baal and other idols.

Purpose. The Book of Judges was written to explain and defend the origin of kingship in Israel by showing the terrible social decay that preceded the establishment of the monarchy.

History and archaeology. Prominent mention is made of a people known as the Philistines in the Book of Judges. While their roots are lost in antiquity, it is thought that they migrated to Canaan from the West, perhaps from as far away as Greece or Crete. Archeological excavations have demonstrated that they were technologically superior to the Hebrews.

Geography. At the time of the judges, Israel was surrounded by hostile nations. The major adversaries are shown on the map below.

Outline of Judges

   I. Causes of decline (chaps. 1—2)
  II. Cycles of oppression (chaps. 3—16)
III. Characteristic sins (chaps. 17—21)

Overview of Judges

Causes of decline (chaps. 1—2). At the end of the conquest, pockets of Canaanite resistance remain in the land (chap. 1). Repeatedly, the author says that Israel does not drive out all the Canaanites. Consequently, a Canaanite presence leads to Canaanite ways being adopted. When the Hebrews adopt the idolatry of the Gentiles (2:11), the Lord gives them into the hands of oppressors (2:14), with temporary relief coming from judges he raises (2:16). [15]

Cycles of oppression (chaps. 3—16). In chapters 3—16, the general pattern of idolatry, oppression, and brief deliverance described at the end of chapter 2 is enlarged and amplified. Six cycles of spiritual decline, foreign oppression, and deliverance by a judge are described. A seventh cycle that involves a Hebrew despot is also noted.

The Judges of Israel

Cycle	Oppressor	Years	Judge	Peace
3:7–11	Mesopotamia	Eight	Othniel	40 years
3:12–30	Moab	Eighteen	Ehud	80 years
4:1—5:31	Hazor	Twenty	Deborah & Barak	40 years
6:1—8:32	Midian	Seven	Gideon	40 years
8:33—10:5	Abimelech (a Hebrew despot)	Three	None	45 years
10:6—12:7	Ammon	Eighteen	Jephthah	31 years
13:1—16:31	Philistines	Forty	Samson	20 years

In addition to these major figures, several minor judges are mentioned: Shagmar (3:31); Tola and Jair (10:1–5); Ibzan, Elon, and Abdon (12:8–15). It is quite likely that many of these cycles overlapped, with different nations oppressing various tribes. Still, the most striking thing is the ease with which Israel fell back into idolatry time after time.

Characteristic sins (chaps. 17—21). By means of graphic stories, the concluding chapters give a deeper glimpse into the depths of moral and spiritual degradation that characterized the period. Foremost among these was idolatry (chaps. 17—18), followed by immorality (chap. 19), and violence (chap. 20—21).

Theological Highlights

Concerning spiritual living. Judges stresses the importance of living by faith in the Lord. It does this by describing the terrible consequences that befell the nation when apostasy reigned.

Christ in Judges

Many Bible teachers see in the judges of Israel *types* or pictures of Christ. They are like Christ in that they deliver from danger and administer justice.

Key Verse

Judges 21:25: "In those days there was no king in Israel; everyone did what was right in his own eyes."

Key Chapter

Judges 2: the causes of national decline.

Message of Judges

This book illustrates the principle found in Galatians 6:7, "Do not be deceived, God is not mocked; for whatever a man sows, that he will also reap."

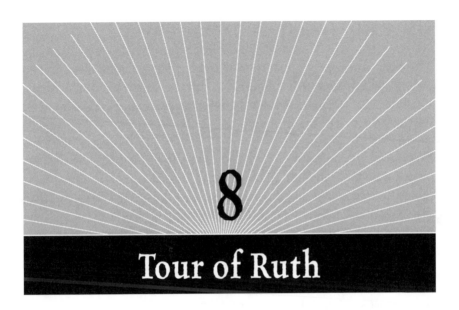

Tour of Ruth

Preview of Ruth

The little book of Ruth, set in the time of the Book of Judges, forms a welcome contrast to that book. It is a love story, telling of a woman's love for God and family. Ironically, Ruth was a Moabite. While Israel turned from God to idols, Ruth turned from idols to God. God amply rewarded her faithfulness through many difficult trials.

Introduction to Ruth

Title. The Book of Ruth is named after its leading character.

Author. Tradition again tells us that the prophet Samuel wrote this book.

Date of writing. The genealogy at the end of the book indicates that it was written after the rise of David (4:22). Assuming a date of composition close to that of Judges, a date of 1050 B.C. seems reasonable.

Theme. Ruth, in contrast to Judges, is a positive book describing a *romance of redemption*. It tells how a convert to the God of Israel, a Moabite widow named Ruth, was redeemed from her widowhood by the kinsman of her late husband.

Purpose. The purpose of Ruth is more elusive. It is often said the purpose was to trace the line of David (4:22). While this is interesting, it seems that a wider purpose was in view—to show that God is merciful to people of faith, regardless of their nationality. The reference to David, the great king, only underscored the greatness of God's mercy in choosing a Moabite to be among Jesus' ancestors.

Geography. The story of Ruth starts in Bethlehem, moves to Moab, then returns to Bethlehem. See map 6, page 40.

Outline of Ruth

   I. Ruth's tragedy (1:1–5)
  II. Ruth's testing (1:6–18)
III. Ruth's triumph (1:19—4:17)
IV. Ruth's descendants (4:18–22)

Overview of Ruth

Ruth's tragedy (1:1–5). The story opens by telling how a Hebrew family from Bethlehem migrates to Moab during a famine. The two sons marry Moabite women. The tragedy of the famine is compounded when the father and sons die, leaving behind three widows.

Ruth's testing (1:6–18). The widowed mother, Naomi, urges her daughters-in-law to return to their fathers' homes. One daughter-in-law does leave, but the other, Ruth, refuses to do so. Instead, she declares her loyalty to Naomi in words that have become immortal. These are found in 1:16–17.

Ruth's triumph (1:19—4:17). Naomi, along with Ruth, journeys back to Bethlehem, arriving at the time of the barley harvest (1:22).

Presumably, they take up residence in the home the family had left years earlier. The next order of business is to secure food. According to the custom of the day, Ruth goes into the fields to glean whatever the reapers leave.

Providentially, Ruth gleans in a field belonging to a near kinsman, Boaz. He kindly sees that she gets enough grain for herself and her mother-in-law. He continues to show her kindness in the later harvest of wheat. Later, Naomi counsels Ruth to appeal to Boaz to redeem (marry) her according to the custom of the day.[16]

Boaz is willing to perform the duty of the kinsman-redeemer. However, he must first obtain the consent of a closer relative. There is a real possibility that the closer relative will want to marry Ruth, for that would give him the use of her late father-in-law's property. As God would have it, the man declines to take Ruth, leaving Boaz free to marry her.

Ruth's descendants (4:18–22). The book concludes by tracing the line of descent from Ruth to David. This might suggest that the intent of the author was to show that the mercy of God was not confined to Hebrews but extended to all people of faith.

Christ in Ruth

Boaz, the kinsman-redeemer, is a type of Christ. As Boaz was related to Ruth by marriage, so Christ is related to us by virtue of the incarnation. And as Boaz willingly paid the price of redemption for Ruth, so Christ willingly paid the price for our redemption. Finally, as Boaz took Ruth as his wife, so Christ looks upon the Church as his bride (cf. Eph. 5).

Key Verses

Ruth 1:16–17: "But Ruth said: Entreat me not to leave you, or to turn back from following after you; for wherever you go, I will go; and wherever you lodge, I will lodge; your people shall be my people, and your God, my God. Where you die, I will die, and there will I be buried. The LORD do so to me, and more also, if anything but death parts you and me."

Key Chapter

Ruth 1: the faith of Ruth shown against a tragic background.

Message of Ruth

The story of Ruth illustrates two later statements found in the Bible. The first is in 2 Chronicles 16:9: "For the eyes of the LORD run to and fro throughout the whole earth, to show Himself strong on behalf of those whose heart is loyal to Him."

The second is in Romans 8:28: "And we know that all things work together for good to those who love God, to those who are the called according to His purpose."

Essentially, the message of Ruth is that God will not fail or forsake those who have placed their faith in him. All things work for our good because we love God and are called according to his purpose.

Tour of First and Second Samuel

Preview of First and Second Samuel

Like Joshua, the books of Samuel are transitional in that they describe how Israel progressed from being under judges or chieftains to being a monarchy. The books get their name from the prophet Samuel, who was the last judge and the kingmaker. First Samuel describes the reign of the first king, Saul, and Second Samuel describes the reign of the second king, David. In Second Samuel we encounter another of the great covenants of the Bible, the Davidic covenant. It figures prominently in Messianic prophecy.

Introduction to First and Second Samuel

Title. The books are named after the prophet Samuel, who is the first major character encountered in the books. Originally one book, they were divided by translators of the Septuagint (the Greek translation of the Hebrew Bible) for ease of handling. The division has been carried over into the English Bible. The same is true for the other "double books" of the Old Testament—Kings and Chronicles. It was simply for convenience that they were divided into double books.

Author. It is not known who wrote the books of Samuel. Certainly, Samuel himself did not, as his death occurred prior to any of the events of Second Samuel. Two possibilities are Nathan or Gad (1 Chron. 29:29) who are said to have written chronicles of the kings.

Date of writing. The period covered in the books is approximately 1100–970 B.C. Composition would have been somewhat later, perhaps around 950 B.C.

Theme. Since they were originally one book, 1 and 2 Samuel share a single theme, *starting Israel's monarchy.* At this point in its history, Israel faced a strong, growing menace in the Philistine people along the sea-coast. Their political cohesiveness and technological sophistication[17] placed increasing pressure upon the Israelites. The people of Israel were of the opinion that the best way to answer the threat was by establishing a strong central monarchy.

Purpose. The purpose behind the writing of the books seems to trace the founding of the Davidic dynasty. They show that David's line was established because he was faithful before God, whereas Saul was not.

History and archaeology. In the thirty-first chapter of 1 Samuel, we are told that the Philistines cut off Saul's head, placed his weapons on display in the temple of Ashtaroth, and fastened his body to the wall of Beth-shan. First Chronicles 10:10 adds that his head was put in the temple of Dagon. The site of Beth-shan has been excavated and both these temples found. Prior to this discovery, critics questioned the historicity of the account since Ashtaroth was a Canaanite goddess and Dagon a Philistine god. Archaeology confirms that the Philistines worshiped both.

Geography. The Philistines occupied the coastal plain along the Mediterranean and constituted the greatest threat to Israel. See map 6, page 40.

Outline of First Samuel

I. Samuel's ministry (chaps. 1—7)
II. Saul's reign (chaps. 8—15)
III. David's selection (chaps. 16—31)

Overview of First Samuel

Samuel's ministry (chaps. 1—7). The book begins by describing the birth of Samuel in answer to the godly petition of his mother, Hannah (1:1–23). Following his weaning, he goes to the tabernacle at Shiloh where he becomes a servant to the high priest Eli (1:24—2:11). The godly character of Samuel contrasts with the depravity of Eli's sons (2:12–36).

God speaks to Samuel concerning the coming fall of the house of Eli, the first of many prophetic revelations given him (3:1–21). The prediction comes to pass when the sons of Eli are killed in battle with the Philistines, and the enemy captures the ark of the Covenant (4:1–11). The news of the loss of the ark so startles Eli that he falls and dies (4:12–22). The Philistines are unable to keep the ark for long because God strikes them with disease (chaps. 5—6). Samuel fills the spiritual leadership void in Israel, calling the nation to repent and exercising judgeship over the people of Israel (chap. 7).

Saul's reign (chaps. 8—15). When Samuel grows old and his sons do not walk in his ways, the people ask for a king (8:1–5). Though the request disturbs Samuel (who sees it as trusting man rather than God), the Lord instructs him to appoint a king (8:6–22). The one chosen is Saul, and Samuel anoints him as the first king of Israel (chaps. 9–10). In his first military campaign against the Ammonites who invaded from the east, Saul wins a great victory (chap. 11). Samuel then makes a farewell speech to the nation (chap. 12). Not long after, Saul fails a spiritual test when he disobeys a specific command from Samuel and usurps the role of the prophet (13:1–12). This act discloses willfulness on the part of Saul that disqualifies him as king (13:13–14). In his place, God will raise up another whose heart is right towards him (13:14). Afterwards, Saul's behavior becomes increasingly rash (13:15—14:52). He furthers his fall by again disobeying God (15:1–19). Samuel rebukes him with some of the best-known words in First Samuel: "Has the LORD as great delight in burnt offerings and sacrifices, as in obeying the voice of the LORD? Behold, to obey is better than sacrifice, and to heed than the fat of rams. For rebellion is as the sin of witchcraft, and stubbornness is as iniquity and idolatry. Because you have rejected the word of the LORD, he also has rejected you from being king" (15:22–23).

David's selection (chaps. 16—31). With Saul rejected by the Lord, Samuel turns to the task of anointing his successor. God guides him to David (16:1–13). Shortly thereafter, David comes into the service of Saul as a court musician (16:14–23). At this point, Saul does not know that David has been chosen as his successor. He pays no attention to him until David courageously slays the imposing Philistine warrior known as Goliath (chap. 17). Thereafter, Saul becomes increasingly jealous and suspicious of the young hero (18:6–16), so he attempts to subvert and destroy David (18:17–30). When that fails, he openly explodes into hostility towards David. The youth flees into the wilderness where he lives as a hunted man (chaps. 19–26). Growing weary of his life as a fugitive, David unwisely becomes the vassal of a lord of the Philistines. The Philistines gather for war against Israel, and only the protests of the other lords against David's presence in their ranks get him out of the predicament (29:1–11). Meanwhile, Saul—failing to get any prophetic word from the Lord—turns to a medium (28:6–10). She channels the spirit of the now dead Samuel, who announces Saul's coming death in battle (28:11–25). The Philistines triumph, and Saul dies in battle (chap. 31).

Outline of Second Samuel

   I. David's triumphs (chaps. 1—10)
  II. David's troubles (chaps. 11—21)
 III. David's achievements (chaps. 22—24)

Overview of Second Samuel

David's triumphs (chaps. 1—10). News of Saul's death is brought to David (1:1–10). Rather than rejoicing as one might expect, David laments the death of Saul and his son, Jonathan (1:11–27). This reveals the purity of David's heart. Afterwards, the men of Judah seek him and make him king over that large tribe in Israel (2:1–8). Meanwhile, one of Saul's remaining sons, Ishbosheth, is made king over the other tribes (2:8–10). For the next seven years, the two groups struggle for supremacy, with David growing in power (2:12–32). When Ishbosheth is assassinated (chap. 4), David becomes king over all the tribes, beginning a forty-year reign (5:1–4).

Following battlefield victories, Israel is established as a major world power (5:7–25; 8:1—10:19). Success does not dampen David's desire for the Lord. He brings the ark of God to Jerusalem, his new capital (chap. 6) and intends to build a temple for the Lord (7:2). While God forbids him to do so (since he is a man of war), he does promise David that his house, kingdom, and throne would endure forever (7:16). This promise (called the Davidic covenant) insured that David would never lack a man to rule (Ps. 89:29). Ultimately, this promise descended upon Jesus (Matt. 1:1).

David's troubles (chaps. 11—21). While David was a godly man, he was not perfect. Late one night, he succumbs to temptation and commits adultery with Bathsheba, the wife of a deployed soldier named Uriah. When she conceives, David tries to cover his deed by recalling Uriah from battle under a false pretense. When Uriah refuses to sleep with his wife while his comrades remain at war, David resorts to homicide. He orders General Joab to place Uriah in the thick of battle where he is fatally wounded. David then takes Bathsheba into his harem (chap. 11). God does not allow David's sin to pass unnoticed but he sends the prophet Nathan who dramatically confronts David. This evokes David's confession. While God forgives David (assuring David's life and salvation), he disciplines him nevertheless (12:1–14).[18] A succession of troubles afflicts David and his family (12:15—21:14). However, as if to show him that he is truly

forgiven, Solomon, David's successor, is born to him and Bathsheba
(12:24–25).

David's achievements (chaps. 22—24). The last three chapters
describe how David writes a song in praise of God, gathers mighty war-
riors, and acquires the property on which the temple would later stand.
These illustrate three areas in which he excelled: hymnody, leadership,
and devotion to God.

Christ in First and Second Samuel. The Davidic covenant
forms the basis for much of the New Testament understanding of
Christ. It is significant that the first verse of the New Testament
describes him as the son (and thus heir to the promises of) David. A frequent term for Jesus is "the Son of David." The conclusion of the Book
of Revelation shows Jesus returning in power as the exalted King of
kings who institutes his reign over the earth, thus fulfilling the promise
to David (Rev. 19:11—20:6). The very term *Christ* (Hebrew, *Messiah*) is a
designation of Jesus as King. The term *the Christ* means "the Anointed."
This refers to anointing the king with oil as the act of investiture. David
himself is a type of Christ: both come from Bethlehem; both are fully
devoted to God; both were initially rejected by Israel; both are shep-
herds to Israel; both build the kingdom.

Key Verses

1 Samuel 15:22—23: recorded on page 50.

Key Chapter

2 Samuel 7: the Davidic covenant.

Message of First and Second Samuel

The books of Samuel teach us that God honors those who honor him.
As noted above (1 Sam. 15:22), this means that God looks for faithful

obedience. Many examples can be found in the books: Hannah, the faithful, obedient parent, is contrasted with Eli, the not-so-faithful priest and negligent father. Samuel, the faithful, obedient child, is contrasted with Eli's faithless and disobedient sons. David, the faithful and obedient shepherd, is contrasted with Saul, the willful and disobedient king. When David transgresses God's command, his fellowship with God is broken until he confesses. In all this, we see that godly living, the type God honors, is living in faithful obedience to the Lord.

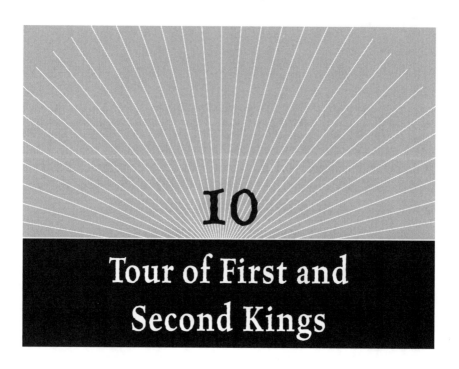

Tour of First and Second Kings

Preview of First and Second Kings

First and Second Kings are just that—a history of the kings that followed David. His immediate successor was his son Solomon, whose wealth and wisdom are legendary. But for all his wisdom, Solomon tolerated and even aided the idolatry of his foreign wives. Because of that, the kingdom broke in two at his death, never again to be reunited. The kings of the resulting kingdoms were no better in combating idolatry, with a few notable exceptions. Judgment fell on the Northern Kingdom when Assyria invaded it in 722 B.C. A similar fate overtook the Southern Kingdom of Judah at the hands of Babylon in 586 B.C. Thus, First and Second Kings trace the fall of the Hebrew nation from the pinnacle of glory to their loss of statehood.

Introduction to First and Second Kings

Title. Originally, First and Second Kings were, like First and Second Samuel, one book. The name, Kings, reflects the content of the books—

the reigns of the various kings of the Northern and Southern Kingdoms. This period of kingship lasted about four hundred years, as did the other periods in Israel's history. The chart below depicts these.

Periods in Israel's History

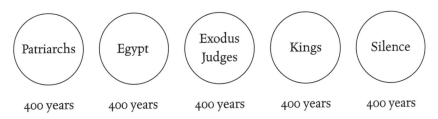

Patriarchs	Egypt	Exodus Judges	Kings	Silence
400 years	400 years	400 years	400 years	400 years

Author. Tradition ascribes authorship to the prophet Jeremiah. The likelihood that he was the author is strengthened by his remarkable absence from the books, an absence made more notable by the prominent mention of other, and in some cases, lesser prophets. The author of Kings used several sources of information. These include the Book of the Acts of Solomon (1 Kings 11:41); the Book of the Chronicles of the Kings of Israel (14:19); and the Book of the Chronicles of the Kings of Judah (14:29). While these books are no longer in existence, their mention assures us that the information within Kings is historically accurate.

Date of writing. These books describe the period of the monarchy from the time of Solomon (970 B.C.), to the division of the kingdom following him, to the fall of Jerusalem to Babylon in 586 B.C., ending with mention of the release of Jehoiachin c. 560 B.C. Since Kings records events as late as 560 B.C., it is likely that the book was written shortly afterwards, possibly around 550 B.C. It is possible that the bulk of the books were completed earlier and the concluding episode recorded by a later editor.

Theme. These books trace the fall of the kingdom. In the true sense of the word, they are tragic, beginning on the high note of Solomon's greatness and ending with the Jews being a dispersed people with no nation of their own. So *kingdoms in decline* is the theme.

Purpose. These books were not intended to merely record political events of the times but to subject them to a spiritual analysis. The emphasis on the Law and the prophets found here suggests that the author's purpose was to show how each king fared depending on his obedience or disobedience to God's Law.

History and archaeology. Archeological finds have clarified or corroborated many points in Kings. Digs at Phoenician temples have shown that the design of Solomon's temple followed the same general pattern. In terms of its decoration with pomegranates, palm trees, and so on, a close correspondence has been shown to other temples of the period. The discovery of the Moabite Stone in 1868 gave the Moabite version of the events recorded in Second Kings 3. Moreover, Omri, King of Israel, is mentioned in Assyrian records a hundred years after his reign.

Geography. During the period of the monarchy, the kingdom of Israel reached its zenith under David and Solomon but then was divided by civil war. The northern tribes formed a separate kingdom, while the tribe of Judah remained loyal to the house of David. In general, the Northern Kingdom is referred to as Israel, with Samaria its capital, and the Southern Kingdom as Judah, with Jerusalem its capital.

Outline of First Kings

   I. Solomon reigns (chaps. 1—11)
  II. The kingdom wanes (chaps. 12—22)

Overview of First Kings

Solomon reigns (chaps. 1—11). David appoints Solomon to succeed him on the throne, and Zadok, the high priest, anoints him (chap. 1). Following the death of his father, Solomon purges the kingdom of his enemies (chap. 2). Realizing his inexperience, he asks God for wisdom to rule (chap. 3). Thereafter, he grows powerful and famous (chap. 4). The crowning achievement of Solomon's reign is the construction of the temple of the Lord (chaps. 5—8). Under his leadership,

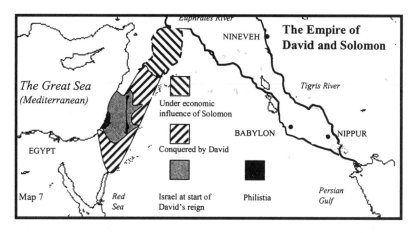

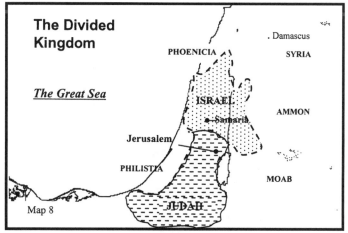

the nation achieves a degree of political stability not known before or after (chaps. 9—10). However, the greatness of Solomon is diminished in his latter years since his many foreign wives[19] turn his heart towards idolatry (chap. 11). This defection from the pure worship of God would have disastrous consequences.

The kingdom wanes (chaps. 12—22). Because of his apostasy, Solomon's kingdom is torn asunder. God raises up an adversary, Jeroboam, to Solomon's son, Rehoboam. Jeroboam establishes himself as king over the ten northern tribes of Israel (chap. 12). Very quickly,

Jeroboam institutes an idol cult, setting a pattern to be followed by every northern king thereafter (12:25—13:34).

The generally wicked deeds of both the northern and southern kings are recalled (chaps. 14—16). As the worship of Baal grows in Israel, God raises up Elijah[20] the prophet (chap. 17). He calls for a famine on the land, which afflicts the unrepentant nation for three years. At the end of those years, Elijah has a contest with the prophets of Baal on Mount Carmel (chap. 18). His demonstration of God's power has some effect on the nation but none on wicked King Ahab and his pagan wife, Jezebel. Elijah must flee for his life to Horeb (Sinai) (chap. 19).

Upon his return, Elijah anoints Elisha to succeed him. The final two chapters describe the continuing wickedness of Ahab and his death in battle.

Outline of Second Kings

I. The deterioration and fall of Israel (chaps. 1—17)
II. The deterioration and fall of Judah (chaps. 18—25)

Overview of Second Kings

The deterioration and fall of Israel (chaps. 1—17). Elijah completes his ministry and is taken into heaven (chaps. 1—2). Elisha then receives the Spirit that was on Elijah and conducts a miraculous ministry (chaps. 2—8). Nevertheless, the spiritual condition of the Northern and Southern Kingdoms progressively grows worse (chaps. 9—16). Then Assyria invades in 722 B.C., destroys the Northern Kingdom, and takes the survivors captive (chap. 17).

The deterioration and fall of Judah (chaps. 18—25). Following the destruction and deportation of the northern tribes, Judah limps along for another 136 years until a similar fate befalls it. While kings Hezekiah (chaps. 18—20) and Josiah (chaps. 22—23) lead the nation in times of revival and spiritual renewal, these are only temporary. Under wicked and weak kings (most notably, Manasseh, chap. 21), the nation continues to move away from God and towards destruction. Finally, Babylon invades and destroys the nation, taking a remnant captive and leaving only the poorest in the land (chap. 25). G. Campbell Morgan summarizes this time as one of "degraded ideals, deadened consciences, and defeated purposes."[21]

Theological Highlights

Concerning God. First and Second Kings reveal four things concerning God. First, God reveals himself to his people so they might know his will. In the time of the kings, many prophets came forward and spoke the Word of God to the nation. Likewise, the Word of God continues to speak to his people today.

Second, God is faithful to his Word. Promises God made to Abraham and David were fulfilled in the reign of Solomon (though not exhaustively). The further fulfillment of his promises may be expected.

Third, God is sovereign. No nation is beyond the scope of his power.

Fourth, God is patient. He endured the rebellion and unfaithfulness of Israel for several centuries prior to bringing the kingdom to a complete end.

Christ in First and Second Kings

Solomon is a type or foreshadowing of Christ. Points of similarity include

- Both are David's sons
- Both have reigns characterized by peace (1 Kings 4:24; Isa. 9:7)
- Both are loved by God (2 Sam. 12:24; Matt. 3:17)
- Both build temples (1 Kings 6; Eph. 2:21)

Key Verses

1 Kings 9:4–5: "Now if you walk before Me as your father David walked, in integrity of heart and in uprightness, to do according to all that I have

commanded you, and if you keep My statutes and My judgments, then I will establish the throne of your kingdom over Israel forever, as I promised David your father, saying, 'You shall not fail to have a man on the throne of Israel.'"

2 Kings 21:14–15: "So I will forsake the remnant of My inheritance and deliver them into the hand of their enemies; and they shall become victims of plunder to all their enemies, 'because they have done evil in My sight, and have provoked Me to anger since the day their fathers came out of Egypt, even to this day.'"

Key Chapters

1 Kings 12: the division of the kingdom.

2 Kings 17: the fall of Israel.

2 Kings 25: the fall of Judah.

Message of First and Second Kings

The books of First and Second Kings warn us that the well-being and prosperity of a nation cannot be divorced from its spiritual life. Under Solomon, the nation enjoyed wealth, power, and good administration. However, all this was lost in the moral and spiritual erosion that took place. Even so, a nation today cannot remain externally strong while at the same time being spiritually weak.

Kings of Israel and Judah

Israel	Judah
Jeroboam (22 years)	Rehoboam (17 years)
	Abijam (3)
Nadab (2)	Asa (41)
Baasha (24)	
Elah (2)	
Zimri (1 week)	
Omri (12)	
Ahab (22)	Jehoshaphat (25)
Ahaziah (2)	
Jehoram (12)	Jehoram (12)
Jehu (28)	Ahaziah (1)
	Athaliah (6)
Jehoahaz (17)	Joash (40)
Jehoash (16)	Amaziah (29)
Jeroboam II (41)	Uzziah (52)
Zechariah (1/2)	
Shallum (1 month)	
Menahem (10)	
Pekahiah (2)	
Pekah (20)	Jotham (16)
Hoshea (9)	Ahaz (16)
	Hezekiah (29)
	Manasseh (55)
	Amon (2)
	Josiah (31)
	Jehoahaz (3 months)
	Jehoiakim (11)
	Jehoiachin (3 months)
	Zedekiah (11)

(Note: Many of the regencies above were overlapping, especially in Judah, where fathers and sons shared a coregency.)

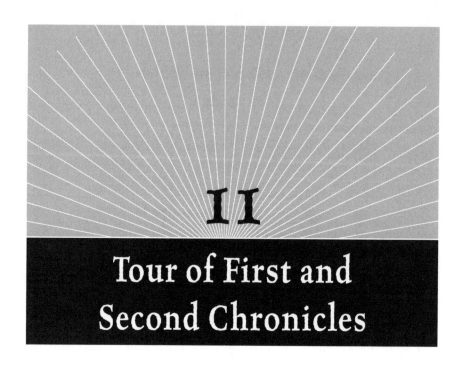

Tour of First and Second Chronicles

Preview of First and Second Chronicles

The books of First and Second Chronicles cover the same time as that of Second Samuel through Second Kings. They differ in that Second Samuel and First and Second Kings are interested in the political history of Israel and Judah, whereas First and Second Chronicles are concerned with the religious history of Judah. Also, the books of Chronicles give more attention to the ministry of the priests and the temple, whereas Samuel and Kings devote more attention to the ministries of prophets.

Introduction to First and Second Chronicles

Author. According to the ancient Jewish writing known as the Talmud, the author of Chronicles was Ezra the scribe. He was among the exiles returning to Judah from Babylon in the fifth century B.C. In writing Chronicles, he originally wrote a single book, which, like the books of Samuel and Kings, was divided by later translators.

Date of writing. Knowing that Ezra returned during the reign of Artaxerxes I (464–423 B.C.; see Ezra 7:1), the writing of Chronicles may be placed around 450 B.C.

Theme. The theme of Chronicles may be stated as *a commentary on Judah*. Of special interest are the kings descended from David that reigned over the Southern Kingdom of Judah. The Northern Kingdom of Israel is only mentioned in passing. Moreover, because the temple was located within Judah, much attention is given to its role in the life of the nation. The chart below summarizes the differences between Samuel, Kings, and Chronicles.

Samuel and Kings verus Chronicles

Samuel and Kings	Chronicles
Focus equally on north & south	Focuses on Southern Kingdom
All kings are of interest	Davidic kings are of interest
Attention to prophetic ministry	Attention to priestly ministry
Little emphasis on the temple	Much emphasis on the temple

Purpose. Chronicles was written to trace the fortunes of Judah, showing that the glory enjoyed under David and Solomon was lost as the kings and people proved increasingly unfaithful to God. The construction and later neglect and loss of the temple are prominent. Given that Chronicles was written when Jews were attempting to reconstruct the temple and reestablish national existence, a further purpose is evident: Chronicles was intended to help them rediscover their spiritual heritage, while avoiding the idolatry of the past. Thus, it placed their tragic loss into a theological perspective.

History and archaeology. The invasion of Shishak as given in 2 Chronicles 12:2–16 is also mentioned in his inscriptions on the temple of Karnak in Luxor, Egypt. The discovery of the Ben-Hadad stele or pillar in 1940 confirmed the chronology of Second Chronicles 16:1–10.

Geography. Chronicles begins in Judah but ends in Babylonia. The last of the Davidic kings, Zedekiah, is overthrown by Nebuchadnezzar of Babylon who takes the survivors into captivity in 586 B.C. They began to return in 536 B.C. when Persia overthrew Babylon. See map 7, page 57.

Outline of First Chronicles

    I. Genealogies from Adam to Saul (chaps. 1—10)
   II. The reign of David (chaps. 11—29)

Overview of First Chronicles

Genealogies from Adam to Saul (chaps. 1—10). Unlike modern people, the returning Jews would have found the extensive genealogical section of interest for at least three reasons. First, it established the family trees of the returning exiles, especially for priests and Levites, thus qualifying them for temple service. Second, it demonstrated that although God had permitted the nation to suffer, he had faithfully maintained the line of David, keeping alive the messianic hope. Third, it illustrated how those who kept faith with God were blessed above others. Thus, Jacob is blessed over Esau and David over Saul.

The reign of David (chaps. 11—29). The chronicler tells us how David came to make Jerusalem his capital (chaps. 11—12). Thereafter, in the pivotal part of the book, it describes how David tried to make Jerusalem the spiritual as well as political capital. He did this first by bringing the ark of the covenant there (chaps. 13—16) and second, by conceiving the idea of building the temple (chap. 17).

While God honored David's desire by promising him that one of his descendants would retain the right to reign (17:11), the honor of building the temple would go to his son (17:12). Thereafter, the book describes his battlefield victories (chaps. 18—20). The placement of this section links the faithfulness of David to his later success—a lesson the chronicler did not want lost on the returnees. The book next tells of the actual preparations David made for the temple in acquiring land and materials for construction (chaps. 21—27). The final chapters contain David's last address to his son Solomon and to the nation.

Outline of Second Chronicles

I. The reign of Solomon (chaps. 1—9)
II. The succeeding kings of Judah (chaps. 10—36)

Overview of Second Chronicles

The reign of Solomon (chaps. 1—9). Israel enters her golden age under Solomon. Wealth increases (1:15), and peace is undisturbed. However, the glory of the age is found in the construction of the temple. Six of the nine chapters describe this project. The significance of this building is that it symbolized the presence of God among the Hebrew people.

The succeeding kings of Judah (chaps. 10—36). Following the death of Solomon, a division occurs in the nation. The ten northern tribes revolt, leaving the Davidic kings with only Judah. With few exceptions, they prove to be ungodly men who do not follow the ways of David. The narrative makes it clear that the fortunes of each king are tied to his walk with God and respect for the temple. Finally, things deteriorate to the point where God sends Babylon against the nation (36:19–21). The book closes on a positive note, telling how once Persia defeats Babylon, the Jews are permitted to return to their land (36:22–23).

Theological Highlights

God's Blessing. Chronicles shows that "God honors those who honor him." In the words of E. M. Bounds in his book, *Power Through Prayer*: "Men are God's method. The Church is looking for better methods; God is looking for better men." Today, as yesterday, when God finds a man or woman whose heart is surrendered to him, he can do great things through that person.

God's Worship

The attention given to the temple in Chronicles shows that worship is central, not peripheral, to the well-being of God's people. In the words of Jesus (John 4:23), God seeks those who worship him "in spirit and truth."

Key Verses

1 Chronicles 17:11–12: "And it shall be, when your days are fulfilled, when you must go *to be* with your fathers, that I will set up your seed after you, who will be of your sons; and I will establish his kingdom. He shall build Me a house, and I will establish his throne forever."

2 Chronicles 7:14: "If My people who are called by My name will humble themselves, and pray and seek My face, and turn from their wicked ways, then I will hear from heaven, and will forgive their sin and heal their land."

2 Chronicles 16:9, "For the eyes of the LORD run to and fro throughout the whole earth, to show Himself strong on behalf of those whose heart is loyal to Him."

Key Chapters

1 Chronicles 17: God's promise to David.

2 Chronicles 6—9: the construction of the temple.

Message of First and Second Chronicles

The promising note on which Chronicles ends suggests a hopeful lesson: The purposes of God will not fail. Despite the unfaithfulness of men and the misfortunes of war, God's plans both for and through his people will be realized. Chronicles shows how he kept alive both a remnant of Israel and the line of David just as promised. Even so, no matter how dark the hour might seem today, God will continue to advance his plan to establish his kingdom.

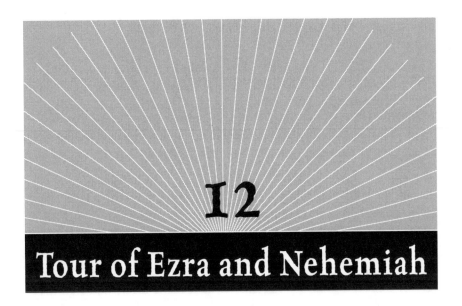

12

Tour of Ezra and Nehemiah

Preview of Ezra and Nehemiah

Following the captivity, a remnant of about fifty thousand Jews left Babylon and journeyed back to their ancestral homeland. Ezra and Nehemiah tell how they reestablished their religious and civil life.

Introduction to Ezra and Nehemiah

Authors. Tradition states that Ezra wrote the book that bears his name, as well as the Book of Nehemiah. In ancient times, these two were circulated as one book. However, the many personal references found in Nehemiah suggest that either Nehemiah authored that book or a diary Ezra used. If Ezra used Nehemiah's diary, that would account for the tradition that he wrote Nehemiah while explaining the personal references in Nehemiah.

Date of writing. Ezra and Nehemiah were written near the end of the Old Testament period, c. 425 B.C.

Themes. Ezra's theme is *the erection of the temple*. The book tells how the returning Jews rebuilt their place of worship. Nehemiah's theme is the new city walls. His concern was for the safety and defense of Jerusalem. With its old walls in ruins, it was in constant danger.

Purposes. The burden of the Book of Ezra is to show how God's plans for the Jews would continue by means of the temple and the Law, despite the loss of kingship. Similarly, Nehemiah was written to demonstrate God's protection of the postexilic community in its efforts to reestablish its national existence.

History and archaeology. Judah both fell and returned in stages. Looking back, we see that the Babylonians made three deportations of the Jews, the last coinciding with the destruction of Jerusalem.

1. In 605 B.C. Nebuchadnezzar, following his defeat of Assyria and Egypt at the Battle of Carchemish, made Judah a vassal state and took a few captives (including Daniel) back to Babylon.
2. In 598 B.C. he returned and reasserted his control, taking Jehoiachin and other nobles to Babylon.
3. Finally, in 586 B.C. Nebuchadnezzar crushed the rebellion of Zedekiah, destroyed Jerusalem, and took the survivors to Babylon.

From 586 to 539 B.C., the Jews lived as exiles in the land of Babylon. However, the Persians (or Medes and Persians) overthrew the Babylonians themselves. The following year, 538 B.C., the emperor Cyrus issued a decree that permitted the Jews to return to their homeland (Ezra 1:2–4). The return, like the exile, was accomplished in stages.

1. In 538 B.C. approximately fifty thousand Jews returned under the leadership of Zerubbabel (presumably the same as "Sheshbazzar the prince of Judah" mentioned in 1:8 and therefore a descendant of David). They successfully rebuilt the temple, although not without opposition and delay.
2. In 458 B.C. Ezra, a scribe, returned with a small entourage of about one thousand with the purpose of reinvigorating the spiritual lives of the returnees.

3. Then in 445 B.C., Nehemiah returned with permission to rebuild the walls of Jerusalem. He completed this task in 52 days (Neh. 6:15), although events of the book cover another thirteen years.

Seventy years? Looking at these dates, it could be asked why the Exile is said to have lasted seventy years, since only forty-seven years elapsed from the destruction of Jerusalem to the first return. The figure of seventy years[22] can be calculated in two ways. One may either subtract the year of the completion of the second temple from the year of the destruction of the first (586–516 = 70), or one may count the years between the first deportation to the laying of the foundation of the second temple (605–535 = 70).

Many archeological finds support the historical nature of these books. Among these are the Cyrus cylinder and Nabonidus chronicle. Both are cuneiform documents that report Cyrus' desire to win favor with people previously taken captive by Babylon. They relate how he gave them the freedom to return to their ancestral homes and to rebuild the temples of their gods. Since Judah provided a buffer state with Persia's not-yet-defeated enemy, Egypt, the goodwill of the Jews would have been of special interest to him.

Geography. The Persian Empire dominated the world from the collapse of Babylon (538 B.C.) to the coming of Alexander the Great (334 B.C.). At its height, it extended west to Greece, east to India, south through Egypt, and north to the Black, Caspian, and Aral Seas.

Outline of Ezra

   I. The exiles return (chaps. 1—2)
  II. The temple is rebuilt (chaps. 3—6)
 III. Ezra returns (chaps. 7—8)
 IV. The people are revived (chaps. 9—10)

Overview of Ezra

The exiles return (chaps. 1—2). In the first year of Cyrus the king, he issues a decree permitting the Jews to return to Judah and

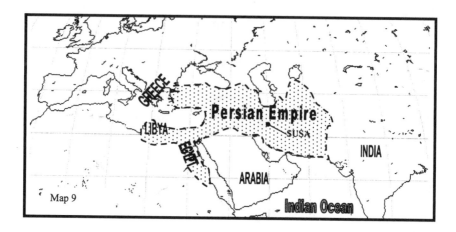

Map 9

rebuild their temple. Out of an estimated two-to-three million Jews then alive, only some fifty thousand elect to leave the security and comfort of their homes in Babylon to make the perilous trip. Those who do so are led by Zerubbabel (Sheshbazzar), a surviving prince of Judah.

The Temple is rebuilt (chaps. 3—6). The first act performed by the returning Jews is the restoration of the altar and the resumption of sacrifices (3:1–3). They proceed to lay the foundation of the temple (3:8–13). However, opposition from Gentiles forces the work to halt for ten years (4:1–5). Then, the prophets Haggai and Zechariah encourage the completion of the task (5:1–2). Again they are opposed, but this time the king of Persia, Darius, supports their efforts, leading to the completion of the temple and the first observance of Passover since the time of King Josiah (6:19–22). Altogether, it took twenty years to complete the temple.

Ezra returns (chaps. 7—8). Some fifty-eight years elapse in the time between chapters 6 and 7. (During this interlude, the events of Esther occur.) The story resumes with the return of Ezra and about one to two thousand other Jews. His motive is to teach the Law (7:10). This second return, eighty-one years after the first, is under the sponsorship of King Artaxerxes I who gives financial support to the effort (7:11–24). Those undertaking the journey begin with a fast to seek God's protection, then proceed to arrive safely in Jerusalem (chap. 8).

The people are revived (9–10). Upon arriving in Jerusalem, Ezra is disturbed to find that Jews are intermarrying with foreign women (9:1–4). Knowing this will lead to idolatry and apostasy, Ezra mourns and prays. A large number of people are moved by his example and agree to end the practice of intermarrying with pagans. Those who have already done so promise to put away their foreign wives. Thus, God spares the nation.

Outline of Nehemiah

I. Nehemiah returns (1:1—2:11)
II. The walls are rebuilt (2:12—7:4)
III. The nation is reformed (7:5—13:31)

Overview of Nehemiah

Nehemiah returns (1:1—2:11). The story opens with Nehemiah in Persia where he is cupbearer to the king (1:11).[23] News about the vulnerability and disgrace of Jerusalem deeply trouble him. For months, he makes this a matter of prayer. Then one day he boldly states his feelings about Jerusalem and requests that the king allow him to return and rebuild the city (actions that could have cost him his life if the king became angry). God grants him favor in the eyes of the king, who gives him permission.

The walls are rebuilt (2:12—7:4). Upon his return to Jerusalem, Nehemiah rallies the people to the task of rebuilding the walls (2:18). However, both external and internal opposition arises (2:19; 4:1–23; 6:1–14, 17–19). The problem of the rich extorting money from the poor further complicates the task (chap. 5). Despite these problems, Nehemiah forges ahead, and the wall is completed in fifty-two days (6:15).

The nation is reformed (7:5—13:31). Once the walls of the city are completed, the need for more people to live within the city becomes apparent. Before they do, a spiritual renewal takes place following a sacred assembly at which Ezra reads the Law, and the people observe the Festival of Booths or the Feast of Tabernacles (chaps. 8—10). Then people begin to move into Jerusalem from the countryside (chap. 11). Finally, with the city repopulated, a formal ceremony is held to rededicate the walls of the city (chap. 12). With the major task completed, Nehemiah makes a trip to Persia (13:6). On his return an indefinite time later, he institutes reforms affecting Jewish relations with Gentiles, provisions for the temple, the Sabbath, and marriage (chap. 13). With these events, that period which we call "the time of the Old Testament" comes to a close. Another four hundred years will pass before the events of the New Testament start to unfold.

Theological Highlights

Concerning providence. Both Ezra and Nehemiah give dramatic examples of God providentially protecting, providing, and enabling.

Concerning the Bible. The power of Scripture to change people is seen in the revival that occurred under Ezra and Nehemiah. Ezra simply reads the Scripture, and people's hearts are pierced and their behavior transformed. While revival cannot be attributed to mechanically reading the Bible, it is doubtful that revival can take place apart from the opening of God's Word.

Key Verses

Ezra 7:10: "For Ezra had prepared his heart to seek the Law of the LORD, and to do it, and to teach statutes and in Israel ordinances."

Nehemiah 2:20: "So I answered them, and said to them, 'The God of heaven Himself will prosper us; therefore we His servants will arise and build, but you have no heritage or right or memorial in Jerusalem.'"

Key Chapters

Ezra 7: the return of the scribe to Jerusalem.

Nehemiah 1: Nehemiah's burden for Jerusalem.

Nehemiah 6: the completion of the walls.

Message of Ezra and Nehemiah

These postexilic books clearly demonstrate that God's plans for his people cannot be frustrated. Even though they were without country, temple, or power, God reestablished them in the land and continued his redemptive program. Today, it may seem that people of faith are being shoved to the margins of society while things deteriorate. Despite this, God is alive and will bring his plans to pass today as then.

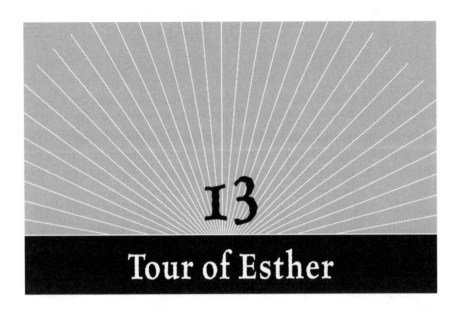

Tour of Esther

Preview of Esther

Esther is unusual among the books of the Bible for it never mentions God. The omission is so glaring that it must have been deliberate, suggesting that God works behind the scenes in the affairs of men. In this story, we find how God used a courageous young woman to save the Jews from annihilation.

Introduction to Esther

Author. While the author of Esther is unknown, there is an old belief that the same Mordecai as mentioned in the book wrote it. Others suggest that Ezra wrote it.

Date of writing. While Esther appears after Ezra and Nehemiah, it may have been written first. The events therein occurred between those recorded in Ezra 1–6 and 7–10. So an approximate date of 460 B.C. can be assigned to Esther, although a later date is entirely possible.

Theme. Esther's theme is escape for the Jews. This book tells how a plot to exterminate the Jews is foiled by Esther and her uncle Mordecai.

Purpose. The purpose behind Esther seems to have been to show God's providence. Though he is hidden, he actively watches over his people. The lack of mention of God only serves to underscore this theme of providence (the hidden working of God in the daily lives of his people).

History and archaeology. The book opens with the mention of a Persian king, Ahasuerus. He is better known by the name Xerxes I, a king who reigned from 485–464 B.C. The fire that destroyed his palace made archeological evidence surrounding Esther scarce. However, a cuneiform text has been found that mentions a high official during the reign of Xerxes named Marduka, presumably the same man as Mordecai in the story. The chart below illustrates the chronological relationship of events in Esther to those in Ezra.

Chronological Relationship of Events in Esther to Ezra

Ezra 1—6 Zerubbabel returns	Esther 1—10 ← 58 years →	Ezra 7—10 Ezra returns

Geography. Events in Esther occurred in the capital of the Persian Empire, Susa. See map 9, page 70.

Outline of Esther

   I. Esther becomes queen (chaps. 1—2)
  II. Haman schemes (chap. 3)
 III. The plot frustrated (chaps. 4—8)
 IV. Purim celebrated (chaps. 9—10)

Overview of Esther

Esther becomes queen (chaps. 1—2). The Persian king Ahasuerus (Xerxes) at a drunken party demands that his queen, Vashti, sacrifice her modesty for the entertainment of the king's guests. When she refuses to do so, she is deposed and the search (something of a beauty contest) begins for a new queen. Esther, an orphaned Jewish girl raised by her uncle Mordecai, is chosen as the new queen.

Haman schemes (chap. 3). Shortly after Esther is made queen, her uncle, Mordecai, gives offense to Haman, the king's counselor.[24] So enraged is Haman that he plots not only the destruction of Mordecai but of all the Jews. By a combination of trickery and bribery, he gains the consent of Xerxes to exterminate them. In so doing, Xerxes does not realize the danger to Esther, for he does not know that she is Jewish.

The plot frustrated (4:1—10:3). Upon learning of the decree against the Jews, Mordecai appeals to Esther to use her position to frustrate the plan (chap. 4). She agrees to do so, although it would mean approaching the king without his first summoning her (an act punishable by death unless the king extends his golden rod). After three days of fasting, Esther approaches the king and asks him to attend a banquet she planned for him and Haman. She loses nerve the first day and requests they come back the next day. Meanwhile, Haman has a gallows built for the special execution of Mordecai (chap. 5). God intervenes by causing the king to honor Mordecai for previous service (chap. 6). This is a harbinger of the downfall of Haman. When the king and Haman come to the second banquet of the queen, she reveals her identity and exposes the plot of Haman. In a stroke of irony, the king commands Haman to be hung on the gallows he had prepared for Mordecai (chap. 7). The king then issues a second edict permitting the Jews to defend themselves from their enemies, thus assuring they would not be exterminated (8:1—9:17).

Purim celebrated. Realizing that this has come from God, the Jews institute the Feast of Purim to celebrate their deliverance (9:18–32).[25] Mordecai becomes second in the kingdom next to Xerxes (10:1–3).

Theological Highlights

Concerning God. Esther is a curious book in that it teaches an immensely important lesson about God without directly mentioning him. He is as hidden in the book as he can be in life. Yet God's hand is obviously at work, returning Haman's evil to him and delivering the Jews from great death. Thus, the book illustrates God's providence.

Christ in Esther. In many ways, Esther foreshadows our Lord Jesus Christ. The chart below illustrates.[26]

Christ's Shadow and Fulfillment in Esther

Shadow	Fulfillment
Esther's three-day period of fasting began during the daylight hours of the first day of Passover, Nisan 14.[27]	Jesus' three-day period of death began around 3:00 P.M. on the first day of Passover, Nisan 14.
Fasting such as Esther's represented affliction and humiliation in the Old Testament, and her change into mourning clothes symbolized a death-like state.	Jesus' three days of death is identified as his period of humiliation or affliction (Phil. 2:8).
Esther's period of fasting, symbolic of death, ended on the third day.	Jesus rose from the dead on the third day.
On concluding her fast but before she presented herself to the king, Esther changed into her royal robes (5:1).	At the time of his resurrection but before his ascension to the Father, Jesus was clothed "in glory" (1 Cor. 15:20, 43)
On the basis of her fast, Esther presented herself to the king who then accepted her into his presence (5:2).	Jesus, on the basis of his sacrificial death, presented himself to the Father and was accepted into the Holy of Holies in heaven (Heb. 9:12, 24).
As a result of Esther's actions, her people were saved, and many Gentiles became Jews (which would require circumcision) (8:17).	Jesus' death provides salvation for "the lost sheep of the house of Israel" (Matt. 15:24), and many Gentiles, through spiritual circumcision, partake of this salvation (Col. 2:11).

Key Verse

Esther 4:14: "For if you remain completely silent at this time, relief and deliverance will arise for the Jews from another place, but you and your father's house will perish. Yet who knows whether you have come to the kingdom for such a time as this?"

Key Chapter

Esther 7: The plot against the Jews is foiled.

Message of Esther

What is a crisis to us is no crisis to God. Neither people nor events can thwart his plans. Therefore, when we encounter evil, we must act boldly while trusting mightily in his unseen presence and ongoing providence.

14

Coming Up Next:
The Poetic Books

The Old Testament and Poetry

The Hebrew Bible contains extensive poetry. Only a handful of books have no poetic sections whatsoever. However, while poetry decorates most Old Testament books, there are five totally poetic books: Job, Psalms, Proverbs, Ecclesiastes, and the Song of Solomon. Whereas the historical books are concerned with the past and the prophetic books with the future, these five are concerned with the present experience of life. Their practical themes make them among the most popular books of the Bible.

Type of Book and Temporal Orientation

Type of Book	Temporal Orientation
History	Past
Poetry	Present
Prophecy	Future

Categories of Hebrew Poetry

The poetic books fall into three categories. The first, which was intended to be accompanied by the harp or lyre, is called *lyric* poetry. This is the predominant type in the Book of Psalms. It is characterized by strong emotional elements. Because the second type teaches principles by which to live, it is called *didactic* (i.e., teaching) poetry. The books belonging to this type are Proverbs and Ecclesiastes. Due to its intense drama, the third category of poetry is appropriately termed *dramatic* poetry. Both the Book of Job and the Song of Solomon belong in this category.

Type of Poetry and Where Found

Type of Poetry	Where Found
Lyric (accompanied by lyre or harp)	Psalms
Didactic (teaching)	Proverbs, Ecclesiastes
Dramatic	Job, Song of Solomon

Characteristics of Hebrew Poetry

Unlike Western poetry that is based on meter and rhyme, Hebrew poetry is based upon a stylistic balance of thoughts. This device is known as *parallelism* because one thought will be balanced or paralleled by a succeeding thought. Several varieties of parallelisms have been identified.

Synonymous parallelism. In this the thought of the first line is restated in the second line. For example, Psalm 24:1:
    The earth is the LORD's, and all its fullness,
    The world and those who dwell therein.
    Notice how the second line essentially repeats the thought of the first.

Antithetic parallelism. This variety is the opposite of the preceding in that the thought of the second line contrasts with the first. An example is found in Psalm 1:6:
    For the LORD knows the way of the righteous,
    But the way of the ungodly shall perish.
    The way of the righteous is set over against the way of the ungodly.

Synthetic parallelism. Here, the second line completes the thought of the first. Proverbs 26:4 illustrates:

Do not answer a fool according to his folly,
Lest you also be like him.

What's wrong with answering a fool in kind? You will be no better than a fool yourself.

Climactic parallelism. This type of parallelism moves to an emotional peak or climax in the second line. Consider Psalm 29:1:

Give unto the LORD, O you mighty ones,
Give unto the LORD glory and strength.

Not until the end of the second line do we know what to give to the Lord. The suspense generated by the first line is resolved in the second.

Emblematic parallelism. This final type of parallelism makes a comparison but without the use of words such as *like* or *as*. A literal rendering of Proverbs 25:25 illustrates:

As cold water to a weary soul,
So is good news from a far country.

Try to classify the following kinds of parallelism. The answers are in the endnotes.[28]

Proverbs 15:17, "Better is a dinner of herbs where love is, than a fatted calf with hatred."

Proverbs 11:22, "As a ring of gold in a swine's snout, so is a lovely woman who lacks discretion."

Psalm 19:2, "Day unto day utters speech, and night unto night reveals knowledge."

Proverbs 10:1, "A wise son makes a glad father, but a foolish son is the grief of his mother."

Psalm 94:3, "LORD, how long will the wicked, how long will the wicked triumph?"

The Books of Wisdom

Job, Proverbs, and Ecclesiastes are sometimes called the "wisdom books" because they offer people down-to-earth wisdom. Unlike much that is called wisdom in the world today, Hebrew wisdom is both practical and God-centered. It assumes that life is best when lived in the fear of the Lord. "The fear of the LORD is the beginning of wisdom, and the knowledge of the Holy One is understanding" (Prov. 9:10).

Overview of the Poetic Books

Job. This is the story of a man who loses all that is precious to him for no apparent reason. While confronting our expectation that life should always be sensible and fair, the book points towards faith and away from doubt when life comes tumbling down.

Psalms. Here is the hymnbook of ancient Israel. Unlike the rest of the Bible where God speaks to people, people speak to God in the Psalms. For this reason, the Psalms are often used as aids to prayer.

Proverbs. Nuggets of wisdom comprise the bulk of this book. It is intended to give the young and the naïve the insights of the spiritually mature.

Ecclesiastes. This volume shows the futility of living with a strictly "under the sun" perspective, a phrase used twenty-nine times. In other words, it illustrates how senseless life is when considered from a strictly earthly point of view.

The Song of Solomon. This is a love story. While often interpreted allegorically as a picture of Christ's love for the church, it probably intends to celebrate the physical and emotional dimensions of marriage.

Composition of the Poetic Books

Most of the poetry books, or large sections thereof, were composed during the reigns of David and Solomon. An exception is the Book of Job, which appears to have been written much earlier.

The Poetic Books

Book	Category	Emphasis	Author
Job	Dramatic	Faith	Unknown
Psalms	Lyric	Prayers	Mostly David
Proverbs	Didactic	Conduct	Solomon
Ecclesiastes	Didactic	Futility	Solomon
Song of Solomon	Dramatic	Marital love	Solomon

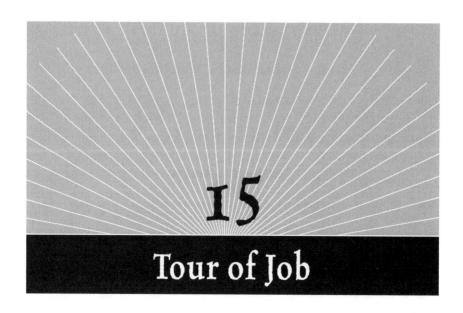

Tour of Job

Preview of Job

Suffering has been called "the atheist's best argument," for nothing else so challenges faith. Yet Job shows that we most need faith when suffering and that faith is refined in suffering.

Introduction to Job

Author. Unknown.

Date of writing. Just as the author is unknown, so is the date of writing. Both the time when the book was written and the time when Job lived are shrouded in mystery. Due to the antiquity of the place names, scholars guess that Job lived either before or during the time of Abraham. The rabbinical view is that the book was written before the time of Moses and that he translated it into Hebrew.

Theme. Jehovah permits suffering. This ancient book explores the ageless problem of suffering. Without directly answering the question, Why do the innocent suffer? it shows that God is sovereign over suffering and deserves our ongoing trust.

Purpose. Job was written to encourage suffering saints to hold fast to their faith in God. While the causes of suffering may be hidden, renewal will come to all who suffer in faith. For Job, that renewal was in this life; for others it may not be until the life to come. In any case, we should faithfully endure, as James 5:11 says, "Indeed we count them blessed who endure. You have heard of the perseverance of Job and seen the end intended by the Lord—that the Lord is very compassionate and merciful."

History and archaeology. While nothing is known with any certainty about when or where the events of Job occurred, something is known about the antiquity of this type of literature. Scholars formerly believed that wisdom literature in the Near East was a late development. For this reason, Job was considered a late work. However, two discoveries have established that wisdom literature enjoyed a very early origin. One work, known as "A Dispute Over Suicide," was composed in Egypt about 2280–2000 B.C. It describes a dialogue between a suicidal man and his soul, which is trying to persuade him that life is better. From another part of the Near East, Babylon, a second story has been found. Termed the "Babylonian Theodicy" and written about 1400–1000 B.C., it contains a dialogue between a suffering man and a friend who attempts to answer his questions. Both works bear a superficial resemblance to Job but draw very different conclusions. If correctly dated, these works establish the fact that wisdom literature existed at or before the time of Moses.

Geography. Because of the antiquity of Job, none of the places named can be identified. Probably he lived somewhere between the Tigris and the Euphrates Rivers.

Outline of Job

I. The dialogue in heaven (chaps. 1—2)
II. The dialogue on earth (chaps. 3—31)
III. The denunciation by Elihu (chaps. 32—37)
IV. The declaration by God (38:1—42:6)
V. The delightful end for Job (42:7–17)

Overview of Job

The dialogue in heaven (chaps. 1—2). Satan appears before God and asserts that the only reason why Job serves God is because God treats him right, not because God is majestic and worthy of worship. (This is like someone telling you that your children only love you for the money they get out of you.) With this assertion, Satan challenges both God's worth and Job's integrity. Therefore, God permits Satan to test Job. A series of calamities befall Job in which he loses his property, his children, and his health. Yet in all of this, Job refuses to accuse God of injustice (2:10). Hearing of his misfortunes, Job's three friends, Eliphaz, Bildad, and Zophar come to comfort him.

The dialogue on earth (chaps. 3—31). The bulk of the book consists of an extended dialogue between Job and his would-be comforters.[29] In three cycles of speeches that grow in intensity and harshness, Job's three "friends" present one argument: God is just, giving men what they deserve. He has given Job suffering; therefore, Job must have done something terrible to have God treat him this way. What they do not know (but the reader does) is that Job's trials were intended to prove his integrity, not punish his sin. As the assault on Job continues, he begins to falter under the weight of the question, *Why is this happening to me?* and he questions the justice of God (31:35–37).

The denunciation by Elihu (chaps. 32—37). With Job's accusers unable to convict him of sin and Job himself questioning how God was running the universe, a new character steps on stage, Elihu (chaps. 32—37). Apparently a younger bystander, Elihu cautions Job's accusers about condemning an innocent man (32:12, 15). He then rebukes Job for concluding that God is unjust and that nothing can be gained by godliness (chaps. 34—35). He goes on to say that God's ways may simply be beyond our comprehension (37:5).

The declaration by God (38:1—42:6). The book reaches its climax when God himself speaks to Job. He does not give Job a straightforward explanation of why tragedy has befallen him. Instead, by reviewing the marvels of nature, God implies that Job should trust him to know what he is doing. By showing his care for nature, God implies his care for Job. The point is not lost, and Job is humbled to the point of repentance (42:6).

The delightful end for Job (42:7–17). After Job learns to trust God even in tragedy, he is blessed again. Only now, he receives back double the possessions he lost and an equal number of children.

Theological Highlights

Concerning God. Job stresses three things about God: his mystery, his sovereignty, and his goodness. While he may seem hidden and remote, letting things run amuck, he is actually in control of every situation, working out his purposes and never ceasing to care for his own.

Concerning Satan. The enemy of man is actively attempting to harm God's people and break the bond of faith between man and God. God's people must resist him by maintaining their faith (1 Pet. 5:8–9).

Concerning man. "Yet man is born to trouble, as the sparks fly upward" (Job 5:7). The Book of Job shows how vulnerable we all are to suffering and tragedy. Jesus warned of the same (John 16:33). The causes of trouble are manifold, some certainly due to our sin, some to the sins of others, some to natural forces at work. God uses troubles as a means of teaching and training his people (Heb. 12:5–6; James 1:2–3). Yet a reward is at our end (James 1:12). So two responses are called for. First, we must dislodge the notion from our thinking that life should be fair because we are Christians. Faith does not come with a guarantee that says "no more problems." Second, we must not allow trials to turn us against God. Rather, they should make us cling all the more to him as we endure. Finally, learning from the example of Job's "comforters," we must be cautious in trying to explain to others why they are suffering.

Concerning the future. The Book of Job indicates that a future of hope and blessing awaits those who trust in God. It speaks of a future physical resurrection (19:25–26). The doubled restoration of Job's possessions hints that whatever faith may cost us here will be amply rewarded there (see Rom. 8:18; 2 Cor. 4:17). Even the fact that God did not double the number of children of Job at the end may hint that the children he had lost were not lost forever but were alive with God and awaiting resurrection.

Christ in Job. The reference in 19:25 to a redeemer who will stand on the earth naturally turns our thoughts to Christ. He, our Redeemer, will return in glory and power at the end of time (Rev. 19).

Key Verses

Job 19:25–26: "For I know that my Redeemer lives, and He shall stand at last on the earth; and after my skin is destroyed, this I know, that in my flesh I shall see God."

Key Chapters

Job 1—2: The dialogue between God and Satan sets the stage for what happens to Job.

Message of Job

Job declares that even when things are terribly bad, they are not hopeless. Beyond suffering, a better life awaits us. So even when life makes no sense, we should hold on to our faith. It will be rewarded.

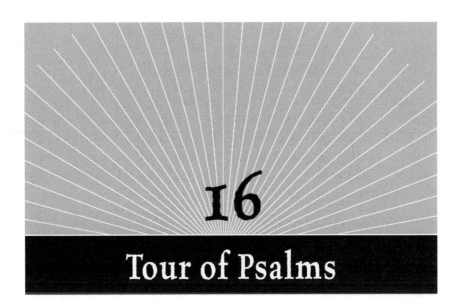

Tour of Psalms

I have been accustomed to call this book, I think not inappropriately, "An Anatomy of all the Parts of the Soul;" for there is not an emotion of which any one can be conscious that is not here represented as in a mirror. Or rather, the Holy Spirit has here drawn to the life all the griefs, sorrows, fears, doubts, hopes, cares, perplexities, in short, all the distracting emotions with which the minds of men are wont to be agitated.[30]

Preview of Psalms

The Book of Psalms is probably among everyone's favorite books of the Bible because, as Calvin remarked, it gives expression to "all griefs, sorrows, fears, doubts, hopes, cares, anxieties," in addition to celebrating the good things the Lord does for his people. It takes these human experiences, shapes them into prayers, and expresses them in poetry. The importance of the Psalms is seen in the multiple quotations from it in the New Testament.

Introduction to Psalms

Author. Most psalms begin with a superscription that mentions the author. David is named as the author of seventy-three psalms, plus two anonymous psalms are attributed to him by the New Testament (Psalms 2 and 95; Acts 4:25; Heb. 4:7). Other psalms are attributed to Asaph (12), Moses (1), Heman (1), Ethan (1), and Solomon (2). Fifty-one are anonymous.

Dates of writing. As might be expected with writings by various people, the dates of composition vary. However, the majority were written during the lifetimes of David and Solomon, broadly dating them around 1050–950 B.C.

Theme. The Book of Psalms, functioning as the hymnbook of Israel, *records praises and petitions* that the people voiced to God in song. In fact, the Hebrews called it the "book of praises."

Purpose. Psalms was meant to give expression to the feelings of people in various, often hurtful, situations in life. Because of this, it has been said that in the rest of the Bible God speaks to man, but in Psalms man speaks to God.

History and archaeology. It was once the scholarly opinion that the Psalms were written following the Exile in Babylon. Some have suggested a date as late as the Maccabean period (167–63 B.C.). However, the discovery at Qumran of a scroll of the Psalms with the same headings and order as found in later manuscripts has forced a revision of this view. Since this scroll was written about 100 B.C., the Psalms must have been extant for quite a bit longer. Further, discoveries at Ras Shamra (Ugarit) reveal that poetry of this type existed from the time of the Exodus.

Terminology. A few obscure terms occur in the superscriptions. *Mizmor* probably indicated a song to be sung to instrumental accompaniment. A *maskil* was most likely a meditative poem. Also in the headings, some psalms are said to be "to the choir director." This indicates a liturgical use of these psalms by temple singers. In the body of several psalms, the term *selah* is found. This may indicate a musical interlude.

Outline of Psalms

I. Book 1: Individual laments are prominent (chaps. 1—41). Mainly by David.

II. Book 2: Individual laments (see below) are prominent (chaps. 42—72). Mainly by David and the "Sons of Korah" (a choir guild).

III. Book 3: Praise and thanksgiving psalms are prominent, along with laments (chaps. 73—89). Mainly by Asaph, a temple musician. Several have a national focus.

IV. Book 4: Thanksgiving and enthronement psalms (see below) are prominent (chaps. 90—106). Mostly by unnamed authors.

V. Book 5: The praise of God is prominent (chaps. 107—150). About evenly divided between David and unknown authors, this book has a wide variety of psalms.

Overview of Psalms

Because of its fivefold division, the Book of Psalms has been called the "Poetic Pentateuch." Rather than being an intentional reflection of the Pentateuch (i.e., the five books by Moses), these five divisions probably reflect stages in the collection of the psalms. Each division ends with a doxology.

Several types of psalms are found in the Psalter. While some psalms are a mixture of types that defies easy classification, it is possible to assign most to one of these types.

Individual laments are a personal cry for help. An example is Psalm 42, which begins on a plaintive note: "As the deer pants for the water brooks, so pants my soul for You, O God. My soul thirsts for God, for the living God. When shall I come and appear before God? My tears have been my food day and night, while they continually say to me, 'Where is your God?'" (vv. 1–3). Finding himself far from home and deeply discouraged, the psalmist recalls better times in which he participated in the joyful worship of the Lord. He expresses his sorrow while doggedly affirming his hope that God would bring him home to worship again. Most laments, like Psalm 42, contain some expression of hope. The most common type of psalm, other individual laments include 3, 4, 5, 7, 10, 13, 17, 25, 26, 27, 28, 31, 35, 43, 54, 55, 56, 57, 59, 61, 62, 63, 64, 69, 70, 71, 77,

86, 88, 102, 109, 120, 140, 141, 142, and 143. We can turn to these psalms for comfort and encouragement when we face personal problems.

National laments bemoan a calamity that has overtaken the nation. An example is Psalm 44, as verses 8–10 illustrate: "In God we boast all the day long, and praise Your name forever. Selah. But You have cast us off and put us to shame, and You do not go out with our armies. You make us turn back from the enemy, and those who hate us have taken spoil for themselves." In contrast to past victories the Lord gave the nation (verses 1–7), now Israel suffers cruel defeat (vv. 8–16). Even so, the psalmist affirms his faith in God and prays that he will awaken and deliver them (vv. 17–26). Other national laments include 60, 74, 79, 80, 83, 90, and 137. National laments can guide us when we pray for our country in times of repentance, war, or crisis.

Penitential psalms express remorse for sin. The best known of these is Psalm 51, written in the aftermath of David's adultery with Bathsheba and the murder of her husband (2 Sam. 11). It begins with a cry for mercy and a confession of sin: "Have mercy upon me, O God, according to Your loving-kindness; according to the multitude of Your tender mercies, blot out my transgressions. Wash me thoroughly from my iniquity, and cleanse me from my sin. For I acknowledge my transgressions, and my sin is always before me" (vv. 1–3). Recognizing the conflict between what he is (a sinner from conception, v. 5) and what God desires him to be (a man of integrity, v. 6), David prays for divine cleansing and restoration to fellowship that he might praise God (vv. 7–15). He does not offer God an animal sacrifice but a heart of repentance (vv. 16–17). The prayer concludes with the request that God build up the nation (thus, not allowing his sin as king to be its undoing, vv. 18–19). Other penitential psalms include 6, 32, and 38. These psalms minister to us when we are broken and sorrowful for personal sin.

Thanksgiving psalms voice appreciation to God. An example is Psalm 30. It begins by saying, "I will extol You, O LORD, for You have lifted me up, and have not let my foes rejoice over me" (v. 1). David describes how the Lord healed him from sickness, for which he offers his ceaseless thanks. Other thanksgiving psalms include 9, 34, 40, 65, 81, 92, 98, 100, 103, 104, 105, 107, 114, 118, and 136. These psalms are helpful when we want to express our appreciation and thankfulness to God.

Praise psalms focus on the greatness and glory of God. Psalm 147 is a good example, which tells us, "Praise the LORD! For it is good to sing praises to our God; for it is pleasant, and praise is beautiful" (v. 1) and proceeds to give multiple reasons why we should praise God. Other praise psalms include 8, 11, 18, 23, 29, 30, 32, 46, 48, 66, 68, 75, 84, 85, 91, 95, 106, 108, 111, 113, 116, 117, 135, 138, 139, 145, 146, 148, 149, and 150. We can incorporate these psalms into our worship to magnify the Lord.

Wisdom psalms give practical advice for living. Psalm 119, the longest psalm with 176 verses, is such. It is written to extol the worth of God's Law. Verse 9 is illustrative of the psalm: "How can a young man cleanse his way? By taking heed according to Your word." (This particular psalm is divided into twenty-two stanzas of eight verses each. Each successive stanza begins with the next letter of the 22-letter Hebrew alphabet. All the verses within that stanza begin with that letter.) Other wisdom psalms include 1, 14, 15, 19, 36, 37, 49, 50, 52, 53, 73, 78, 82, 94, and 112. These psalms are beneficial in times of meditation.

Travelers (pilgrims) going to Jerusalem for a festival sang **pilgrim psalms.** They are also called *Songs of Ascent* since the people ascended (went up) to Jerusalem. These are found from Psalm 120 to 134. In Psalm 122, the pilgrim anticipates his arrival in the city: "I was glad when they said to me, 'Let us go into the house of the LORD.' Our feet have been standing within your gates, O Jerusalem!" (vv.1–2). These psalms remind us that in our pilgrimage through life, we need the Lord.

Royal psalms give attention to Israel's king. Psalm 21 is one such psalm, probably written to express the king's gratitude of the king for a victory over his enemies. Other royal psalms include 20, 45, 89, 101, and 144. These psalms offer guidance in praying for leaders and in meditating on Christ (but see below).

Messianic psalms are a special class of the preceding type. They speak of things that go beyond the contemporary king to the Messiah or Christ. Outstanding among these are Psalms 2, 16, 22, 24, 72, and 110. The last celebrates the union of the offices of king and priest in the Lord's anointed as seen in verses 2 and 4: "The Lord shall send the rod of Your strength out of Zion. Rule in the midst of Your enemies!" (v. 2); "The Lord has sworn, and will not relent, 'You are a priest forever according to the order of Melchizedek" (v. 4). The New Testament Book of Hebrews cites the psalm some four times in chapters 5, 6, and 7.

Enthronement psalms celebrate the reign of God. An example would be Psalm 93 where the first two verses declare: "The LORD reigns,

He is clothed with majesty; the LORD is clothed, He has girded Himself with strength. Surely the world is established, so that it cannot be moved. Your throne is established from of old; You are from everlasting." Other enthronement psalms are 47, 93, 96, 97, 98, and 99. These psalms lend themselves to praise and worship.

Imprecatory psalms call for a curse upon the enemies of God and of God's people. Psalm 35 illustrates. It begins with a plea for help: "Plead my cause, O LORD, with those who strive with me; fight against those who fight against me" (v.1). Thereafter, it describes the injustices done by these enemies and reiterates the plea that God destroy them. Many Christians wonder how such seemingly vindictive psalms found their way into the Bible. Should we not pray instead for our enemies' salvation and forgiveness? Yes, we should, but at the same time we should pray that justice and righteousness might prevail, which is what the imprecatory psalms seek. Mercy and justice are not incompatible in the work of God. And if we commit the matter of justice to God rather than taking it in our own hands, then we are emotionally free to pray for our enemies and to show them good. Other imprecatory psalms include 58, 69, 83, and 109.

Theological Highlights

Concerning praise and thanksgiving. The Book of Psalms has much to teach us concerning the worship of God. He is worthy of our praise since he created all things and he alone is our Savior. We should be mindful of this and express our consequent joy in praise. Likewise, the cultivation of gratitude expressed in thanksgiving should be a deliberate undertaking and given prominence in his worship.

Concerning confession and comfort. The God whom we worship forgives sin and aids his people. Troubled hearts have found relief from the burden of sin and worry in the psalms.

Christ in Psalms. Many psalms are prophetic of Christ and are applied to him in the New Testament. Examples include Psalms 2, 45, and 72, which concern Messiah's reign; Psalms 22 and 69, which tell of

Messiah's suffering; Psalm 16:10, which predicts his triumph over death; and Psalm 110, which foretells Messiah's priesthood and kingship.

Key Verse

Psalm 1:6: "For the LORD knows the way of the righteous, but the way of the ungodly shall perish."

Key Chapters

Psalm 1: the two ways of life.

Psalm 2: the installation of God's King.

Psalm 23: the Good Shepherd.

Psalm 51: forgiveness after great sin.

Message of Psalms

Psalms shows the importance of relating life to God. From God comes strength in times of trial. In a real sense, the Psalms form a book of prayer. By their example, we learn much about the role and form prayer should take in our own lives.

Psalms for Times of Need

When you are tempted to turn away from God, read Psalm 1.
When evil may seem to triumph, read Psalm 2.
When facing the end of life, read Psalm 16.
When you need comfort, read Psalm 23.
When you are troubled, read Psalm 34.
When you are ill, read Psalm 41.
When you feel discouraged, read Psalms 42 and 43.
When you wish to confess sin, read Psalm 51.
When life seems unfair, read Psalm 73.
When your life feels out of control, read Psalm 139.
When you wish to praise God, read Psalm 147.

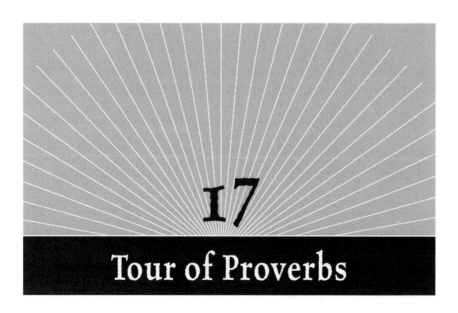

Tour of Proverbs

Preview of Proverbs

A. T. Pierson defined a proverb as "a wise saying in which a few words are chosen instead of many, with a design to condense wisdom into a brief form both to aid memory and stimulate study. Hence, Proverbs are not only 'wise sayings,' but 'dark sayings'—parables, in which wisdom is disguised in a figurative or enigmatic form like a deep well, from which instruction is to be drawn, or a rich mine, from which it is to be dug. Only profound meditation will reveal what is hidden in these moral and spiritual maxims."[31]

The Book of Proverbs is like a house with the key hanging by the front door. It begins by telling us what it intends to do: to make wise the simple (1:1–7). It follows with an extended appeal to the young to pursue wisdom (wisdom being personified in chapters 8 and 9). The bulk of the book consists of pithy sayings by Solomon compiled during his reign (chaps. 10—24). Additional sayings of Solomon, added during the time of Hezekiah, follow (chaps. 25—29). The sayings of the mysterious figures, Agur and Lemuel, conclude the book (chaps. 30—31).

Introduction to Proverbs

Author. Solomon is the primary author of Proverbs. Later sections are attributed to "the wise" (22:17; 24:23), to Agur (chap. 30), and King Lemuel (31:1–9). Who these were is unknown. Some speculate that "Lemuel" may have been a nickname for Solomon, but this is unproven. The last item in the book, the praise of the virtuous woman (31:10–31), is anonymous.

Date of writing. The majority of the book was composed during the reign of Solomon, 970–930 B.C. Additions during the time of Hezekiah were made about 700 B.C.

Theme. Proverbs is concerned with those tricky situations encountered in daily life. If not handled wisely, issues like relationships, words, and money can cause harm. Consequently, the theme of this book is *prudence for life*. Many subjects are developed in the book, but always a choice must be made between wisdom and foolishness.

Purpose. Proverbs tells us its purpose (1:2–4): "To know wisdom and instruction, to perceive the words of understanding, to receive the instruction of wisdom, justice, judgment, and equity; to give prudence to the simple, to the young man knowledge and discretion." In brief, it was intended to help young and naïve people acquire wisdom and moral judgment.

History and archaeology. Wisdom literature like that found in Proverbs was common in the ancient world. Parallels have been found in both Egypt and Mesopotamia, dating as far back as the late third millennium B.C., about the time of Abraham.

Types. Three types of proverbs are found.

- The *contrastive* proverb presents a truth by way of contrast. An example is found in Proverbs 14:30: "A sound heart is life to the body, but envy is rottenness to the bones." Characteristic of such proverbs is the use of the word *but* between the thoughts of the first and second lines.
- The *completive* proverb introduces a thought in the first line that is finished or completed in the second. Proverbs 16:3 illustrates: "Commit your works to the LORD, and your thoughts will be established." The word *and* is often used between the first and second lines.
- Finally, the *comparative* proverb makes a comparison between something in the first line and something in the second. It uses the word *than* between the lines. For example, Proverbs 15:16 says, "Better is a little with the fear of the LORD, than great treasure with trouble."

Outline of Proverbs

  I. Purpose of Proverbs (1:1–7)
 II. Parental appeal (1:8—9:18)
III. Pithy sayings (chaps. 10—29)
 IV. Parting thoughts (chaps. 30—31)

Overview of Proverbs

Purpose of Proverbs (1:1–7). As already noted, Proverbs begins with a statement of purpose: to make wise the simple. The essence of wisdom is found in a reverent relationship with God (v. 7). Only fools despise God's instruction. The entire book stresses that God has all the answers to life's problems. Nothing is hidden from his knowledge. Therefore, the beginning of wisdom is to reverence and fear God.

Parental appeal (1:8—9:18). Proverbs is written as an address from a father to his son (1:8). In this section are ten fatherly discourses.

1. The first, 1:8–19, deals with the enticement of worthless friends: "My son, if sinners entice you, do not consent" (v. 10). Wicked men meet a wicked end.

2. The second discourse, 1:20–33, presents the imperative of wisdom. Wisdom personified calls to people, and their response determines their fate: "For the turning away of the simple will slay them, and the complacency of fools will destroy them; but whoever listens to me will dwell safely, and will be secure, without fear of evil" (vv. 32–33).

3. Discourse three, 2:1–22, stresses that wisdom should be sought as treasure for "when wisdom enters your heart, and knowledge is pleasant to your soul, discretion will preserve you; understanding will keep you" (vv. 10–11).

4. Along similar lines, discourse four, 3:1–35, argues for wisdom's benefit: "For her proceeds are better than the profits of silver, and her gain than fine gold" (v. 14).

5. Next, in the fifth discourse, 4:1–27, the father contrasts two ways of living—the way of the wise and the way of the wicked: "But the path of the just is like the shining sun, that shines ever brighter unto the perfect day. The way of the wicked is like darkness; they do not know what makes them stumble" (vv. 18–19).

6. In the sixth discourse, 5:1–23, the wisdom of marriage and fidelity is presented: "Drink water from your own cistern, and running water from your own well" (v. 15).

7. Discourse seven, 6:1–35, mentions potential pitfalls, including sloth, dishonesty, selfishness, and adultery.

8. Then eighth in 7:1–27 sounds a warning about the temptation of the adulteress: "For she has cast down many wounded, and all who were slain by her were strong men. Her house is the way to hell, descending to the chambers of death" (vv. 26–27).

9. In the next to the last discourse, 8:1–36, Wisdom makes an impassioned appeal: "Does not wisdom cry out, and understanding lift up her voice? She takes her stand on the top of the high hill, beside the way, where the paths meet. She cries out at the gates, at the entry of the city, at the entrance of the doors: 'To you, O men, I call, and my voice is to the sons of men'" (vv. 1–4).

10. Finally, 9:1–18 stresses that we help or hurt ourselves by choosing wisdom or folly: "If you are wise, you are wise for yourself, and if you scoff, you will bear it alone" (v. 12).

Pithy sayings (chaps. 10—29). The bulk of the book consists of either two or four-line capsules of wisdom. The majority (chaps. 10—24) are by Solomon, with an addition by scribes of Hezekiah (chaps. 25—29). Themes include wisdom, foolishness, diligence, friends, words, and the family. For example, 10:8 contrasts wisdom to folly in terms of teachability: "The wise in heart will receive commands, but a prating fool will fall." A man's wisdom will show itself in his attentiveness, whereas a fool is only interested in spouting off. Concerning diligence, 11:27 has this to say about diligently seeking good: "He who earnestly seeks good finds favor, but trouble will come to him who seeks evil." In other words, what you seek for others is what you will get yourself. To encourage us to select friends carefully, 13:20 says, "He who walks with wise men will be wise, but the companion of fools will be destroyed." We become like our friends. Many proverbs deal with the power of words, such as 15:1, "A soft answer turns away wrath, but a harsh word stirs up anger." Words can be water or oil on fiery emotions. Family living gets its share of attention in proverbs like 17:1: "Better is a dry morsel with quietness, than an house full of feasting with strife." Peace in a household is more desirable than abundance.

Parting thoughts (chaps. 30—31). The last two chapters are by individuals named Agur and Lemuel, about whom nothing is known. Agur (chap. 30) is a keen observer of life who draws lessons from its wonders. Lemuel (31:1–9) passes along some advice for kings. Chapter 31:10–31, portraying the virtuous wife, is anonymous but well loved. It celebrates the unique contribution of a wife and mother to a household. She is a trusted partner (v. 11), who manages her home (v. 15) and knows how to make and handle money (vv. 16–19, 24), yet is considerate of the less fortunate (v. 20). In all, she earns the praise of her family (vv. 28–31).

Key Verse

Proverbs 1:7: "The fear of the LORD is the beginning of knowledge, but fools despise wisdom and instruction."

Key Chapters

Proverbs 8—9: the speech of Wisdom.

Message of Proverbs

From God comes wisdom for life's difficult situations. Those who live in contact with God, accepting instruction from him, will experience blessing in this life as well as the life to come.

> *Take the proverbs of other nations, and we shall find great numbers founded upon selfishness, cunning, pride, injustice, national contempt, and animosities. The principles of the Proverbs of Solomon are piety, charity, justice, benevolence, and true prudence. Their universal purity proves that they are the word of God.*
>
> —Matthew Henry

18

Tour of Ecclesiastes

The strength and happiness of a man consists in finding out the way in which God is going, and going that way, too. — Henry Ward Beecher[32]

Preview of Ecclesiastes

There is an old saying, "Two things can make someone unhappy: not having what he wants and having what he wants." The experience of the writer of Ecclesiastes illustrates this maxim. Whatever he wanted, he was able to get, only to find any satisfaction was fleeting. This leads him on a search for the secret of a satisfying life, a secret he shares in his conclusion.

Introduction to Ecclesiastes

Author. While the book does not explicitly name its author, it does leave clues strongly suggesting that it was Solomon. He was the son of David, king in Jerusalem (1:1, 12); he was a great builder (2:4); he was greater than any of the kings before him (2:9); and he wrote many proverbs (12:9). That would make this the second of three books traditionally ascribed to King Solomon. Ecclesiastes is thought to have been written when he was an older man who could truly say, "Been there, done that." Thus, it offers the wisdom of a lifetime.

Dates of writing. The book must fall within the reign of Solomon from 971–931 B.C. Assuming it was written in his later years, we can date Ecclesiastes to approximately 935 B.C. Critics who deny Solomonic authorship usually do so on the claim that the type of Hebrew employed is similar to that used after the Exile. But recent studies show it is a unique literary Hebrew, so there is no conclusive reason to late-date the book.

Theme. The book of Ecclesiastes states its theme in 1:2 and 12:8: "Vanity of vanities, all is vanity." Moreover, it uses the refrain "under the sun" about twenty-nine times. Further, Solomon repeatedly speaks of what he saw or had seen. Thus, he is dealing with life not as understood through divine revelation but only through human observation. The frequently recurring term *vanity*, often in conjunction with *under the sun*, is a Hebrew term meaning "fleeting" or "vaporous." So the vanity to which it refers is a godless, "this world only" pursuit of life. We might say that it refers to the hollowness of secularism. Therefore, the theme of Ecclesiastes might be stated as the emptiness of life when lived without consideration for God and the hereafter. Solomon is deliberately vague concerning the afterlife (3:19–21). As Christians who view life through the resurrection of our Lord and the promise of the life to come, we would not say that life is empty. However, knowing that this is how the godless view life helps us to understand many of their actions.

Purpose. In a world where much seems senseless and nothing quite satisfies our longings, Solomon wanted to show the necessity of living by faith. Life can best be pursued with an orientation toward God and the life to come.

History and archaeology. Literature like that exemplified in Ecclesiastes was known in other parts of the ancient Near East. From

Egypt comes a text known as the Words of Ahikar, a sage who wrestles with emotions and thoughts similar to Solomon's.

Outline of Ecclesiastes

   I. The vanity of life (1:1–2)
  II. Various vanities (1:3–11)
 III. The verification that all is vanity (1:12—6:9)
 IV. Advice for living in this vain world (6:10—12:14)

Overview of Ecclesiastes

The author begins by setting forth his theme: Life under the sun is filled with vanity (1:2). He briefly illustrates his point (1:3–11). Knowing that some people think they have found the secret of happiness, the preacher demolishes the idea that lasting happiness can be found in anything the world offers (1:12—6:9). It is not . . .

- In achievement (1:12–15)
- Nor in wisdom and knowledge (1:16–18)
- Nor in wealth and pleasure (2:1–11)
- Nor in wise behavior (2:12–18)
- Nor in labor (2:18—6:9)

Death brings the wise and the foolish to a common end. Oppression, political turmoil, rote religion, and accumulated wealth ultimately fail us (4:1—6:9). This being the case, the preacher then gives his counsel for living in this disappointing world (6:10—12:14). His final verdict is that one should fear God and always keep in mind that he will judge our deeds (12:13–14).

Theological Highlights

A fundamental question of philosophy is, why are we here? By underscoring the essential meaningless of life when lived without faith or an eternal perspective, Ecclesiastes shows that the secular person has no answer to the question.

Key Verses

Ecclesiastes 12:13–14: "Let us hear the conclusion of the whole matter: Fear God and keep His commandments, for this is man's all. For God will bring every work into judgment, including every secret thing, whether good or evil."

Key Chapter

Ecclesiastes 12: concluding admonitions.

Message of Ecclesiastes

Life as experienced by many today is meaningless. Therefore, having no higher purpose, people rush into the pursuit of pleasure in an attempt to fill the void within. As in the days of Solomon, so it is today. Such efforts are self-defeating. Only with faith that transcends this life can genuine meaning and satisfaction be found.

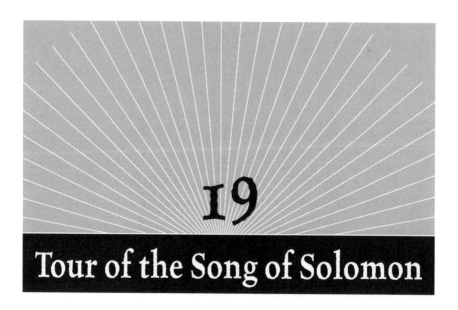

Tour of the Song of Solomon

Preview of the Song of Solomon

Known by various names ("Canticles," the "Song of Songs," and the "Song of Solomon"), this book has also been variously interpreted. Some see it as a celebration of marital love; others see it as an allegory describing God's love for Israel or Christ's love for the church. While applications can be made to the divine love for God's people, the details of the story suggest that a literal interpretation as a love poem is best. In it we see that sex is a joy and blessing designed by God for a husband and wife.

Introduction to the Song of Solomon

Author. The book itself attributes authorship to Solomon. A common suggestion is that he wrote the song as a young man in love.

Date of writing. The Song of Solomon might be dated c. 960 B.C., early in the reign of Solomon.

Theme. The Song of Solomon is a story of romance and marriage, filled with passionate expressions of longing. Its earthy theme might be stated as *sexually expressed love.*

Purpose. The last poetic book has a vastly different purpose. While many interpreters understand the intention of the song to be an allegorical expression of the love of God for Israel or the love of Christ for the church, the plainest understanding of the writer's purpose seems to be that he wished to elevate the beauty of sex in marriage.

History and archaeology. With respect to the song, neither history nor archaeology has been able to clarify the significance of calling the bride the "Shulammite." The term remains a puzzle. However, references to places in both the north and the south of Israel suggest that the song was written prior to the division of the kingdom following the death of Solomon.

Outline of the Song of Solomon

   I. Love begins (1:1—3:5)
  II. The marriage of the lovers (3:6—5:1)
 III. The maturing of love (5:2—8:7)
 IV. Meditation on and affirmations of love (8:8–14)

Overview of the Song of Solomon

The song begins with the Shulammite describing her love to the "daughters of Jerusalem" (either members of Solomon's harem or a chorus, 1:1–8). Then the lover expresses his great love for the Shulammite, praising her beauty (1:9–10). Further descriptions of their courtship follow as the lover and the Shulammite dialogue, with dramatic interjections by the daughters of Jerusalem (1:11—3:5). The day of the wedding is described, with much emphasis on the physical delight they find in each other (3:6—5:1). Thereafter, the dialogue describes the adjustments and growth of love within the marriage (5:2—8:7). We see that love is not always easy and, without commitment, would likely not endure. The concluding verses offer the reflection of the Shulammite on her relationship with Solomon and their final affirmation of love for one another.

Theological Highlights

Concerning God. Many Bible teachers apply the story of Solomon and the Shulammite to God and his people. The love and devotion of the king for the bride is compared to the love of God for the redeemed. There may be some justification for such an interpretation since the church is described as the bride of Christ (Rev. 19:6–9).

Concerning humankind. The song corrects two extreme views of sex. On the one hand, it rebuffs the idea that sexual relations are inherently dirty. On the other hand, it rebukes the idea of sex without commitment. It elevates the place of both sex and marriage in human society. The song points to the way of meaningful sexual expression: committed marriage. While marriage has its ups and downs (as did that of the lover and the Shulammite), it can mature into a permanently enriching relationship.

Key Verse

Song of Solomon 8:7: "Many waters cannot quench love, nor can the floods drown it. If a man would give for love all the wealth of his house, it would be utterly despised."

Key Chapter

Song of Solomon 4: expressions of love.

Message of the Song of Solomon

The song reminds us that God intended for husbands and wives to experience romantic love.

20

Coming Up Next: The Prophetic Books

This next section of the Old Testament can be further subdivided into the Major Prophets (so-called because their works are longer) and the Minor Prophets (not less important but shorter). There are five books in the Major Prophets: Isaiah, Jeremiah, Lamentations, Ezekiel, and Daniel. The remaining twelve books constitute the Minor Prophets.

The Office of Prophet

The office of prophet had its origin in Moses (Deut. 18:15; 34:10). The Hebrew term for prophet comes from an Akkadian verb, *nabu*, meaning, "to call." Thus, the root idea of a prophet is that of a person called by God to deliver the message of God.

The Functions of Prophets

Prophets had four major functions:

1. To encourage trust in God
2. To remind the people to be faithful
3. To kindle hope for the future
4. To verify the true message of God from false messages by fulfilled predictions (Deut. 18:22)

Times of the Prophets

The ministries of the prophets ranged from about 840 B.C. (Obadiah) to 420 B.C. (Malachi). The prophets fall into three groups, depending on when they prophesied.

Preexilic Prophets (those that ministered before the Babylonian Exile)	Exilic Prophets (those that ministered during the deportations and Exile)	Postexilic Prophets (those that ministered after the Babylonian Exile)
840–586 B.C.	**605–538 B.C.**	**520–420 B.C.**
Obadiah	Ezekiel	Zechariah
Joel	Daniel	Haggai
Jonah		Malachi
Amos		
Hosea		
Isaiah		
Micah		
Nahum		
Zephaniah		
Habakkuk		
Jeremiah		

Christ in the Prophets

Of special interest to Christians are prophecies of Christ. A few are listed below:

1. His birthplace. Micah 5:2, "But you, Bethlehem Ephrathah, though you are little among the thousands of Judah, yet out of you shall come forth to Me the One to be Ruler in Israel, whose goings forth are from of old, from everlasting."
2. His virgin birth. Isaiah 7:14, "Therefore the Lord Himself will give you a sign: Behold, the virgin shall conceive and bear a Son, and shall call His name Immanuel."
3. His triumphal entry on a donkey. Zechariah 9:9, "Rejoice greatly, O daughter of Zion! Shout, O daughter of Jerusalem! Behold, your King is coming to you; He is just and having salvation, lowly and riding on a donkey, a colt, the foal of a donkey."
4. Suffering abuse. Isaiah 50:6, "I gave My back to those who struck Me, and My cheeks to those who plucked out the beard; I did not hide My face from shame and spitting."
5. Time of his execution. Daniel 9:24–26, "Seventy weeks are determined for your people and for your holy city, to finish the transgression, to make an end of sins, to make reconciliation for iniquity, to bring in everlasting righteousness, to seal up vision and prophecy, and to anoint the Most Holy. Know therefore and understand, that from the going forth of the command to restore and build Jerusalem until Messiah the Prince, there shall be seven weeks and sixty-two weeks; the street shall be built again, and the wall, even in troublesome times. And after the sixty-two weeks Messiah shall be cut off, but not for Himself; and the people of the prince who is to come shall destroy the city and the sanctuary. The end of it shall be with a flood, and till the end of the war desolations are determined."
6. Was buried in a rich man's grave. Isaiah 53:9, "And they made His grave with the wicked—but with the rich at His death, because He had done no violence, nor was any deceit in His mouth."
7. Israel will yet mourn for him. Zechariah 12:10, "And I will pour on the house of David and on the inhabitants of Jerusalem the Spirit of grace and supplication; then they will look on Me whom they pierced. Yes, they will mourn for Him as one mourns for his only son, and grieve for Him as one grieves for a firstborn."

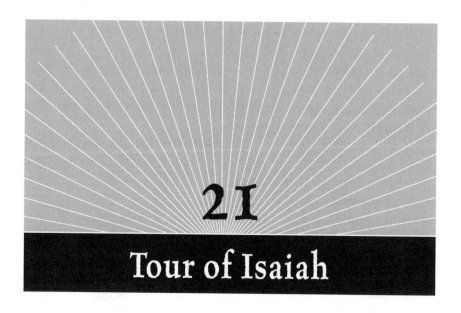

Tour of Isaiah

Preview of Isaiah

The Book of Isaiah is probably the best loved of the prophetic books. His name means "the Lord saves," and he has much to say concerning the subject of salvation. Because of this, Isaiah's role in the Old Testament has been compared to that of Paul's in the New. One finds that it has sixty-six chapters just as the Bible has sixty-six books. Moreover, it divides into two major parts of thirty-nine chapters and twenty-seven chapters, just as the Bible divides into thirty-nine Old Testament books and twenty-seven New. Even the emphases of these two divisions are similar to those of the Old and New Testaments respectively, the first sounding messages of judgment while the latter proclaims salvation. For these reasons, the Book of Isaiah is often called the "Bible in miniature."

Introduction to Isaiah

Author. Isaiah, son of Amoz (1:1). The reigns of the kings mentioned establish the greater part of his ministry in the latter half of the eighth century B.C. Until the nineteenth century, authorship of this book was a matter of agreement among both Jews and Christians. However, with the rise of critical scholarship, critics claimed that three different figures wrote the book. Isaiah supposedly wrote chapters 1—39 in the eighth century B.C.; a "Deutero-Isaiah" wrote chapters 40—55 in the middle of the sixth century B.C.; and a "Trito-Isaiah" wrote chapters 56—66 late in the sixth century B.C. Those who argue for multiple authors say that the historical setting, the literary style, and the theology of these divisions are so different as to demand multiple authors. Conservative scholars argue for the unity of the book on all three issues.

Date of writing. Holding that the book was written by Isaiah alone, a date of around 700 B.C. or slightly later may be assigned to it.

Theme. Israel's judgment and salvation. A message of judgment predominates the first thirty-nine chapters of the book. However, the latter part of the book foresees a time of national and global salvation. The word *salvation* occurs some twenty-six times in the book. For this reason, Isaiah is called the "evangelical prophet."

Purpose. Isaiah wrote to warn the nation of impending judgment due to its idolatry. Yet he also wrote so that when the Babylonian tragedy befell the nation, the captives could hope that the nation still had a future through God's salvation.

History and archaeology. The most important archeological find of the twentieth century was the discovery in 1947 of a complete scroll of Isaiah among the Dead Sea Scrolls. Copied between 125 and 100 B.C., and one thousand years older than any previously known scroll of Isaiah, it agrees in all essential respects with later scrolls. This demonstrates the great care taken by scribes in transmitting the Old Testament through the centuries.

Outline of Isaiah

I. The judgment of God (chaps. 1—39)
   A. Preface: Present sin in contrast to future glory (chaps. 1—5)
   B. Prophecies against Judah and Israel (chaps. 6—12)

    C. Prophecies against neighboring countries (chaps. 13—23)
    D. Prophecies against the world (chaps. 24—27)
    E. Six woes upon Israel and Judah (chaps. 28—33)
    F. The day of vengeance (chap. 34)
    G. The joy of the redeemed (chap. 35)
    H. The invasion of Sennacherib (chaps. 36—39)
II. The salvation of God (chaps. 40—66)
    A. The greatness of God (chaps. 40—48)
    B. The servant of God (chaps. 49—57)
    C. The kingdom of God (chaps. 56—66)

Overview of Isaiah

The judgment of God (chaps. 1—39)

Preface: Present sin in contrast to future glory (chaps. 1—5). The opening chapters of the book paint its themes in broad strokes. The present wickedness of the nation (chap. 1) will give way to the future glory of Zion (2:1–4). This alternation between the what-is versus the what-will-be continues, with interjections of the judgment that will put an end to the evil age and usher in the age of righteousness (3:13—4:6, for example, is such an interjection).

Prophecies against Judah and Israel (chaps. 6—12). In this section of the book, Isaiah warns the northern and southern Kingdoms of coming judgment. A "rod" to be used by God will be Assyria (10:5), the nation that destroyed the Northern Kingdom in 722 B.C. and nearly destroyed the Southern. Yet even in this section, Isaiah looks ahead to the time when God's King will reign (9:6–7) and his kingdom will be established upon the earth (chap. 11).

Prophecies against neighboring countries (chaps. 13—23). The prophet denounces eleven different nations for various sins against God, against Israel, and against neighboring countries. Foremost among the wicked nations is Babylon (chaps. 13—14). While Assyria greatly overshadowed it during Isaiah's time, Babylon became the power that overthrew Jerusalem in 586 B.C.

Prophecies against the world (chaps. 24—27). In what is called the "little Apocalypse" (in contrast to the "big" Apocalypse, the Book of Revelation), Isaiah predicts a global judgment that will befall the world. The establishment of God's kingdom will follow this terrible time on earth and the removal of death itself (25:8).

Six woes upon Israel and Judah (chaps. 28—33). Various sins of the people lead to a six-fold pronunciation of woe[33] upon them. These sins include drunkenness (28:1–8), a refusal to listen to God (28:12), trust in falsehood (28:15), lip service (29:13), defiance (29:15), unholy alliances (30:1–2), and rejection of prophecy (30:12). Such things seal their fate.

The day of vengeance (chap. 34). Looking to the end times, Isaiah foresees an eventual destruction of the nations' armies in a final great slaughter. Compare this passage to Joel 3:13–15 and Revelation 14:18–20; 16:13–16; and 19:17–21.

The joy of the redeemed (chap. 35). Following the overthrow of world powers, a time of rejuvenation and restoration for Israel is seen. The blind receive sight, the lame are healed, and the scattered remnant of Israel gathered. This passage may be compared to Zechariah 14.

The invasion of Sennacherib (chaps. 36—39). The first major division of Isaiah (chaps. 1—39) concludes with a historical interlude with an account of the Assyrian invasion under Sennacherib. Following the deliverance of King Hezekiah and the people of Judah, the king's illness and recovery is described. Woven into the story is a visit by envoys from Babylon who come to congratulate Hezekiah. This gives Isaiah the opportunity to predict that the destruction, which the nation had just escaped, would yet engulf them in a future invasion by the Babylonians.

The salvation of God (chaps. 40—66)

The greatness of God (chaps. 40—48). The second major part of Isaiah (chaps. 40—66) begins with a description of God's greatness. He will prove to be the ultimate source of Israel's deliverance. Repeatedly, the writer stresses the folly of turning from him, the one true God, to idols.

The servant of God (chaps. 49—55). These chapters describe a figure known as the servant of the Lord. Several so-called "Servant Songs" describe him (42:1–9; 49:1–9; 50:4–11; 52:13—53:12). These are prophetic of the Lord Jesus Christ. Other verses in this section refer to the nation of Israel as God's servant, also. Attention must be paid to the context to determine if the reference is to Christ or the nation.

The kingdom of God (chaps. 56—66). The book reaches a climax with the prophet's vision of the ultimate coming of God's kingdom on earth. True repentance—evidenced by a practice of justice, mercy, and righteousness—is rewarded with salvation. The time of salvation will be preceded by deep darkness (60:1–3). When the kingdom does arrive, Israel's fortunes will be renewed (61:4—62:12). The Savior will come as the Conqueror (63:1–6). In light of God's coming mercies to Israel, the prophet then recalls his previous mercies (63:7–14). The ingratitude of the nation causes him to offer a prayer of penitence (63:15—64:12). The Lord replies that he will repay those who have done evil but will bless those who are his true servants, even bringing them into a new heaven and earth (65:1—66:24).

Theological Highlights

Concerning God. Isaiah has an exalted view of the Lord. He presents him as the Creator who, while distinct from his creation, is actively involved in its affairs. A special burden of Isaiah is to present the Lord as the one true God. The uniqueness of God is stressed in the following passages: 42:8; 43:10–11, 13; 44:6–8, 24–25; 45:5–6, 12, 18, 22; 46:9.

It is instructive to see the names that Isaiah gives to God. He uses the covenant name of God, *Yahweh* (translated "the Lord"), more than three hundred times. Fifty-two times he refers to God as "the Lord Almighty"; ten times as "the Lord, the Lord Almighty" (literally, "the Master, Yahweh of Hosts"); "the God of Israel" twelve times; "the Holy One of Israel" twenty-five times; and "the Redeemer" thirteen times. Collectively, these names stress the presence, power, faithfulness, and holiness of God.

Concerning judgment and salvation. The Lord visits both judgment and salvation upon humankind. When people turn to falsehood and their ways become corrupt, God will judge them. This is the message of chapters 1—39. However, God is not content to merely judge; he will graciously redeem. Central in the work of redemption or salvation is the Suffering Servant of Isaiah 53.

Christ in Isaiah

Many prophecies of Christ are to be found in Isaiah. These include

- his virgin birth (7:14)
- his ministry in Galilee (9:1–2)
- his rule and name (9:6)
- his kingdom reign (11:1–16)
- his miraculous ministry (35:5–6)
- his rejection and atoning death (53:1–12)

Key Verses

Isaiah 53:6: "All we like sheep have gone astray; we have turned, every one, to his own way; and the LORD has laid on Him the iniquity of us all."

Isaiah 57:15: "For thus says the High and Lofty One who inhabits eternity, whose name is Holy: 'I dwell in the high and holy place, with him who has a contrite and humble spirit, to revive the spirit of the humble, and to revive the heart of the contrite ones.'"

Key Chapter

Chapter 53: the Suffering Servant.

Message of Isaiah

In today's society, many people have extreme views of God. Some think that God is too loving to call sin into account. Others think God so hates sin that he is reluctant to have any dealings with us. The former extreme encourages unholy living. The latter extreme strips the Christian life of all joy and peace. Isaiah gives the balance needed to rightly relate to God. Certainly, God is to be honored and revered above all else in life. His people do attempt to walk in his ways. However, the knowledge of his compassion and mercy should encourage us that forgiveness and hope are ever available.

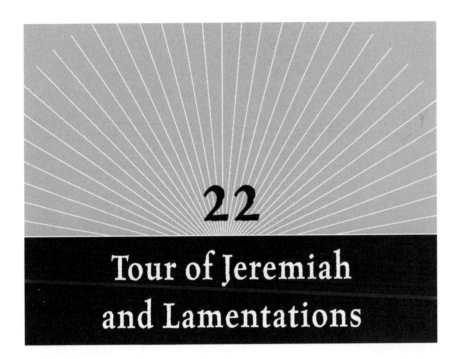

22

Tour of Jeremiah and Lamentations

Preview of Jeremiah and Lamentations

Jeremiah is known as the "weeping prophet." He wept because the message of impending judgment that he delivered was heavy, and the people of Judah were unresponsive. False prophets, corrupt priests, wayward kings, and idolatrous neighbors all opposed him. Not wanting to be a prophet in the first place, Jeremiah sometimes fell into periods of depression. But he could not contain the message that burned within him. Like Christ after him, Jeremiah was totally faithful to God despite his circumstances or feelings.

Introduction to Jeremiah and Lamentations

Author. Jeremiah, a priest from the town of Anathoth, is given as the author of the book bearing his name. On the other hand, Lamentations is anonymous. The ancient and unbroken tradition among the Jews was that he also authored the latter work. That he was capable of so doing is seen in the fact that he authored a lament at the time of King Josiah's death (2 Chron. 35:25).

Date of writing. Jeremiah exercised his ministry from 627 to 586 B.C., perhaps slightly later. Conservative scholars believe that his prophetic book took shape in stages. The first stage was the scroll later burned by King Jehoiakim in 36:11–26. The second stage was the rewrite of the book ordered by God in 36:28–32. The final (and present) form of the book probably took shape under the hand of Baruch, Jeremiah's scribe, because it has reference to events that most likely happened after Jeremiah died. Thus, the final composition of the book probably occurred around 560 B.C. As for Lamentations, it has the appearance of having been written in the immediate aftermath of the destruction of Jerusalem by the Babylonians, giving it a date of 586 B.C.

Themes. The Book of Jeremiah sounds an alarm. Because it warns of the imminence of destruction, the theme may be expressed as *Judah's last warning*. The theme of Lamentations, simply stated, is *the lament for Jerusalem*.[34] It is the cry of a broken heart over the unimaginable tragedy that befell the holy city.

Purpose. Initially, Jeremiah's purpose was to call Judah back from the brink of destruction. When it became obvious that his warning would go unheeded, his purpose changed to giving hope of a better tomorrow, as seen in the promise of a new covenant (31:31–34) and the reaffirmation of the unchangeableness of God's covenants with David and Abraham, which ensured a return to the land (33:19–26).

As might be imagined, the purpose of Lamentations was to express the author's grief.

History and archaeology. In a famous battle at Carchemish, Babylon defeated the combined armies of Assyria and Egypt in 605 B.C. Thereafter, it sought to subjugate Judah, deporting prisoners in 605, 598, and again in 586 B.C. following Judah's destruction. In the latter part of the 586 B.C. war on Judah by Nebuchadnezzar, only three fortified cities remained: Jerusalem itself, Azekah, and Lachish. In the rubble of Lachish, archeologists found twenty-one letters written during the time of war. Several remarks in the letters illuminate matters spoken of in the Book of Jeremiah.

Outline of Jeremiah

   I.   The prophet's call (chap. 1)
  II.   Prophecies concerning Judah (chaps. 2—45)
 III.   Prophecies concerning various nations (chaps. 46—51)
 IV.   Postscript (chap. 52)

Overview of Jeremiah

The prophet's call (chap. 1). The first chapter is devoted to telling how a young, reluctant Jeremiah became a prophet. God ordained his ministry prior to his birth. It was to be a sober ministry, pronouncing judgment on Judah for her idolatry and her neighbors for their own misdeeds.

Prophecies concerning Judah (chaps. 2—45). The bulk of the book consists of prophecies delivered by Jeremiah to the leaders and people of Judah. The arrangement of the material is topical rather than chronological. Buried in the messages of doom is the bright promise that God will someday put into effect a new covenant that would supersede the covenant made through Moses (31:31–34). Two key features of this new covenant are that it would affect a change of heart among God's people and result in the forgiveness of sins. Luke 22:20 records the inauguration of this covenant at the Last Supper. Other New Testament references to it include 2 Corinthians 3:6 and Hebrews 8:7–13.[35]

Prophecies concerning various nations (chaps. 46—51). The prophet singles out nine nations surrounding Judah. They were guilty of furthering the suffering of the Jews in one way or another. The gist of the messages against them is that they would drink of the same cup that Judah had been forced to drink from, the cup of judgment and destruction.

Postscript (chap. 52). Perhaps written by Baruch, chapter 52 describes the fall of Jerusalem for the second time in the book (see also chap. 39). It suggests that God had not forgotten the Jews by telling of the release of King Jehoiachin from his imprisonment in Babylon.

Outline of Lamentations

   I. Jerusalem's devastation (chap. 1)
  II. Jerusalem's destruction (chap. 2)
 III. Jeremiah's lament (chap. 3)
 IV. Judah's loss (chap. 4)
  V. Judah's prayer (chap. 5)

Overview of Lamentations

Lamentations consists of five mournful songs expressing the horror of Judah's tragedy. The first four songs are in the form of an acrostic where each succeeding verse begins with the next letter of the Hebrew alphabet. Since there were twenty-two letters in the Hebrew alphabet, each chapter has twenty-two verses, except for chapter 3 where three verses begin with each letter for a total of sixty-six verses. To heighten the sense of mourning, Lamentations employs what scholars call a limping meter that gives it the cadence of a funeral dirge.

Theological Highlights

Concerning God. The character of God is seen through the prophet Jeremiah. His is both deeply offended by sin, yet is grieved when He must judge His people. His sovereignty is such that no national policies can outmaneuver Him. His power is so great that no nation escapes accountability.

Christ in Jeremiah and Lamentations. In 23:5 and 33:15, the prophet foresees the coming of a Branch of David (i.e., a descendant of David, the Messiah). By means of him, God's promises to Israel and Judah will be fulfilled. He will establish righteousness and justice upon the earth (33:14–17). Christians see this as a prophecy of Jesus who will bring it to fulfillment in his second coming.

Key Verses

Jeremiah 7:23: "But this is what I commanded them, saying, 'Obey My voice, and I will be your God, and you shall be My people. And walk in all the ways that I have commanded you, that it may be well with you.'"

Lamentations 3:22–23: "Through the LORD's mercies we are not consumed, because His compassions fail not. They are new every morning; great is Your faithfulness."

Key Chapters

Jeremiah 31: the new covenant.

Lamentations 3: one ray of hope—God is good.

Message of Jeremiah and Lamentations

The enduring message of Jeremiah is that sin breeds destruction. Neither men nor nations can escape the judgment of God against sin. When judgment falls, it is ruinous. Therefore, the wise take warning and choose to live righteously before him.

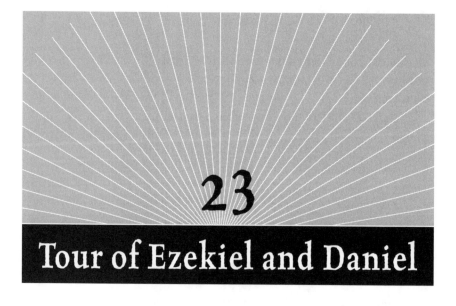

Tour of Ezekiel and Daniel

Preview of Ezekiel and Daniel

Both Ezekiel and Daniel ministered during the time of the Babylonian Exile. Daniel was taken to Babylon in 605 B.C., Ezekiel in 598 B.C. (see notes under Ezra, history and archaeology). Ezekiel's ministry was among the Judean captives. Daniel's ministry was in the court of Babylon, and when Babylon was overthrown, in the court of the Persians. God, providing vivid insights as to what the future held, gave both men visions and dreams.

Introduction to Ezekiel and Daniel

Authors. The authors are traditionally believed to have been the men whose names the books bear. Ezekiel was of the family of Aaron, Israel's first high priest, making him a priest, since the office was inherited. However, Daniel was of royal blood (Dan. 1:3). Ezekiel paid tribute to Daniel's righteousness and intelligence (Ezek. 14:14, 20; 28:3).

Dates of writing. The Book of Ezekiel was written c. 570 B.C. Because Daniel lived to see the overthrow of Babylon, his book was written about 537 B.C.[36]

Themes. The Book of Ezekiel is concerned with what might be termed expectations for Israel. He explores the near future, then the more distant future for the nation. Daniel writes about God's decree for the future. He predicts the broad course of human events leading up to the climatic arrival of the kingdom of God.

Purpose. Ezekiel's purpose was twofold. In the early part of his book, he writes to convince the Jews in exile that their expectations of a quick return to Judah were futile. They needed to prepare for a lengthy exile. In the latter part of the book, presumably after the fall of Jerusalem in 586 B.C., he writes to give the forlorn exiles hope for the future. Daniel's purpose was to emphasize the sovereignty of God over the nations. That is, he wrote to demonstrate that world events did not take place haphazardly but within the scope of God's plan to eventually inaugurate his kingdom.

History and archaeology. Ezekiel tells us that he was "by the river Chebar" when the word of the Lord came to him (Ezek. 1:1). The Chebar was the "grand canal" of the Babylonians, stretching from Babylon through the city of Nippur to the southeast. Near Nippur, the remains of a large Jewish colony have been found, perhaps the place where the prophet lived.

Archaeology has demonstrated that things in Daniel once thought to be historical errors are in fact accurate. Prime among these is the mention of Belshazzar as the king of Babylon at the time it fell. Ancient historians named Nabonidus as the last king of Babylon. However, it has been discovered that Nabonidus was the father of Belshazzar and made his son his coregent. Afterwards, Nabonidus left the city and went on an extended campaign in Arabia, leaving his son the de facto king. Knowing this clarifies his offer to make Daniel the third-highest ranking ruler in the kingdom (Dan. 5:16).

Geography. Babylon (where Daniel resided), and Nippur (near where Ezekiel resided) are shown on map 7, page 57.

Outline of Ezekiel

I. Prophecies of judgment (chaps. 1—32)
    A. God's judgment on the Jews (chaps. 1—24)
    B. God's judgment on Gentiles (chaps. 25—32)
II. Promises of restoration (chaps. 33—48)
    A. Ezekiel appointed to be a watchman (chap. 33)
    B. The coming true Shepherd (chap. 34)
    C. The rebirth of the nation (chaps. 35—37)
    D. The victory of the nation over invaders (chaps. 38—39)
    E. The future temple (chaps. 40—48)

Overview of Ezekiel

Prophecies of judgment (chaps. 1—32)

God's judgment on the Jews (chaps. 1—24). Chapters 1 to 3 describe Ezekiel's dramatic call to a prophetic ministry. God appears to him in the fifth year of King Jehoiachin's captivity (1:2), which would have been 593 B.C. The Lord sits enthroned above four living creatures, surrounded by a burning radiance. The awestruck prophet is commissioned to speak to the nation in the name of the Lord. Symbolic of internalizing God's message, the prophet is given a scroll to eat (2:9—3:3). Thereafter, he is God's watchman, responsible for sounding an alarm for the exiles.

Those Jews who had gone into exile in either 605 or 598 B.C. held the opinion that the exile would be short. Ezekiel warned them of the tragedy that would befall the nation (which it finally did in 586 B.C.). He dramatized his message by acting out several signs.[37] These were like skits performed to illustrate the point of a message. The substance of his message was that the ongoing idolatry and corruption of Judah would result in the destruction of the nation.

God's judgment on Gentiles (chaps. 25—32). All the nations around Judah either furthered her disaster or hoped to profit thereby. So the prophet delivers a message that they, too, would experience doom for the evil they had done. One of these messages concerns Tyre, a city-state on the Mediterranean noted for its trade. After speaking to the prince of Tyre (28:2), the prophet redirects his message to the king of Tyre (28:11–19). These remarks may refer to Satan for the following reasons:

- The "king of Tyre" was in Eden, the Garden of God.
- He was the anointed cherub who covers (i.e., covers God's throne).
- He was perfect until iniquity arose within him, causing him to be cast from God's mountain (mountain being symbolic for the seat of power, in this case, heaven).

If this interpretation is correct, then it suggests that operating behind earthly tyrants are satanic powers.

Promises of Restoration (chaps. 33—48)

The latter part of the book presumably follows the fall of Jerusalem in 586 B.C. It is intended to give hope to the survivors that restoration of the nation would someday come. There are two main thrusts to this section: God will give the nation new life (chaps. 33—39) and establish a new temple-centered order in his coming kingdom (chaps. 40—48).

Outline of Daniel

I. Historical events (chaps. 1—6)
   A. Daniel's dedication (chap. 1)
   B. Nebuchadnezzar's dream (chap. 2)
   C. The fiery furnace (chap. 3)
   D. Nebuchadnezzar's second dream (chap. 4)
   E. Belshazzar's feast (chap. 5)
   F. Daniel in the lion's den (chap. 6)

II. Future events (chaps. 7—12)
- A. Five coming kingdoms (chap. 7)
- B. The kingdoms of Persia and Greece (chap. 8)
- C. The prophetic timetable for Israel (chap. 9)
- D. Battles between the kings of the north and south (10:1—11:35)
- E. The final conflict and arrival of the kingdom (11:36—12:13)

Overview of Daniel

Historical events (chaps. 1—6). In the first six chapters, Daniel is introduced and his credentials as a prophet are established. Deported to Babylon in 605 B.C. while a young man, Daniel demonstrates his loyalty to God by refusing to eat Babylonian food that is forbidden to Jews by God's Law (chap. 1). He is subsequently blessed and achieves a position in the court of King Nebuchadnezzar. Not long afterward, Daniel demonstrates an ability to interpret dreams. The king has a dream that disturbs him, but he cannot recall it. God enables Daniel to tell him what the dream was and that it concerned four great kingdoms that would rule the world (chap. 2). For this, Daniel and his friends, Shadrach, Meshach, and Abed-nego, are promoted.

Sometime later, the devotion of Daniel's three friends is tested. The king erects a statue and orders everyone to worship it. When the three refuse, Nebuchadnezzar orders them thrown into a fiery furnace (probably a brick kiln). Through the flames, the king sees a fourth man in the furnace like the Son of God (3:25). When the three emerge unscathed, Nebuchadnezzar promotes them.

Unfortunately, while Nebuchadnezzar is impressed with the God of the Jews, he is not humble before him. He takes pride in his achievements. Even when warned that judgment has been decreed upon him, he does not turn from his pride. Therefore, he is given the mind of a beast and loses his throne for a time. Eventually, God grants him repentance, and he is restored (chap. 4).

Despite all that God did during the reign of Nebuchadnezzar, the king who follows him two generations later, Belshazzar, persists in idolatry. He holds a blasphemous feast while the city of Babylon is under siege by the Medo-Persians. A hand appears and writes his condemnation upon a wall. That night, the city falls (chap. 5).

Under the new administration, Daniel continues to prosper. By now an old man, his enemies attempt to trap him in some crime. They induce King Darius to forbid petitioning any god or man but him for thirty days. He foolishly passes such a law. Daniel continues to worship the Lord, is discovered, and cast into a den of lions. That night an angel of the Lord rescues him. When the king finds him alive the next morning, he orders the enemies of Daniel, along with their families, to be thrown to the lions (chap. 6).

Future events (chaps. 7—12). God gives Daniel a remarkable series of visions that concern future events having a major bearing on Israel and the arrival of God's kingdom. In the seventh chapter, four great world empires are predicted.[38] These correspond to the four seen in Nebuchadnezzar's vision of chapter 2, namely, Babylon, Persia, Greece, and Rome. In chapter 8, two of these four (Persia and Greece) are given special attention. The conquest of the Persian Empire by Alexander the Great is foreseen.

Chapter 9 outlines Israel's future. Special attention should be paid to verses 24–27. The seventy weeks are understood as weeks of years. Therefore, sixty-nine weeks equal 483 years. This was to be the time between the decree to restore Jerusalem (issued under Nehemiah) and the crucifixion of Christ. The seventieth week is the final seven years of tribulation yet to engulf the earth.

Chapters 10 through 12 depict a climatic struggle between kings to the north and south of Israel. Verses 1–35 of chapter 11 clearly refer to events that transpired during the period between the Old and New Testament. Verses 36 and following look beyond to a similar struggle to occur at the climax of history. This will involve the person commonly known as the Antichrist.

Theological Highlights

Concerning God. Ezekiel reveals three things about God: He will not compromise with sin; he will judge men for their sins; yet he grieves over the necessity of judgment. Both Ezekiel and Daniel underscore the sovereignty of God, showing him in control of all things.

Daniel further shows the faithfulness of God towards those who are uncompromising in their stand for him. Both Daniel (chap. 6) and his three friends (chap. 3) are delivered from death sentences imposed upon them for their refusal to budge from the worship of the Lord.

Concerning the future. Both Daniel and Ezekiel anticipate a time of restoration for the people of God. When history concludes and the kingdom of God arrives, those who persevere in their faith will be resurrected and receive their inheritance.

Christ in Ezekiel and Daniel

Ezekiel predicts the reunification of Israel under one Davidic King and Shepherd. Daniel gives the time of the first coming and death of Christ (9:24–27).

Key Verses

Ezekiel 36:24–27: " For I will take you from among the nations, gather you out of all countries, and bring you into your own land. Then I will sprinkle clean water on you, and you shall be clean; I will cleanse you from all your filthiness and from all your idols. I will give you a new heart, and put a new spirit within you; I will take the heart of stone out of your flesh and give you a heart of flesh. I will put My Spirit within you and cause you to walk in My statutes, and you will keep My judgments and do them."

Daniel 2:44: "And in the days of these kings the God of heaven will set up a kingdom which shall never be destroyed; and the kingdom shall not be left to other people; it shall break in pieces and consume all these kingdoms, and it shall stand forever."

Key Chapters

Ezekiel 37: the vision of the dry bones, depicting Israel's future hope.

Daniel 9: the prophetic timetable for Israel.

Message of Ezekiel and Daniel

The books of Ezekiel and Daniel were composed at a time when the hope of godly people in Israel was at low ebb. The nation and temple had been destroyed, the survivors were captives in a strange land, and the future held no promise. Yet both prophets spoke of coming times of restoration and renewal. The near fulfillment of their prophecies occurred in the sixth and fifth centuries B.C. when the Jews were allowed to return and rebuild. The further fulfillment awaits the end of history.

Today the people of God confront situations in the world that seem hopeless. The prophets continue to renew hope with their vision of the arrival of God's kingdom in the end.

The Major Prophets in Review

Prophet	Times	Audience	Emphasis
Isaiah	740–680 B.C.	Judah	Salvation
Jeremiah	627–580 B.C.	Judah	Judgment
Ezekiel	593–571 B.C.	Exiles	Restoration
Daniel	605–535 B.C.	Exiles	Sovereignty

Preview of the Minor Prophets

Place of Ministry	Preexilic Prophets	Postexilic Prophets
Northern Kingdom	Jonah	
	Amos	
	Hosea	
Southern Kingdom	Obadiah	Haggai
	Joel	Zechariah
	Micah	Malachi
	Nahum	
	Habakkuk	
	Zephaniah	

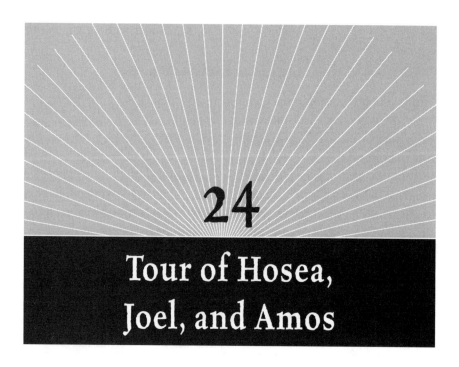

24

Tour of Hosea, Joel, and Amos

Preview of Hosea, Joel, and Amos

The so-called Minor Prophets have major things to say. However, their arrangement is a mystery, not following any discernable pattern. Hosea, the first book in the twelve, ministered in Israel during the second half of the eight century B.C., making him a contemporary of Isaiah and Micah in Judah. It is said that his marriage was his message in that, at God's direction, he took a wife who was just as unfaithful to him as Israel was to the Lord. The first three chapters describe their tragic marriage.

Joel, whose name means "Yahweh is God," is a mystery. Nothing is known of him beyond his writing. He has the distinction of being one of the earliest of the Minor Prophets if conservative dating is correct, his ministry being assigned to the ninth century B.C. He is sometimes called the "prophet of Pentecost" for he predicted the events of Acts 2. He also predicted "the day of the Lord."

Amos was a shepherd from Judah whose ministry was in Israel. God called him to prophesy at Israel's idolatrous sanctuary at Bethel. He prophesied during a time of great social extremes—comfortable prosperity and grinding poverty. His message was directed against the wealthy who were exploiting the poor. Merchants were dishonest, and the judicial system favored the rich. Prosperity blinded the upper class regarding the sickness of their society.

Introduction to Hosea, Joel, and Amos

The Minor Prophets.   Due to the brevity of their works, the last twelve prophetic books are known as the Minor Prophets. The Jewish people treated them as one book that they called the "Twelve." All of them together are about the same length as Isaiah. Beginning with Obadiah (tenth century B.C.), their ministries extended to Malachi (fifth century B.C.). The order in which they occur is not the order in which they were written. The reason for their arrangement is unknown.

Authors.   The books are named for the men who wrote them. Aside from what can be learned in the books themselves, nothing is known about these authors.

Dates of writing.   The approximate dates of writing for these authors are as follows: 729 B.C., Hosea; 835 B.C., Joel (since the enemies mentioned in Joel are the Philistines, Phoenicians, Egyptians, and Edomites, rather than Assyria and Babylon); 755 B.C., Amos.

Themes.   The theme of Hosea is *the harlotry of Israel*. His own adultery-devastated marriage illustrates the relationship of Israel to God. The theme of Joel is *judgment on Judah*. The prophet foresees the catastrophe of the coming day of the Lord. Amos' theme is *apostasy brings judgment*. Social evils and pagan worship spell doom for Israel. Norman Geisler points out that they share a common concern for national restoration under Christ.[39]

Purposes. Primarily, each of these books was written to warn the Hebrew people of the dire consequences that awaited them if they did not turn from their idolatry and return to the Lord. Sadly, their warnings were not heeded. Yet the positive promises with which each book concludes indicates that a secondary purpose was to encourage people of faith that no matter how black the times, a better day was coming.

History and archaeology. In the eighth century B.C., the time of Hosea and Amos, the Northern Kingdom enjoyed a period of increased prosperity and some military success. However, this only blinded them to their spiritual poverty. Therefore, the nation continued its downward slide until destroyed by Assyria in 722 B.C. Ostraca[40] has been found at Samaria, the capital of the Northern Kingdom, bearing the name *Baal*, the primary god of the Canaanite pantheon.

Geography. Following the death of Solomon, the kingdom of Israel split into two warring factions. The Northern Kingdom, called Israel, had its capital at Samaria. The Southern Kingdom, called Judah, had Jerusalem as its capital. See map 8, page 57.

Outline of Hosea

   I. The faithless wife and the faithful husband (chaps. 1—3)
  II. The faithless nation and the faithful God (chaps. 4—14)

Overview of Hosea

The faithless wife and the faithful husband (chaps. 1—3).
God directs Hosea to marry an adulterous woman named Gomer. Three children are born to them and given names intended to be signs to Israel: Jezreel ("God scatters"), Lo-ruhamah ("not pitied"), and Lo-Ammi ("not my people"). Similarly, God will scatter and reject Israel without pity. Gomer leaves Hosea and finds other lovers. However, they reject her, and she is forced by economic necessity to sell herself as a slave.

Despite her degradation, Hosea redeems and restores her as his wife, picturing how God will treat Israel.

The faithless nation and the faithful God (chaps. 4—14). The experience of God with Israel parallels that of Hosea to Gomer. Just as Hosea loves Gomer, God loves Israel despite her unfaithfulness. Unfortunately, Israel has become hardened to God's appeals. Having violated his laws, they stand guilty before the Lord. Though God wants to redeem them (7:1, 13), they persist in their rebellion. Therefore, the nation will experience dispersion (chaps. 9—10). Yet because of God's endless love, he will eventually save them and bring back his erring people.

Outline of Joel

 I. The devastation of the land by locusts (1:1–20)
 II. The devastation of the land by invaders (2:1–17)
 III. The deliverance and blessings to come (2:18—3:21).

Overview of Joel

The devastation of the land by locusts (1:1–20). The opening chapter of Joel describes a plague of locusts that has devastated the land. The harvest has been ruined and everything stripped bare. To make matters worse, the land is in the grip of a drought.

The devastation of the land by invaders (2:1–17). The natural calamity that has befallen the land is an illustration of a coming, greater devastation. An army will invade the land in "the day of the Lord," causing unparalleled destruction. Still, the people have time to repent (2:12–17). Unfortunately, they do not do so, and this will lead to the later Babylonian invasion.

The deliverance and blessings to come (2:18—3:21). However, a future time of material and spiritual blessing will come (2:18–32), including the outpouring of the Holy Spirit (2:28; cf. Acts 2:16–18). In the last days, Israel will again be invaded when God gathers all nations of the world to the Valley of Jehoshaphat for a day of slaughter (cf. Rev. 16:12–; 19:11–21).[41] Afterwards, God's people will experience blessing and renewal (Joel 3:18–21).

Outline of Amos

I. Eight oracles (chaps. 1—2)
II. Three sermons (chaps. 3—6)
III. Five visions (chaps. 7:1—9:10)
IV. Promise of restoration (9:11–15)

Overview of Amos

Eight oracles (chaps. 1—2). God calls Amos, a resident of Judah, to preach in and against the Northern Kingdom of Israel. His prophecy opens with eight oracles directed against the seven nations around Israel and lastly against Israel itself. Each of these begins by saying, "For three transgressions . . . and for four." It is as though God is saying that the fourth is the "last straw." Every nation is ripe for judgment. Seven times, God says that he will send "fire," a symbol of judgment.

Three sermons (chaps. 3—6). Each beginning with the phrase, "Hear this word," Amos delivers three blistering sermons. The first (chap. 3) pronounces judgment; the second (chap. 4) exposes the crimes of the people; the third (chaps. 5-6) calls for repentance. Failure to repent will bring wailing and woe.

Five visions (7:1—9:10). The prophet next describes five visions of coming judgment on Israel. Due to the prophet's intercession, God relents concerning the first two. The third vision shows that Israel is like a crooked wall when God's plumb line is held next to it (7:7–9). In the only narrative section of the book, Amaziah, the priest presiding over the idolatrous worship at Bethel,[42] rebukes the prophet. Amos, however, stands his ground and gives two further visions. In the fourth, he sees Israel as a basket of ripe fruit, symbolizing their ripeness for judgment. In the fifth, he sees judgment beginning with the destruction of the sanctuary at Bethel, resulting in the dispersion of the northern tribes among the nations.

Promise of restoration (9:11–15). The closing verses of the prophecy look beyond the coming trouble and turmoil to a day of restoration. A king from the house of David[43] will once again reign, and the nation will enjoy untold abundance and peace.

Theological Highlights

The danger of superficial religion. Hosea rebukes a people that are united to God in name only. In practice, they turn to other gods. Likewise, Amos condemns the practice of religion at Bethel that, despite its ritual, has no contact with the true and living God. These dangers of a halfhearted, formal-but-dead religion continue to present themselves today.

The coming day of the LORD. Joel 2:1–11 and Amos 5:16–20 both speak of a terrible time of destruction known as the "day of the Lord." Equivalent to the Great Tribulation spoken of by Christ (Matt. 24) and John (Rev. 6:1—18:24), the day of the Lord is the time when God finally comes crashing into history to exercise judgment. It is a sobering warning that mankind will be accountable to God.

The coming of the Spirit. Joel predicts the outpouring of the Holy Spirit upon all flesh (2:28–29). Peter cited this prophecy in explanation of the events of the day of Pentecost (Acts 2) when the Holy Spirit descended with power upon the church. Ideally, the Christian life is intended to be a life characterized by the Spirit with respect to his fruit (Gal. 5:22–23) and filling (Eph. 5:18).

Social justice. Amos denounces those who oppress the poor (Amos 2:6–7; 4:1). God expects his people to exercise compassion towards the poor and to uphold their rights to life and property.

The coming kingdom. Each of these books ends with a prediction of the coming kingdom of God. It will bring peace and plenty, and evil will be no more. This hope is intended to sustain the people of God during times of adversity.

Key Verses

Hosea 4:1: "Hear the word of the LORD, you children of Israel, for the LORD brings a charge against the inhabitants of the land: 'There is no truth or mercy or knowledge of God in the land.'"

Joel 2:28–29: "And it shall come to pass afterward that I will pour out My Spirit on all flesh; your sons and your daughters shall prophesy, your old men shall dream dreams, your young men shall see visions. And also on My menservants and on My maidservants I will pour out My Spirit in those days."

Amos 5:24: "But let justice run down like water, and righteousness like a mighty stream."

Key Chapters

Hosea 1—3: The prophet's marriage illustrates the relationship between God and Israel.

Joel 2: This chapter contains both the prediction of the day of Pentecost and the coming day of the Lord.

Amos 5: God calls his people to repent or to face judgment.

Message of Hosea, Joel, and Amos

The first three Minor Prophets speak to us of the importance to love God and our neighbors. To scorn the love of God (as in Hosea) or to be selfishly indifferent to our neighbors (Amos) is to invite the judgment of God (all three).

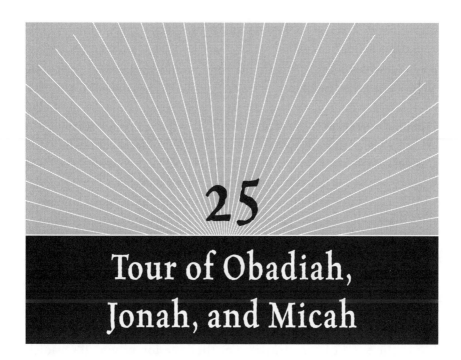

Tour of Obadiah, Jonah, and Micah

Preview of Obadiah, Jonah, and Micah

The next three Minor Prophets include the shortest Old Testament book (Obadiah), the "fishiest" book (Jonah), and a book best known for predicting the place of Christ's birth (Micah). But there is much more to these than first meets the eye. They present timeless messages about God's sovereignty, mercy, and justice.

Introduction to Obadiah, Jonah, and Micah

Authors. Nothing is known of the prophet Obadiah other than that his name means "servant of the Lord." He holds the distinction of writing the shortest book of the Old Testament. Jonah, the unwilling prophet, was a historical person (2 Kings 14:25). Legend has it that he was the son of the widow of Zarepath that Elijah raised from the dead (1 Kings 17:17–24). Micah was a contemporary of Isaiah, and his prophecy contains striking similarities to the larger work. His name is a question, "Who is like the Lord?"

Dates of writing. Opinion is divided on the date of Obadiah. It was clearly written in the aftermath of an invasion of Jerusalem where the invaders divided up the spoils (v. 11). This does not seem to fit the mass destruction of the Babylonian invasion, so perhaps it refers to the invasion of the Arab–Philistine force mentioned in 2 Chronicles 21:16–17. If so, this would place the date of composition around 846 B.C. Jonah, on the other hand, was written around 760 B.C., given the time of his life and historical events happening in the city of Nineveh that are thought to have a bearing on the details of his story. Micah must be dated close to the time of his contemporary, Isaiah, c. 700 B.C.

Themes. Obadiah's message is directed towards Edom, Judah's neighbor to the southeast. At the time of the invasion of which Obadiah speaks, Edom allied herself with the invaders, rather than offering support to her neighbor. Therefore, a simple way to remember the theme of Obadiah is "O bad Edom."

God called Jonah to preach to Israel's nemesis, Assyria (the capital of which was Nineveh). Jonah did not want to do this, for he feared they would repent (which they did) and escape judgment (which he wanted to fall on them). He needed to learn about God's mercy even upon the undeserving. So the theme of his book is *Jehovah is merciful.*

Micah writes out of a concern for the poor and oppressed. His message reflects this burden for social justice. Therefore, his theme might be phrased as *make society just.*

Purposes. Obadiah wrote with the purpose of showing that God would judge those who harmed his people (cf. Gen. 12:3). Jonah was written to show that God's grace extends to all people. Micah wrote to voice God's displeasure with social injustice.

History and archaeology. Through the centuries, there was an ongoing feud between Israel and Edom that provides the backdrop to Obadiah. The roots of this feud reach back to the patriarchal period.

Isaac had two sons, Esau and Jacob. Each became the head of a people: Esau, the father of the Edomites, and Jacob (renamed Israel), the father of the twelve tribes of Israel. Esau bore a grudge towards Jacob that his heirs perpetuated. They clashed often as the following verses show:

- Numbers 20:20–21, "So Edom came out against them with many men and with a strong hand. Thus Edom refused to give Israel passage through his territory; so Israel turned away from him."
- 1 Samuel 14:47, "So Saul established his sovereignty over Israel, and fought against all his enemies on every side, against Moab, against the people of Ammon, against Edom, against the kings of Zobah, and against the Philistines. Wherever he turned, he harassed them."
- 2 Samuel 8:14, "He also put garrisons in Edom; throughout all Edom he put garrisons, and all the Edomites became David's servants. And the LORD preserved David wherever he went."
- 1 Kings 11:14, "Now the LORD raised up an adversary against Solomon, Hadad the Edomite; he was a descendant of the king in Edom."
- 2 Chronicles 20:22 (Mt. Seir = Edom), "Now when they began to sing and to praise, the LORD set ambushes against the people of Ammon, Moab, and Mount Seir, who had come against Judah; and they were defeated."
- 2 Chronicles 21:8, "In his days Edom revolted against Judah's authority, and made a king over themselves."

During the general time of the story of Jonah, it is known that a series of catastrophes occurred in Nineveh that may have disposed the people to heed the warnings of a foreign prophet. Moreover, it is now known that the metropolitan area of Nineveh outside the walls of the administrative district was almost sixty miles in circumference. Hence, the statement that it required a three-day journey (Jon. 3:3).

Geography. The countries addressed by these prophets are Israel, Edom, and Nineveh (Assyria). See map 6, page 40, and map 7, page 57.

Outline of Obadiah

I. Edom's judgment (vv. 1–14)
II. Judah's restoration (vv. 15–21)

Overview of Obadiah

Obadiah begins his prophecy with a prediction that Edom, then feeling so secure, will cease to exist as a nation. Because of the aid she rendered to Israel's enemies (v. 11) and the advantage she took of Judah's helplessness (v. 12), she will be invaded and swallowed up. However, the Jews will experience deliverance (v. 17) and occupy the land of Edom (v. 19). The reason Obadiah gives is the sovereignty of God: "Then saviors shall come to Mount Zion to judge the mountains of Esau, and the kingdom shall be the LORD's" (v. 21).

Outline of Jonah

I. Jonah disobeys God and deserves to die (chap. 1)
II. God rescues Jonah who gives thanks for his mercy (chap. 2)
III. Jonah preaches that disobedient Nineveh deserves to die unless it repents (chap. 3).
IV. Nineveh repents, and Jonah resents God's mercy (chap. 4).

Overview of Jonah

In disobedience to God's call, Jonah attempts to flee. His flight is cut short by a terrible storm. When the sailors aboard the ship realize that he is responsible for their plight, Jonah admits that he deserves to die. Therefore, they hurl him into the sea (chap. 1). Mercifully, God rescues Jonah from death by having him swallowed by a large fish[44] (1:17). From within the fish, he repents and eloquently thanks God for sparing his life. Thereafter, the fish vomits Jonah onto dry land.

In the third chapter, Jonah warns that disobedient Nineveh will face judgment unless it repents. When the city does repent, Jonah becomes angry and resentful of the mercy God has shown (4:1–3). God then teaches Jonah, who has himself received mercy, that he delights in showing mercy (4:4–11). In other words, those who are shown mercy should not begrudge mercy to others.

Outline of Micah

I. The disobedient nations (chaps. 1—2)
II. The disobedient rulers (chaps. 3—5)
III. God's case against his people (chaps. 6—7)

Overview of Micah

Micah begins by condemning the sins of Israel and Judah. Because of their unfaithfulness to God, both kingdoms will be overthrown. Nevertheless, God will gather a remnant and bring them back (2:12–13). The prophet turns his attention to the princes, false prophets, and priests who abuse the poor, mislead the nation, and prostitute their office.

Chapters 4 and 5 provide a message of hope, describing the future kingdom of God. His focus narrows to the coming King in whom the nation will find peace (5:2–5).

In the sixth chapter, God presents his case against the ungodly nation. He will strike the nation for its lack of repentance. However, a day will come when Israel does repent, and God will forgive (chap. 7).

Theological Highlights

The sovereignty of God (Obadiah). Because of the wrong done to Judah by Edom, Obadiah predicted that God will someday destroy Edom (which he did by means of the Nabataens in the fifth century B.C.). God does not ignore the wrongs done by nations any more than those done by individuals.

The mercy of God (Jonah). Jonah emphasizes the mercy of God towards those who repent. In his willingness to forgive Nineveh, a picture is given of the heart of God. He does not desire to punish but to forgive.

The justice of God (Micah). The Book of Micah shows God's concern for social justice. In a day when there was much oppression of the poor and empty religious ritual, he calls for a piety that shows itself in kindness and justice (6:8).

Christ in Jonah and Micah

Jonah's escape from the belly of the fish after three days pictures Jesus' resurrection (Matt. 12:39–40). Micah 5:2 predicts Bethlehem as the place of his birth.

Key Verses

Obadiah 21: "Then saviors shall come to Mount Zion to judge the mountains of Esau, and the kingdom shall be the LORD's."

Jonah 4:11: "And should I not spare Nineveh, that great city, in which are more than one hundred and twenty thousand persons who cannot discern between their right hand and their left—and much livestock?"

Micah 6:8: "He has shown you, O man, what is good; and what does the LORD require of you but to do justly, to love mercy, and to walk humbly with your God?"

Key Chapters

Jonah 4: God teaches Jonah a lesson about mercy.

Micah 6: God threatens to judge Israel for her social injustice.

Message of Obadiah, Jonah, and Micah

These books preserve a balance between God's justice and mercy. On the one hand, God is a just God who will deal with people as their deeds deserve (as seen in Obadiah). On the other hand, he is merciful towards those who repent and will show them his compassion (as seen in Jonah). And he urges those who profess faith in him to be like him in these respects.

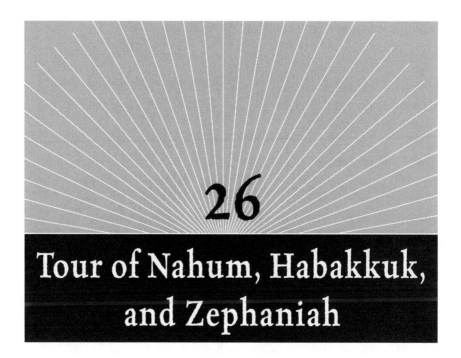

26

Tour of Nahum, Habakkuk, and Zephaniah

Preview of Nahum, Habakkuk, and Zephaniah

A famous sermon by R. G. Lee about judgment was titled, "Pay Day, Someday." The next three prophets echo this, each talking about national and international judgment. But each looks at God's judgment of nations a bit differently. Nahum shows that it operates on the basis of retributive justice; Habakkuk shows that God is righteous when he judges; and Zephaniah shows the finality of judgment on the day of the Lord.

Introduction to Nahum, Habakkuk, and Zephaniah

Authors. Conservative scholars believe the men who wrote these books are those whose names they bear. It is possible that Nahum's hometown of Elkosh (1:1) became known as the city of Capernaum mentioned in the New Testament, since the latter means "the village of

Nahum." The musical notations in Habakkuk 3:1, 19 suggest that he may have been a temple musician. A distinctive feature of Zephaniah is that his own genealogy is traced back to King Hezekiah, making him a member of the nobility.

Dates of writing. The Book of Nahum was written sometime after the fall of the Egyptian city of No-Amon (Thebes), mentioned in 3:8. This city was sacked by the Assyrians in 663 B.C. Since Nineveh fell in 612, the Book of Nahum would have been written between those two events. So a date about 650 B.C. seems likely. Habakkuk seems to have been written before the first Babylonian invasion (605 B.C.), but after the time Babylon had become a menace (following the fall of Nineveh in 612 B.C.). So a date of 607 B.C. can be assumed for Habakkuk. Finally, Zephaniah prophesied during the reign of King Josiah (640–609 B.C.). If he was associated with the revival that took place under Josiah in 621 B.C. (2 Chron. 34), then he delivered his message around 625 B.C.

Themes. As hinted in the opening statement of the book, Nahum's message concerns *Nineveh's coming judgment.* The cruel oppression of her neighbors and failure to maintain the repentance that took place at the preaching of Jonah has brought God's patience to an end. Habakkuk's burden concerns the need for *holiness in judgment.* He cannot understand why God uses a people worse than the Jews (i.e., the Babylonians) to judge the Jews. This seems to violate God's holiness. Finally, Zephaniah foresees the coming of wrath upon Jerusalem and Judah. He predicts the dreadful day of the Lord. So his theme might be stated as *Zion's frightful day.*

Purposes. Nahum effectively states his purpose in 1:3: to show that the Lord will punish the guilty. Habakkuk's purpose was to show that a righteous God could use unrighteous people to accomplish his purposes. Zephaniah wrote to warn the nation of the severity of judgment if it persisted in its idolatry.

History and archaeology. The seventh century B.C. witnessed the collapse of Assyria and the rise of Babylon on the world scene. Under the leadership of Nabopolassar, the Babylonians first succeeded in destroying the capital city of the Assyrian Empire, Nineveh, in 612 B.C. Then the last vestiges of Assyrian power were obliterated when Nebuchadnezzar defeated an Assyrian–Egyptian coalition in the Battle of Carchemish in 605 B.C. This left Babylon the undisputed master of the world.

Outline of Nahum

   I. The decree of Nineveh's fall (1:1–8)
  II. The completeness of Nineveh's fall (1:9–15)
 III. The description of Nineveh's fall (2:1—3:4)
  IV. The inescapability of Nineveh's fall (3:5–19)

Overview of Nahum

Nahum begins with a description of God that explains the inevitability of judgment (1:1–8). He then predicts that Nineveh will be destroyed, a matter of good news and peace for all who hear (1:10–15).[45] The next two chapters describe the fall of Nineveh. She will be helpless in the day of her distress.

Outline of Habakkuk

   I. Habakkuk's first question (1:1–4)
  II. God's first answer (1:5–11)
 III. Habakkuk's second question (1:12–17)
  IV. God's second answer (chap. 2)
   V. Habakkuk's song of praise (chap. 3)

Overview of Habakkuk

The book begins with Habakkuk's first question to God: Why doesn't he do something about the wickedness in Judah (1:2–4)? God replies that he is going to send the Babylonians (1:5–11). This only gives rise to another question: How can God use people worse than the Jews to punish the

Jews without compromising his righteousness (1:12—2:1)? God replies that Babylon, too, will be judged, thus upholding his righteousness (2:2–20). Habakkuk concludes with a prayer in which he praises God and vows to trust him, come what may (3:1–19).

Outline of Zephaniah

  I.   Judgment in the day of the Lord (1:1—3:8)
 II.   Salvation in the day of the Lord (3:9–20)

Overview of Zephaniah

The book largely concerns the coming of God's wrath in the day of the Lord. Not only will it affect Judah but also the nations about her (2:4–15). Jerusalem in particular is ripe for judgment, for the city where God caused his name to dwell is filled with falsehood and injustice (3:1–7). Indeed, his day of wrath will ultimately encompass all the earth (3:8). Yet, beyond judgment, a time of blessing will come when the King of Israel, the Lord, will be in Judah's midst and restore her fortunes (3:9–20).

Theological Highlights

The judgment of God.   Each of these books stresses that men and nations are subject to God. If they ignore his commands and spurn his mercy, then judgment is not a question of "if" but "when."

The importance of faith and hope.   Habakkuk and Zephaniah both stress the necessity of facing uncertain and difficult days with faith and hope. Without denying the reality of suffering that befalls godly people, both prophets point to the Lord as the source of strength while waiting for better days to come.

Key Verses

Nahum 1:7: "The LORD is good, a stronghold in the day of trouble; and He knows those who trust in Him."

Habakkuk 2:4: "Behold the proud, his soul is not upright in him; but the just shall live by his faith."

Zephaniah 2:3: "Seek the LORD, all you meek of the earth, who have upheld His justice. Seek righteousness, seek humility. It may be that you will be hidden in the day of the LORD's anger."

Key Chapters

Nahum 1: This chapter announces the Lord's judgment on Nineveh.

Habakkuk 3: The prophet's song celebrates the majesty of God and the prophet's resolve to trust him.

Zephaniah 3: This chapter announces two distinct parts to the day of the Lord, judgment and restoration.

Message of Nahum, Habakkuk, and Zephaniah

Nations are accountable to the Lord. Each of these prophets stresses this message in slightly differing ways. So the social injustice and moral transgressions of our society are matters for public concern. Neither our military might nor our economic prosperity can prevent our nation from going into decline or even ceasing to exist should we persist in ignoring the Lord.

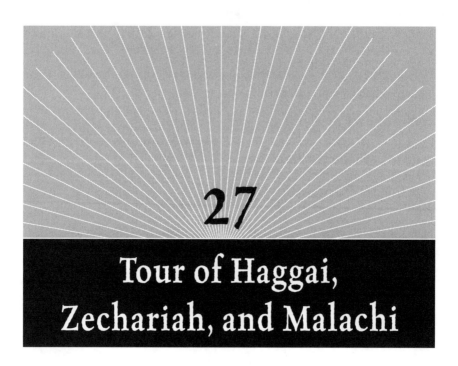

Tour of Haggai, Zechariah, and Malachi

Preview of Haggai, Zechariah, and Malachi

The remaining three prophets all preached in the days following the Jew's return from Babylon in 536 B.C. New circumstances and new problems faced the remnant. No longer was idolatry the problem it had been. Now a halfhearted approach to the worship of the Lord was the concern. These prophets rallied the faithful to a renewed zeal.

Introduction to Haggai, Zechariah, and Malachi

Authors. Strong tradition supports the authorship of these books by the men whose names they bear. Critics sometimes try to assign chapters 9–14 of Zechariah to someone else on the basis that it has a different style and tone than the first part of the book. However, the change in subject matter can account for this.

Malachi was written about one hundred years later than Haggai and Zechariah. The lack of any mention of his prophetic ministry in Nehemiah or of Nehemiah in his book suggests that he followed Jerusalem's great governor. This makes him the last of the Old Testament writers.

Dates of writing. Both Haggai and Zechariah date to the latter part of the sixth century before Christ. An approximate time of writing would be 520 B.C. Malachi was written about 420 B.C.

Themes. The theme of Haggai is *the house of God*. He exhorts the Jews returning from the Exile to complete the reconstruction of the temple. The theme of Zechariah may be stated as *Zion's remnant saved*. He encourages the Jewish returnees by assuring them that their labors will not be in vain. God does indeed have a future for them. Finally, the theme of Malachi can be phrased as *make righteous ways*. He deplores the spiritual backsliding that characterizes the Jewish nation in the generations following the revival under Haggai and Zechariah.

Purposes. Haggai and Zechariah prophesy in the postexilic period, the time following the seventy years of captivity in Babylon. When Jerusalem falls to Babylon in 586 B.C., the beautiful temple of Solomon is destroyed. Work to rebuild it begins in 535 B.C. following the first return of Jews under Zerubbabel (Ezra 3). However, the opposition of the enemies of the Jews (Ezra 4) halts the reconstruction. Then, after a delay of some fifteen years, Haggai and Zechariah encourage the people, with the result that the work is resumed (Ezra 5:1–2). It takes another four years to finish the work, but by 515 B.C., after seventy years without a temple, the Jewish people once again have a place for worship. In contrast to Zechariah who speaks of more than the temple, Haggai speaks predominantly about the temple. Malachi, who follows 100 years after Haggai and Zechariah, intends to revive the nation. Following the revival under Nehemiah, the Jews had again fallen into half-hearted obedience. The vigorous preaching of Malachi rebukes them for the purpose of perfecting their obedience."

History and archaeology. In 538 B.C., the Medes and Persians defeated the Babylonians. Thereafter, they permitted the exiled Jews to return to their ancestral land, the same as they did for other captive peoples. It was during this time that the Samaritans of the New Testament found their origins. They had been settled in the Northern Kingdom of Israel by the Assyrians and had intermarried with the few remaining Israelites. Their religion was a mixture of paganism and historic Israelite religion. Ezra 4–6 tells how they hindered the construction of the temple.

Outline of Haggai

    I. The call to rebuild God's house (chap. 1)
   II. The future glory of God's house (2:1–9)
 III. The blessings for helping build God's house (2:10–19)
 IV. The blessing on Zerubbabel for rebuilding God's house (2:19–20)

Overview of Haggai

Because the people have neglected the house of God, God withholds his blessing from them. Once the temple is completed, the people can anticipate a future blessing of great magnitude as described in 2:6–9. It awaits a future fulfillment at the time of the second coming of our Lord.

Outline of Zechariah

    I. The call to repentance (1:1–6)
   II. The eight night visions (1:7— 6:8)
 III. The crowning of Joshua the priest (6:9–15)
 IV. The question concerning fasts (7:1—8:23)
   V. The coming King and kingdom (9:1—14:21)

Overview of Zechariah

While Zechariah does have an immediate concern with the rebuilding of the temple (1:16; 4:9), he puts these concerns into a much larger context: The people should rebuild because God has a great future for the nation. God will return to Zion and dwell in her midst (8:3), and the remnant of the people will be blessed so that they might be a blessing (8:13). But before that final gathering of the remnant, times of distress will come upon the nation (9:1—14:15). The Lord will usher in a final victory, though, and establish Jerusalem as the spiritual center of the earth (14:18–21).

Outline of Malachi

   I. The love of God for the nation (1:15)
  II. The sins of the priests (1:6—2:9)
 III. The sins of the people (2:10—3:17)
  IV. The day of the Lord (4:1–6)

Overview of Malachi

Through the skillful use of questions and answers, Malachi calls the nation to account for its backsliding ways. They cheat God with respect to his offerings and tithes (1:7–8; 3:8). Priests corrupt the Law (2:8). Men enter mixed marriages (2:11) while divorcing their wives (2:14). And they deny the value of serving God. In all these ways, the Jewish people have departed from the way of the Lord as presented in the Law of Moses (4:4). For this reason, blessing has been withheld and judgment looms (3:1–3; 4:1). But those who fear the Lord can look forward to a day of renewal and victory (4:2–3).

Christ in Haggai, Zechariah, and Malachi. These three books collectively contain nearly a dozen prophecies that Christians have historically interpreted as applying to Christ. He is seen as the following:

- The Desire of all nations (Hag. 2:7)
- God's Servant the Branch (Zech. 3:8; 6:12)
- The King-Priest (Zech. 6:12–13)
- The Savior-King coming on a donkey (Zech. 9:9; see John 12:14)

- The Cornerstone (Zech. 10:4)
- The Pierced One (Zech. 12:10; see John 19:37)
- The stricken Shepherd (Zech. 13:7)
- The Lord who will stand on the Mount of Olives (Zech. 14:3–4)
- The Messenger of the covenant (Mal. 3:1)
- The Sun of Righteousness (4:2)

Key Verses

Haggai 2:7: "'And I will shake all nations, and they shall come to the Desire of All Nations, and I will fill this temple with glory,' says the LORD of hosts."

Zechariah 9:9: "Rejoice greatly, O daughter of Zion! Shout, O daughter of Jerusalem! Behold, your King is coming to you; He is just and having salvation, lowly and riding on a donkey, a colt, the foal of a donkey" (see Matt. 21:1–5).

Malachi 3:1: "'Behold, I send My messenger, and he will prepare the way before Me. And the Lord, whom you seek, will suddenly come to His temple, even the Messenger of the covenant, in whom you delight. Behold, He is coming,' says the LORD of hosts."

Key Chapters

Haggai 2, Zechariah 14, and Malachi 4: Each of these chapters present a prophetic hope of ultimate victory and glory for the nation of Israel."

Messages of Haggai, Zechariah, and Malachi

Haggai confronts believers with a big question: Can they expect God's blessing if they ignore his purposes for them? God's priority was the building of the temple in Haggai's day. Failure to address that priority resulted in a loss of blessing. The question to be asked today is what is God's purpose for the church and are we fulfilling that purpose?

Zechariah, by drawing attention to the ultimate establishment of the kingdom of God on earth, encourages God's people to be faithful through difficult times that will surely precede the Lord's coming. Knowing the end that awaits us makes the sacrifice worthwhile.

The message of Malachi concerns the danger of spiritual apathy and indifference. A merely formal religion—going through motions without an accompanying desire to honor and obey the Lord—is unacceptable to him.

28

Introduction to the New Testament

He Kaine Diatheke (*Latin*, Novum Testamentum) *literally means "The New Covenant." The Greek word* diatheke *speaks of a last will and testament that came into effect upon the death of the testator. The New Covenant was ratified with the blood of Christ, and a person enters into that covenant relationship when he comes to God on His terms. This redemptive covenant is a unifying theme that bind the books of the New Testament together.* [46]

The Old Testament Foundation

The study of the New Testament is severely limited without some knowledge of the Old Testament. A foundation for the New is laid in the Old. Therefore, a brief overview of the Old Testament is appropriate before we study the New Testament.

In the Old Testament, the story is told of how God created the world and revealed himself to mankind. It begins by describing how God created the universe *ex nihilo* (out of nothing) and placed Adam in an ideal environment where he would act as God's governor over creation (Gen. 1—2). But Adam and Eve failed to trust and obey God. The judicial consequence of disobedience was the curse on humans and their works (Gen. 3). Thus, because they set their wills against God, they were separated from God.

In his plan to overcome this separation, God called Abram (subsequently changed to Abraham) and made him three promises.

- The promise of a land (Gen. 12:1; 13:14–15; 15:18–21)
- The promise of a great nation (Gen. 12:2; 17:4–6)
- The promise of blessing to him and through him to the world (Gen. 12:3; 22:18)

From Abraham's descendants grew the nation of Israel. After spending four hundred years as slaves in Egypt, they made their exodus under Moses. Through Moses, God gave his Law to Israel, the core of which was the Ten Commandments (Exod. 20). This constituted God's covenant with Israel. Thereafter, Israel occupied the land of Canaan as God had promised to Abraham.

Centuries passed in which the kings and people of Israel became progressively more unfaithful to God. This occasioned the prophetic prediction of a great King from the line of David who would reign and the implementation of a new covenant that would change people's hearts by placing the Spirit of God within them (Jer. 31:31–34, 33:14–15; Ezek. 36:24–27; 37:24–28). Sadly, Israel departed so far from God that he allowed the nation to be destroyed and the people to go into captivity in Babylon. After seventy years, a remnant returned to rebuild the fallen nation (Ezra; Nehemiah).

The story of the Old Testament draws to a close with a sense of anticipation. The promised King or Messiah (in Greek, *Christ*, both meaning "the Anointed [King]") was yet to come. The change of covenants was yet to take place. The New Testament would continue the unfolding of these predicted events.

Changes between the Testaments

More than four hundred years passed between the ministry of Malachi that concluded the Old Testament and the birth of Christ that opened the New Testament. During those so-called "intertestamental" years, vast changes occurred that set the stage for the events and writings of the New Testament.

Political changes

During the four centuries before Christ, power shifted from East to West. In the time of the Old Testament, the dominant world powers were eastern: Egypt, Assyria, Babylon, and Persia. Power shifted West with the conquest of the East by Alexander the Great in the fourth century before Christ. This brilliant military leader came from Macedonia, a Greek-speaking country on the northern perimeter of Greece.

Following his death, Alexander's empire fragmented into four smaller kingdoms. In turn, these were absorbed into the Roman Empire that underwent its greatest expansion in the three centuries before Christ. The Romans entered Jerusalem under Pompey in 63 B.C. In 40 B.C. the Roman senate declared Herod "the king of the Jews." He loyally served Rome until his death in 4 B.C. While Roman rule was oppressive, it did create peace throughout the Mediterranean world. This *pax Romana* allowed the gospel to spread more easily in the first century after Christ.

Language changes

Through his conquests, Alexander extended the Greek language and culture throughout the East. The type of Greek spoken from his day to the third century after Christ (a period of six hundred years) was known as Koine (meaning "common") Greek. This became the language of trade and literature throughout the ancient world. Educated Romans widely used Greek, and even the people of Judea and Galilee had a working knowledge of Greek due to trade and the proximity of Greek-speaking communities to the east of the Jordan River.

The everyday language spoken by the Jews who returned from Babylon in 538 B.C. and continuing through the time of Christ was Aramaic. This Semitic language was adopted from the Babylonians. It is similar to Hebrew in the way that Spanish is similar to Portuguese. By Jesus' day, Hebrew had become a liturgical language employed in worship, much as Latin was in the Catholic church until the 1960s.

Religious changes

Major religious changes took place in the four hundred years between the testaments. This was the time when religious parties came into existence. The chart below summarizes.

Religious Parties in the New Testament Period

Group	A Distinct Belief	New Testament	Place in Society
Pharisees	Resurrection	Mentions	Common People
Sadducees	No resurrection	Mentions	Aristocratic
Essenes	No temple worship	Not mentioned	Communal life

Another major religious change that occurred in the intertestamental period was the translation of the Old Testament from Hebrew into Greek. This, the first known translation of Scripture, is called the *Septuagint* (meaning "the seventy") because it supposedly took seventy scholars seventy days to make seventy identical translations. This translation (often abbreviated LXX) was the Bible of the early church. Its influence is also seen in the New Testament where the apostle Paul sometimes quoted from it.

A third religious change that took place in the intertestamental period was the loss of confidence among pagan peoples in the gods of Greece and Rome. The intense religious search that followed provided fertile soil for the gospel (the "good news" of Christ).

The Growth of the New Testament

Altogether, the New Testament contains twenty-seven books. At first, these circulated independently of one another. However, from a very early time, Christians began to share, copy, and make collections of these writings (see, for example, Col. 4:16). By the end of the fourth century after Christ, the present twenty-seven books enjoyed universal recognition as the New Testament.

The primary factor determining whether or not a document was included in the New Testament (that is, recognized as having the status of Scripture) was authorship. Ancient Christians carefully determined if a book was written by an apostle of Christ or by someone closely associated with an apostle (such as Mark or Luke). Many works that falsely claimed to be apostolic (such as the Gospel of Peter and the Gospel of Thomas) were rejected. A few books (Second Peter and Revelation among them) were regarded with caution by some who doubted their genuineness. However, a majority of ancient Christians never doubted the twenty-seven books.

The Arrangement of the New Testament

The New Testament books fall into three categories: history, letters, and prophecy.

Historical books. Five books belong in this category: the four Gospels (*gospel* means "good news") and the Acts of the Apostles. The Gospels (Matthew, Mark, Luke, and John) interpret the life of Christ. While they are historical, they are highly selective in what they present (for instance, only one episode from the boyhood of Jesus is mentioned, and a disproportionate amount of space is given to the last week of Jesus' life). These four books are further subdivided. The first three are called the *synoptic* (meaning "seeing together") Gospels. They have much material in common, almost identical wording in many cases, and follow a similar outline of the life of Christ. Yet each has some unique material. Two possible explanations for their similarity is that either the authors worked from a common oral tradition or else they had documents available to them which have since been lost.

John's Gospel differs significantly from the other three. It is much more reflective; it never mentions the baptism of Jesus; it mentions three Passover festivals during the time of Christ's ministry, whereas the Synoptics mention only one; and it devotes more attention to the ministry of Jesus in Judea than in Galilee—the reverse of the Synoptics. The chart below compares the four Gospels.

Comparison of the Four Gospels

Matthew	Mark	Luke	John
Synoptic	Synoptic	Synoptic	Supplementary
To Jews	To Romans	To Greeks	To the church
Jesus as King	Jesus as Servant	Jesus as Son	Jesus as the Word
Prophetic	Practical	Historical	Spiritual
53 O.T. quotes	36 O.T. quotes	25 O.T. quotes	20 O.T. quotes

The Acts of the Apostles (or "Acts" for short) continues the story from the time of Jesus' ascension into heaven to the establishment of the church in Rome. It describes the birth of the church on the day of Pentecost, tells of its early growth in Jerusalem, and gives the highlights of Paul's missionary journeys.

The letters. Also known as "epistles," the twenty-one letters of the New Testament fall into two categories: those by Paul and those by other writers. The thirteen letters by Paul come first (Romans–Philemon). They are named after their recipients. The eight remaining letters (Hebrews–Jude) are named after their authors, the one exception being Hebrews. While some people think Paul wrote Hebrews, it is so unlike anything else he wrote that it is always included in the eight so-called General Epistles. In both the Pauline and General Epistles, letters are arranged according to their length, starting with the longest. The letters of the New Testament apply Christian faith to life.

The prophetic book. Only one book is purely prophetic in the New Testament, the Book of Revelation. This concluding work of the New Testament looks down the path of time to the ultimate triumph of Christ and the establishment of his kingdom over the world.

Message of the New Testament

The New Testament speaks to us about the fact that Jesus the King has come, bringing forgiveness of sins and the promise of eternal life to all who believe in him. To be rightly related to life, we must be rightly related to him. Such a relationship is one of faith leading to obedience.

The ABC'S of Intertestamental History

	Political	Religious	Cultural
A	Alexander the Great, 333–323 B.C.	Academic Judaism (scribes & lawyers)	Aegean (Western) orientation
B	Breakup of Alexander's Empire, 323 B.C.	Bible translated to Greek (LXX, the Septuagint)	Bilingual world
C	Conflict between Ptolemaic & Seleucid kings, 198–167 B.C.	Contempt for the temple by Seleucids	Colonization of East by Greeks
D	Deliverance by the Maccabees, 167 B.C.	Deuterocanonical books written; development of religious parties	Destruction of Carthage, 146 B.C., by Rome
E	Entry into Jerusalem by Romans under Pompey, 63 B.C.	Essenes produce the Dead Sea Scrolls; expectation of Messiah builds	Ease of travel increases as Rome builds roads, stops pirates

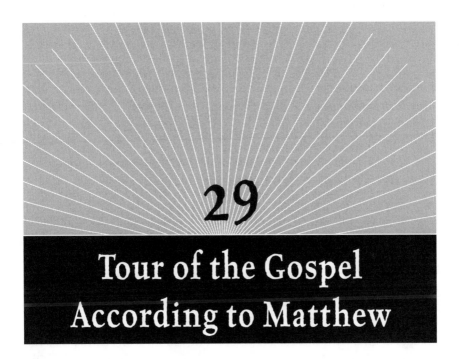

29

Tour of the Gospel
According to Matthew

Preview of Matthew

Four hundred years passed from the ministry of Malachi to the opening pages of Matthew. The world's attention was directed to Rome where Caesar Augustus reigned supreme. Judea was a minor province in the vast Roman Empire. Yet here an event unnoticed by the world took place that would forever change the world—Christ was born. Matthew links his life and death to the prophecies of the Old Testament in solemn testimony to this glorious event, showing how Israel's Messiah is the Savior of all nations. Matthew also places great emphasis on Jesus' teaching ministry, with five great discourses by Christ in the book (chaps. 5—7, 10, 13, 18, 24—25).

Introduction to Matthew

Author. Matthew Levi (Matt. 9:9; Mark 2:14), a Roman tax collector by trade.[47] His collaboration with the Romans would cause the Jews to despise him. However, his position required literacy, a fact that supports the ancient tradition that attributes the authorship of the first Gospel to him. Further support for his authorship is seen in the fact that the first Gospel has more references to money and more types of money than any other Gospel.

Date of writing. Around A.D. 60. Support for this is seen in that the destruction of Jerusalem predicted in chapter 24 is not recorded as having happened. Jerusalem was destroyed by Rome in A.D. 70, suggesting that this Gospel was written before that time.

Exemplary Old Testament Predictions in Matthew

Theme. Messiah has come. Recalling that *Messiah* (Greek, "Christ") had reference to the promised King, it is important to note that the first Gospel begins with the declaration that it is about Jesus Christ (i.e., the King), the Son of David. Thereafter, Matthew draws heavily upon Old Testament prophecies to demonstrate that Jesus is the Promised One. For example, note the following Old Testament citations.

Exemplary Old Testament Predictions in Matthew

Passage in Matthew:	Old Testament Prediction:
Matthew 1:22–23	Isaiah 7:14
Matthew 2:5–6	Micah 5:2
Matthew 4:12–16	Isaiah 9:1-2
Matthew 21:2–5	Zechariah 9:9

Purpose. Matthew seems to have written with two major purposes in mind. Primarily, he wished to show the Jewish people that Jesus was their Messiah. As a necessary part of this, he also desired to connect the events of Christ's life to the predictions made about the Messiah in the Old Testament.

History and archaeology. The Gospel according to Matthew covers the years from 6 B.C. to A.D. 33. At the outset, Caesar Augustus ruled the Roman Empire. Upon his death in A.D. 14, Tiberius became Caesar. The vassal king of the Jews under Augustus was Herod the Great, who died in 4 B.C. His kingdom was divided among his three sons, Archaelus, Philip, and Antipas. Archaelus was subsequently removed by Rome and replaced with procurators appointed by Rome. The best known of these was Pontius Pilate who governed Judea from A.D. 26 to 36. An inscription discovered at Caesarea Maritima in this century mentions both Pilate and Tiberius. This is the only archeological evidence of Pilate ever found. During this period, the dislike of Roman rule fueled an intense messianic expectation among the Jewish people.

Geography. The Gospel of Matthew, after mentioning the flight to Egypt by Joseph and Mary with the baby Jesus, devotes most of its attention to Jesus' ministry in Galilee. Nazareth, Jesus' boyhood home, and Capernaum, his ministry headquarters, were there.

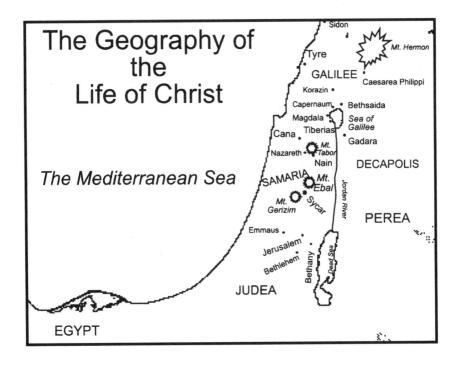

Outline of Matthew

I. The preparation of the King (1:1—4:11)
II. Jesus' ministry in Galilee (4:12—18:35)
III. Jesus' ministry in Judea and Jerusalem (19:1—25:46)
IV. Jesus' suffering and resurrection (26:1—28:20)

Overview of Matthew

The preparation of the King (1:1—4:11). Matthew begins by tracing the descent of Jesus from two of the Old Testament's greatest figures: Abraham and David. This is significant, for through Abraham had come the promise of blessing to the world, and David was promised a descendant who would rule the nations of the earth (Ps. 2:8). Thus, Matthew links these two vital promises in the one person of Jesus. By undergoing baptism (chap. 3), Jesus identifies with the ministry of his forerunner, John the Baptist. Thereafter, he proves his moral perfection by withstanding the temptations in the wilderness (4:1–11).

Jesus' ministry in Galilee (4:12—18:35). After describing the baptism and temptation of Jesus, Matthew briefly describes Jesus' return to Galilee and the selection of disciples (4:12–22). There follows a sample of Jesus' teaching (chaps. 5–7), called the Sermon on the Mount. The background to the sermon is the call to repent (i.e., to change one's mental focus) and to follow him, trusting in his power (4:17–25).

The first portion of this sermon describes the spiritual conditions of his followers that promise them blessing. Jesus hereby shows that ordinary people can indeed experience the fullness of his kingdom. Turning the prevailing philosophy of the day on its head, he asserts that it is not the rich and the well-to-do who are blessed but those who humbly seek the ways of God. The balance of the Sermon on the Mount demonstrates that righteousness begins within. Apart from transformed hearts, we cannot attain righteousness. The problem with the righteousness of the scribes and Pharisees (5:20) was that it was all for show—a pursuit of religious respectability. So Jesus did not intend to give stricter laws than Moses gave but to correct the externalism of the day by pointing to the need of inward transformation that takes place in true repentance.

The topics in the sermon have an order. Christ starts with anger and contempt (5:21–26), for that is where most human moral failure begins. Anger and contempt are most often behind marital discord that leads to adultery and divorce (5:27–32). Likewise, anger, contempt, adultery, and divorce lead to deception, retaliation, and hatred (5:33–48). In short, Jesus shows that to be truly good, we must pursue from the heart that which is good for our neighbors.

Having answered in chapter 5 the two fundamental questions of who is blessed and who is good, Jesus deals in chapter 6 with two main obstacles to blessing and goodness. These are the desire for approval and the misguided pursuit of wealth. Then, in chapter 7 he shows how we can help others attain kingdom righteousness. We do this first of all by leaving off condemnation and trying to force our "pearls" upon them. Such behavior also stems from anger and contempt. Instead, we engage in appeal—asking them (and God) instead of trying to direct them. This, after all, is how we want to be treated (7:1–12). The remainder of chapter 7 issues three warnings. First, we must diligently seek the way of Christ, for the old way of religious respectability is easy to travel (vv. 13–14). Second, we must be wary of people who talk religiously but do not evidence the fruit of righteousness as described in the sermon (vv. 15–20). Third, we must not be content with merely knowing what Jesus taught; we must obey it (vv. 21–27). His sermon is a way of life.

The authority of Jesus is demonstrated by ten miracles (chaps. 8—9). By sending his disciples into the cities and villages of Israel (chap. 10), Jesus extends his message to the entire nation. However, it becomes evident that the nation as a whole will reject him (chaps. 11—12). This leads him to cloak his teaching in parables that he interprets to his disciples (chap. 13) as he becomes more intimate with them (chaps. 14—18).

Jesus' ministry in Judea and Jerusalem (19:1—25:46). Jesus enters Judea (19:1) and Jerusalem (21:1) where opposition becomes intense. After confrontations with the religious leaders in Jerusalem, he gives his famous discourse on the end times known as the Olivet Discourse (chaps. 24—25). The first part deals in a general way with the times between his first and second comings (24:1–14). Then, with the introduction of the abomination of desolation (24:15), he instructs his disciples regarding the Great Tribulation. He pointedly teaches that he will return physically and visibly (24:30). The balance of chapters 24 and 25 stresses the need to live with watchfulness and readiness.

Jesus' sufferings and resurrection (26:1—28:20). Just prior to the Passover feast, Judas agrees to betray him (26:14–16). Following trials before the Sanhedrin and Pilate, Jesus is crucified (chap. 27). On the Sunday morning following the Friday crucifixion, Jesus appears to the women who have come to his tomb. He then reveals himself to his disciples and gives them what is known as the Great Commission (Matt. 28:18–20). Four things believers are commanded to do in the Great Commission include going to all nations where we are to make disciples, baptize, and teach the gospel.

Theological Highlights

Concerning Scripture. Jesus taught that the Scriptures will endure until all things in them are fulfilled (5:18). Looking at Jesus' declaration here concerning Scripture and his use of an Old Testament passage in 22:31–32 (where his argument rests upon one word, "am"), it is clear that he viewed Scripture as possessing authority extending to the very words used.

Concerning God. God is the God of the living (22:32), meaning that he preserves the lives of his followers after death. Thus, Jesus taught the reality of life after death. Further, Jesus taught that God is entitled to complete love and loyalty (22:37).

Concerning the church. Jesus will build his Church upon the confession that he is the Christ (16:18).

Key Verse

Matthew 28:18–20: "And Jesus came and spoke to them, saying, 'All authority has been given to Me in heaven and on earth. Go therefore and make disciples of all the nations, baptizing them in the name of the Father and of the Son and of the Holy Spirit, teaching them to observe all things that I have commanded you; and, lo, I am with you always, even to the end of the age.' Amen."

Key Chapters

Matthew 5—7: the Sermon on the Mount.

Message of Matthew

In our troubled world, Matthew reminds us that God plans to establish his kingdom. For the time, it spreads as a spiritual kingdom of those who receive the message of Jesus. Christians today are to be busy in spreading the message that the Messiah has come.

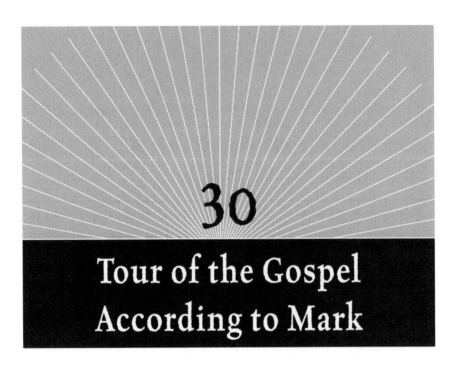

30

Tour of the Gospel According to Mark

Preview of Mark

Mark is a book recounting the deeds of Jesus. No less than half the recorded miracles of Christ (eighteen of thirty-six) are found in this book. Over and over, Mark tells us that "straightway" Jesus did something. In contrast to Matthew, Mark only gives slight attention to Jesus' teaching.

Introduction to Mark

Author. John Mark, an early disciple from Jerusalem (Acts 12:12) and companion of Paul and Barnabas on their first missionary journey. For some unknown reason, he quit the mission and returned to Jerusalem (Acts 13:13). The cousin of Barnabas (Col. 4:10), he traveled with him following his separation from Paul (Acts 15:37–40). Whatever differences Mark had with Paul were short-lived, for we find him mentioned not only in Paul's letter to the Colossians but also in Philemon (v. 24) and 2 Timothy 4:11. He also became close to the apostle Peter who described him as his "son" (1 Pet. 5:13), perhaps suggesting that he led Mark to Christ. Tradition[48] holds that what Mark wrote was the gospel as preached by Peter at Rome. For a possible connection of Mark to Jesus, see Mark 14:51–52.

Date of writing. A.D. 67 or earlier. Traditional statements do not make it clear if Mark wrote before or after the death of Peter. A date somewhere in the middle of the first century seems likely since the Rufus mentioned by Paul in Romans 16:13 is quite likely the same man mentioned in Mark 15:21.

Theme. Man's Servant-Savior. The best expression of Mark's theme is found in 10:45, "For even the Son of Man did not come to be served, but to serve, and to give His life a ransom for many." Notice the twofold but related purposes of Christ: on the one hand, service; on the other, salvation. Compassion for mankind is the unifying factor between these two. The theme is supported by the abundant examples of Christ's works or service and the disproportionate space given to his final week (almost 40 percent of the book) in which he wrought salvation.

Purpose. Apparently, Mark's purpose was to interpret the significance of Christ's life to a Roman audience. Reasons include that Mark alone uses some Latin terms (Latin being the language of the Romans); he explains Jewish customs unfamiliar to Romans; and he identifies Simon of Cyrene (15:21) as the father of Rufus, a member of the church at Rome (cf. Rom. 16:13).

Textual problems. Mark's conclusion has been the source of unending controversy. The oldest manuscripts do not contain 16:9–20. Altogether, three different endings of Mark are found among the manuscripts. It may be that the longer ending reflects an attempt by some to give a smoother conclusion to the book. However, it is also possible that the oldest manuscripts currently possessed were made from a corrupt copy in which the longer ending had been lost.

History and archaeology. The Book of Acts (28:15) attests to the fact that Christianity was established in Rome prior to the apostle Paul's first imprisonment (c. A.D. 60). It is likely that some visitors from Rome who were in Jerusalem on the day of Pentecost (Acts 2:10) did the first preaching of the gospel there. Despite horrible persecutions under Nero that claimed the lives of both Peter and Paul, the Christian community continued to grow as inscriptions in the catacombs show. Therefore, a need for a written account of the Gospel would have existed in Rome from early in the Christian era.

Geography. In common with Matthew and Luke, Mark gives more attention to Jesus' ministry in Galilee than in Judea. See map 10, page 165.

Outline of Mark

  I.   Jesus' baptism and temptation (1:1–13)
 II.   Jesus' ministry in Galilee (1:14—9:50)
III.   Jesus' ministry in Judea and Jerusalem (10:1—13:37)
 IV.   Jesus' death and resurrection (14:1—16:20)

Overview of Mark

Jesus' baptism and temptation (1:1–13). Without any reference to the birth of Jesus, Mark begins his narrative with the story of Jesus' baptism and temptation, events that inaugurated his public ministry.

Jesus' ministry in Galilee (1:14—9:50). A rapidly moving account of Jesus' selection of his disciples and the beginning of his ministry in Galilee follows the temptation story. One episode of special importance is the healing of a paralytic man (2:1–12). Jesus uses this as a demonstration of his authority to forgive sins, an authority that make him equal with God. An early reaction to Jesus sets in among the Pharisees that would eventually lead to his death (3:6). The following chapters alternate between the miracles of Jesus and short accounts of his teaching, with opposition to him growing all the while.

Jesus' ministry in Judea and Jerusalem (10:1—13:37).
From chapter 10 onward, the action shifts from Galilee to Judea and
Jerusalem (10:1). The disciples mistakenly interpret his advance to
Jerusalem as the prelude to earthly glory, even though he had spoken
to them of his coming death (10:32–41). Jesus corrects their ideas and
ambitions by pointing to himself as a model of servant-leadership
(10:45). Though he enters Jerusalem like a king (11:1–10), he would
shortly die as a criminal.

Jesus' death and resurrection (14:1—16:20). Betrayal leads
to the arrest, trials, and crucifixion of Jesus. However, death was not the
end of his story. The Sunday after the crucifixion found the tomb empty
and Jesus risen (16:1–8).

Theological Highlights

Concerning Christ. Mark records two statements by Christ that
his adversaries understood as claims to deity. The first was the authority
to forgive sins (2:10). The second was that he was Lord of the Sabbath
(2:28). Since God gave Israel the Sabbath, this title would normally have
been reserved for God.

Jesus also manifested a foreknowledge of his death. "For He taught
His disciples and said to them, 'The Son of Man is being betrayed into
the hands of men, and they will kill Him. And after He is killed, He will
rise the third day'" (Mark 9:31; see also 10:32–34, 45; 14:8, 24–25).

Concerning man. What makes people unclean in the eyes of God?
More than their deeds defile them. Jesus taught that their spiritual
defilement extends to the depths of their hearts where evil desires are
conceived (7:20–23). The very character of humankind is flawed.

Concerning salvation. Jesus described his death as a *lutron anti
pollon*, a ransom in the place of many (10:45). The word translated *ransom* referred to money paid to obtain the freedom of slaves. *Anti* has the
idea of one person taking the place or becoming the substitute for

another. So, with these words, Jesus taught what has come to be known as "substitutionary atonement." This is the idea that in his death Jesus substituted himself as the object of God's justice so that "the many" (those who believe in him) could be set free from the guilt and power of sin.

Key Verse

Mark 10:45: "For even the Son of Man did not come to be served, but to serve, and to give His life a ransom for many."

Key Chapter

Mark 2: Forgiveness and healing of the paralytic.

Message of Mark

Mark speaks to the tendency within each of us to minimize the seriousness of our spiritual conditions. By showing that the root of sin is imbedded deeply in our hearts (7:20–23), the gospel enables us to move from self-deception to self-understanding. At the same time, the willingness of Jesus to serve us, sinners though we are, gives us hope that we can be set free from what we are to what he can make us to be.

Herod the Great and His Descendants

Herod the Great
7–4 B.C., Matt. 2:1–17; Luke 1:5

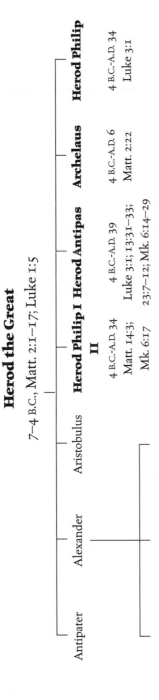

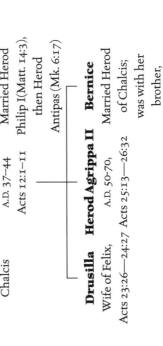

Antipater

Alexander

Aristobulus

Herod Philip I II
4 B.C.–A.D. 34
Matt. 14:3;
Mk. 6:17

Herod Antipas
4 B.C.–A.D. 39
Luke 3:1; 13:31–33;
23:7–12; Mk. 6:14–29

Archelaus
4 B.C.–A.D. 6
Matt. 2:22

Herod Philip
4 B.C.–A.D. 34
Luke 3:1

Herod of
Chalcis

Herod Agrippa I
A.D. 37–44
Acts 12:1–11

Herodias
Married Herod
Philip I(Matt. 14:3),
then Herod
Antipas (Mk. 6:17)

Drusilla
Wife of Felix,
Acts 23:26—24:27

Herod Agrippa II
A.D. 50–70,
Acts 25:13—26:32

Bernice
Married Herod
of Chalcis;
was with her
brother,
Acts 25:13; 26:30

Names in **Boldface** mentioned in passages cited; dates are those of reign

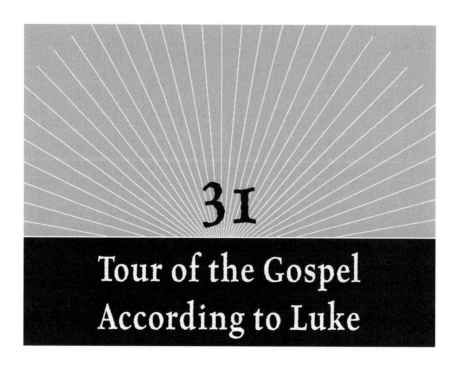

31

Tour of the Gospel According to Luke

Preview of Luke

More than any other Gospel writer, Luke emphasized that the gospel was for everyone, whether Jew or Gentile, rich or poor, male or female. He showed himself to be a capable historian, giving us not only the most comprehensive account of the life of Christ but also the account of the birth and growth of the church in his sequel to this Gospel, the Acts of the Apostles.

Introduction to Luke

Author. Luke was "the beloved physician" (Col. 4:14) and traveling companion of the apostle Paul. An early and unbroken tradition specifically states that Luke wrote not only the third Gospel but also the Book of Acts.[49] The listing of Paul's fellow workers in Colossians

4:10–14 indicates that Luke was a Gentile. This would make him the only non-Jewish author of Scripture. His writing style reveals a devotion to detail and an accuracy that one would expect from a physician.

Date of writing. Since Luke's second work (Acts) concludes with Paul's first Roman imprisonment but does not mention his second imprisonment, it seems likely that both volumes were completed prior to the second imprisonment in A.D. 66. So perhaps the book was written around A.D. 60. The fact that there is no mention of the fulfillment of the predicted destruction of Jerusalem (Luke 19:41–44) further supports a date of composition prior to A.D. 70 when that destruction occurred.

Theme. Light of the world. The third Gospel presents Jesus not simply as a national Savior for the Jews but a universal Savior for all men. Several passages develop the idea that Jesus was to be the Savior of the Gentiles as well as the Jews (2:32; 3:23–38; 4:25–27; 24:47).

Purpose. As a Gentile, Luke wanted to show that Jesus came to bring salvation to all men, not simply to the Jewish people. This was a novel idea to many Jews of that day. His second purpose was to give an accurate, consecutive account of the life of Christ (1:1–4).

History and archaeology. Before the advent of modern archaeology, it was fashionable among critics to dismiss Luke's claims to historical accuracy. Several discoveries (such as inscriptions that confirm the accuracy of 3:1 referring to Philip and Lysanias as tetrarchs) have confirmed him as a careful and trustworthy writer.

Geography. In common with Matthew and Mark, Luke devotes most attention to Jesus' ministry in Galilee. See map 10, page 165.

Outline of Luke

I. Prologue (1:1–4)
II. Jesus' birth and childhood (1:5—2:52)
III. Jesus' preparation for ministry (3:1—4:13)

VII. Jesus' Galilean ministry (4:14—9:50)
  V. Jesus' journey to Jerusalem (9:51—19:27)
 VI. Events in Jerusalem (19:28—21:38)
VII. Jesus' sufferings and resurrection (22:1—24:53)

Overview of Luke

Prologue (1:1–4). Luke opens his Gospel in a unique way with an address to Theophilus (perhaps a wealthy Roman who sponsored Luke's work).

Jesus' birth and childhood (1:5—2:52). Luke proceeds to give his account of the birth of Jesus. He also includes the account of the baby Jesus being presented at the temple. Luke alone among the evangelists tells us something about the boyhood of Jesus: "And Jesus increased in wisdom and stature, and in favor with God and men" (2:52).

Jesus' preparation for ministry (3:1—4:13). Following a brief description of the preaching of John the Baptist, Luke gives his account of Jesus' baptism and genealogy,[50] tracing all the way to Adam. Unlike Adam, Jesus overcomes the tempter, showing his moral fitness.

Jesus' Galilean ministry (4:14—9:50). Luke proceeds, in common with the other synoptic Gospel writers, to describe the Galilean ministry of Jesus. The power of Jesus over both the natural and supernatural realms lends authority to his teaching.

Jesus' journey to Jerusalem (9:51—19:27). Luke presents actions and teachings of Jesus on the final journey to Jerusalem.

Events in Jerusalem (19:28—21:38). Once in Jerusalem, Jesus encounters the hostility of the religious establishment (19:47), which leads to his prediction of the destruction of Jerusalem. The various factions in Jerusalem attempt to discredit Jesus with their questions about taxes and the afterlife, but the Lord confounds them. The section ends with Luke's version of the Olivet Discourse (21:5–36)

Jesus' sufferings and resurrection (22:1—24:53). Soon after, Judas betrays him (22:1–6). Following His arrest and trials, Jesus is put to death (23:26–56). On the first day of the following week, Jesus appears to the disciples (24:1–36). After convincing them that he was not a ghost but truly risen from the dead (24:37–42), he charges them to witness to all nations. Twice (24:27, 44) he explains that he is at the center of all Old Testament writings. His sufferings and the forgiveness of sins would form the substance of their witness (24:45–49). Taking them to Bethany to the east of Jerusalem, Jesus then ascends into heaven (24:50–53).

Theological Highlights

Concerning Scripture. Two statements by Jesus recorded in the Gospel of Luke reveal his understanding of the limits of the Old Testament. The first is 11:51, where he makes a statement about the murders from Abel to Zechariah. It is tantamount to saying "from the first murder in the Bible to the last," since the former is recorded in Genesis 4 (first book in the Jewish arrangement of the Old Testament) and the second in Second Chronicles 24 (last book in the Jewish arrangement of the Old Testament). The other is 24:44 where Jesus mentions the Law, the Prophets, and the Psalms, referring to the threefold arrangement of the Jewish Scriptures. While combining some books that today are separated, this Jewish arrangement of the Old Testament included the present thirty-nine books and no more. Thus, it does not appear that Jesus considered the apocryphal books part of the Bible.

Concerning the Holy Spirit. Luke mentions the Holy Spirit more than any other Gospel writer. He notes that the Holy Spirit was the active agent in the conception of Jesus (1:35). Luke alone speaks of Jesus being full of the Holy Spirit (4:1). He is also the only Gospel writer to record the promise that the Father would give the Holy Spirit to those who ask for him (11:13).

Concerning salvation. The statement of Jesus in 19:10 that he came "to seek and to save that which was lost" is descriptive of the need of those who are without God in the world. Like sheep lost in the wilderness, they are in danger and hence, needing to be saved by being brought back into the fold. Early in the book, Luke makes it clear that such salvation included Gentiles (i.e., non-Jews, 4:25–27).

Concerning prayer. Luke contains many examples of Christ praying and teaching on prayer.

Key Verse

Luke 19:10: "For the Son of Man has come to seek and to save that which was lost."

Key Chapter

Luke 15: parables of salvation.

Message of Luke

If Christianity is the faith of Jesus Christ, and if Jesus Christ himself instructed his disciples to proclaim his message to "all nations" (24:47), then Christians must maintain a missionary mind-set. To conclude that Christianity is "our religion" and be content to let other people have "their religion" is not tolerance so much as abdication of responsibility towards Christ. Those who know Christ are under orders to make him known.

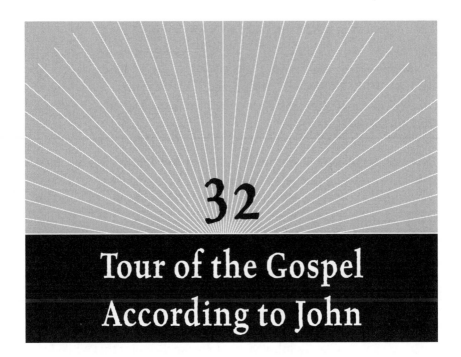

32

Tour of the Gospel According to John

Preview of John

In this, the most reflective of the four Gospels, John the apostle probes the identity of Jesus, the Son of God. In so doing, he shows us that the Christ who saves is a divine person, equal to the Father. Chapters 13—17, known as the Upper Room Discourse, are unlike anything in the Synoptic Gospels.

Introduction to John

Author. The apostle John, mentioned anonymously as "the disciple whom Jesus loved" (13:23; 19:26; 21:7, 20). This unnamed disciple can be identified as John by the process of elimination. Irenaeus[51], writing early in the second century, reported that John not only wrote the fourth Gospel, but that he wrote it while residing in Ephesus.[52]

Many people confuse the apostle John with the John called "the Baptist." While they were both named John, they were two different people. The latter was a prophet whose ministry prepared the way for the coming of Jesus (1:6–8, 19–34).

Date of writing. If written near the end of John's life, an approximate date of A.D. 90 can be assigned to the book. A first-century date of composition was strengthened by the finding in Egypt of a papyrus fragment of the Gospel that can be dated to about A.D. 125, the technical name of which is (p^{52}).

Theme. Jesus is God. No other Gospel writer goes to such lengths as John in establishing the deity of Jesus Christ. Beginning with the first verse, "In the beginning was the Word, and the Word was with God, and the Word was God," John carefully builds his case (1:18; 8:58; 9:38; 10:30; 12:40–41; 20:28). Clearly, John wishes to make the point that while Jesus was a man, he was God in the form of a man. The identification of Jesus as "the Word" in the prologue of the book was intended to say that Jesus was the expression of God to man. While John is careful to maintain a distinction between the Father and the Son, he is equally emphatic that the Son shares the deity of the Father.

Purpose. John gives his purpose for writing this Gospel in 20: 31, "But these are written that you may believe that Jesus is the Christ, the Son of God, and that believing you may have life in His name." Thus, he had a dual purpose for writing, that we might believe and that we might have life.

Textual problems. The earliest manuscripts of the Gospel of John do not contain 7:53—8:11, the story of the woman caught in adultery. It is possible that this story was not part of the original manuscript of John but a later addition. In all probability, it is an authentic episode from the ministry of Jesus.

History and archaeology. The discovery of a fragment of John (p^{52}) in a small village in Egypt from very early in the Christian era indicates the popularity and wide circulation of this document. It also destroys those critical theories that argue that the idea of the deity of Jesus was a later development and was not part of the beliefs of the infant church.

Geography. In contrast to the Synoptic Gospels, the Gospel of John concentrates on the ministry of Jesus in Judea rather than Galilee. It alone describes his journey through Samaria where he conversed with the woman at the well (4:1–42). See map 10, page 165.

Outline of John

I. Prologue (1:1–18)
II. Jesus' miraculous ministry (1:19—12:50)
III. Jesus' Upper Room Discourse (13:1—17:26)
IV. Jesus' death and resurrection (18:1—20:31)
V. Epilogue (21:1–25)

Overview

Prologue (1:1–18). In words reminiscent of Genesis 1, John introduces Jesus as the Word. The term was used among some Greek philosophers to refer to the organizing principle of the universe. Among Jews, it would evoke thoughts of God's creative power. Four things are affirmed about the Word in verses 1–3: He was in the beginning; he was with God; he was God; and as God, he made all things.

Jesus' miraculous ministry (1:19—12:50). Having established his theme in the first verse (that Jesus is divine), John describes the introduction of Jesus by John the Baptist. The forerunner proclaims him to be "the Lamb of God who takes away the sin of the world!" (1:29). This dual claim that Jesus is both divine and the sin-bearer is supported by *seven* miracles, *seven* sermons, and *seven* "I AM" statements (which recall the name of the Lord, Exod. 3:14). The chart below locates these.

Seven Signs, Sermons, and "I Am" Sayings in John

Sign	Sermon	"I AM" Saying
Water to wine, 2:1–11	New birth, 3:1–21	"I AM the Bread of Life," 6:35, 41, 48, 51
Nobleman's son, 4:46–54	Water of Life, 4:1–42	"I AM the light of the world," 8:12
Paralyzed man, 5:5–18	Equality with Father, 5:19–47	"I AM the door," 10:2, 7, 9
Multiplication of bread and fish, 6:1–15	Bread of life, 6:22–66	"I AM the good shepherd," 10:11–14
Walking on water, 6:16–21	The promised Spirit, 7:1–52	"I AM the resurrection and the life," 11:25
Healing of blind, 9:1–7	The light of the world, 8:12–59	"I AM the way, the truth, and the life," 14:6
Lazarus raised, 11:1–44	The Good Shepherd, 10:1–21	"I AM the vine," 15:1, 5

Yet despite all the evidence of the signs and the persuasive nature of his words, the nation largely refused to believe in Jesus (12:37).

Jesus' Upper Room Discourse (13:1—17:26). Thereafter, Jesus becomes increasingly intimate with the twelve disciples, giving them the example of service by washing their feet and making the remarks known as the "Upper Room Discourse." He includes in his remarks the distinguishing feature of a disciple: "By this all will know that you are My disciples, if you have love for one another" (13:35). Chapter 17 records Jesus' prayer on behalf of his disciples.

Jesus' death and resurrection (18:1—20:31). Following the Passover meal, Judas betrays him to the authorities, and Jesus is condemned to death. On the cross, he cries, "It is finished!" (19:30) and dies. The body of the Lord is buried by Joseph of Arimathea in his tomb with the help of Nicodemus (19:38–42). Then, on the first day of the week, Mary Magdalene discovers the stone rolled away from the tomb. Peter and "the other disciple" investigate and find it empty. They do not know what to make of this until Jesus appears. Even Thomas, who doubted the initial reports of the resurrection, is convinced upon seeing Jesus (20:26–28).

Epilogue (21:1–25). In the final scene of this Gospel, Jesus commands Peter to feed his sheep as the appropriate expression of love for him. The Gospel then concludes with the statement that Jesus did too many other things to be written about.

Theological Highlights

Concerning God. Jesus lays the foundation for the doctrine of the Trinity by identifying himself with the Father, yet maintaining a distinction between himself, the Father, and the Spirit (see especially 14:26 and 16:13).[53]

Concerning Christ. As noted, this Gospel goes to great lengths to demonstrate the deity of Christ.

Concerning salvation. The basis for salvation that Jesus gives is faith in him (3:16). Because of the repeated emphasis on this, the Gospel of John is sometimes referred to as the "Gospel of belief." He alone is the way to experience salvation (14:6).

Concerning the Holy Spirit. The Holy Spirit proceeds from the Father to bear witness to Jesus (15:26). This witness includes convicting the world of sin, righteousness, and judgment (16:8). The Spirit is the believers' Helper who will abide in them forever (14:16–17).

Key Verse

John 3:3: "Jesus answered and said to him, 'Most assuredly, I say to you, unless one is born again, he cannot see the kingdom of God.'"

Key Chapters

Chapters 13—17: the Upper Room Discourse.

Message of John

"What does God expect of me?" This is the most personal and significant question one can ask. John answers that question both succinctly and decisively: God expects faith in Jesus his Son. Moreover, John assures us that although Jesus has gone, we are not alone. Through the Holy Spirit, Jesus continues with us, bearing fruit in all who will abide in him (15:1–17).

Summary of the Teachings of Jesus Christ

The forms of Jesus' teaching

- Hyperbole: Matt. 5:29–30
- Sharp contrasts: Matt. 7:24–27
- Puns: Matthew 16:18
- Proverbs – Matt. 7:1, 6
- Hebraic poetry (parallelism): Luke 6:26–28 (synonymous parallelism); Mark 8:35 (antithetic parallelism); Luke 9:48 (step parallelism)
- Parables: Matt. 13; Luke 15–16

Themes in the teaching of Jesus

God

- God is Father (Matt. 6:9)
- God is merciful (Luke 15:11–32)
- God is gracious (Matt. 20:1–16)

The kingdom

- It is present (Matt. 12:28)
- It awaits completion (Matt. 8:11)

His identity

- He is Messiah (Matt. 16:16)
- He is the Son of God (John 5:25–26)
- He is the Son of Man (Luke 5:24)

People

- Must repent (Matt. 4:17)
- Must love God (Matt. 22:37-38)
- Must love their neighbors (Matt. 22:39)
- Must have faith in Jesus (John 6:29, 40)

Eternity

- Jesus will judge all people (Matt. 7:22–23)
- Some will experience eternal condemnation (Matt. 25:41–46)
- Some will receive eternal reward (Matt. 19:27–29; 25:34)

Chronology of the Life of Christ

Birth - December 5 B.C. or January 4 B.C.

Evidence:

- Prior to death of Herod the Great (died March/April, 4 B.C.)
- After the census of Quirinius (likely between 6 and 4 B.C.)
- About 30 years prior to the fifteenth year of Tiberius, 5 or 4 B.C.)

Commencement of ministry Summer or autumn, A.D. 29

Crucifixion Passover, A.D. 33

Ascension Pentecost, A.D. 33

The Importance of Jesus' Claims

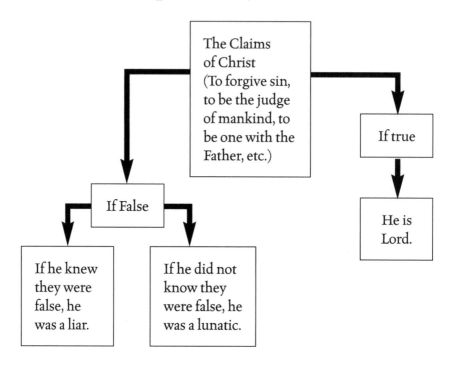

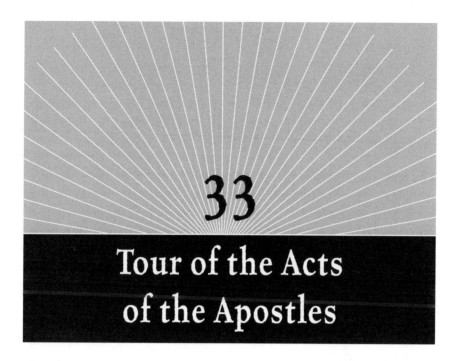

33

Tour of the Acts of the Apostles

Preview of Acts

In this companion volume to his Gospel, Luke continues the story of Christianity from the ascension of Christ to Paul's arrival in Rome. We discover how the Holy Spirit came and empowered the apostles to be bold and effective witnesses to Christ. In so doing, the Spirit led them to carry the Gospel beyond the racial confines of Israel to people of every nation.

Introduction to Acts

Author. Luke, who also authored the third Gospel. In terms of size, these two volumes make up nearly 25 percent of the New Testament. Because he engaged in careful research (Luke 1:3) and was an eyewitness of much of what he wrote about (note the "we" sections, 16:11 and following), he must be considered a reliable historian.

Date of writing. On or near A.D. 61. This date is based upon the likely chronology of Paul's life. His first imprisonment (mentioned at the end of this book) would have been about that time. The failure to mention any events subsequent to that time (such as the deaths of Peter and Paul or the destruction of Jerusalem) strengthens the likelihood of this date.

Theme. The apostles preach Christ. Almost 20 percent of Acts consists of the speeches and sermons of the apostles and other early leaders of the church. The book tells how their devotion to the proclamation of the Gospel (the "good news") carries Christianity from its beginnings in Jerusalem to the hub of the Roman Empire, Rome itself. Bruce Metzger notes the following points that formed the core of apostolic preaching in Acts:

(1) The promises of God made in the Old Testament days have now been fulfilled, and the Messiah has come.
(2) He is Jesus of Nazareth, who
    (a) Went about doing good and executing mighty works by the power of God;
    (b) Was crucified according to the purpose of God;
    (c) Was raised by God from the dead;
    (d) Is exalted by God and given the name "Lord";
    (e) Will come again for judgment and the restoration of all things.
(3) Therefore, all that hear the message should repent and be baptized.[54, 55]

Purpose. Given the structure and progress of the work, Luke's purpose was to give an account of the westward expansion of the church. Its progress closely follows the outline given in 1:8. But a second purpose woven into the book was to show the activity of the Holy Spirit that enabled the apostles to overcome great odds and extend the Gospel beyond the borders of Judea and Galilee. The many references to the Holy Spirit have led some to suggest that a better title would be the "Acts of the Holy Spirit."

History and archaeology. A hundred years ago, scholars did not believe Luke was a good historian. But as more discoveries have been made, a complete reversal of that opinion has occurred. For example, Luke's correct use of the titles of Roman officials (asiarchs, politarchs, praetors, procurators, consuls, kings) has been demonstrated repeatedly. While these titles changed from place to place and time to time, Luke never once used them incorrectly.

Geography. Luke writes about events that took place in thirty-two countries, fifty-four cities, and nine Mediterranean islands. Great attention is given to Paul's missionary work. The maps below trace his journeys.

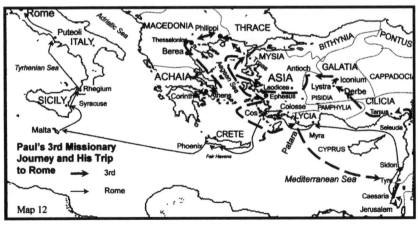

The first missionary journey is found in Acts 13 and 14. Paul went to Crete, then on to Galatia before returning to Antioch in Syria.

The second missionary journey is found in Acts 15:40—18:22. It went as far as Macedonia in Europe.

The third missionary journey is described in 18:23—21:15. Following this, Paul was arrested in Jerusalem and went to Rome as a prisoner.

Outline of Acts

   I. The preparation for witness (1:1–26)
  II. The witness in Jerusalem (2:1—7:60).
 III. The witness in Judea and Samaria (8:1—12:25)
 IV. The witness to the Roman world (13:1—28:31)

Overview of Acts

The preparation for witness (1:1–26). Acts begins in the city of Jerusalem. The resurrection of Jesus occurred forty days earlier. Now, as he appears to the apostles one final time, he charges them to wait for the gift of the Holy Spirit who would enable them to be his witnesses even to the ends of the earth (1:3–11). Following the ascension of Jesus into heaven, the apostles, his mother Mary, and other disciples (a group numbering about 120) spend the next ten days in prayer (1:12–26).

The witness in Jerusalem (2:1—7:60). The days of prayer are climaxed on the day of Pentecost (meaning "fiftieth day," originally a harvest festival occurring fifty days after Passover). The Holy Spirit descends in power upon the apostles and other followers (2:1–4). Immediately, they proclaim Christ, and the fellowship grows to about three thousand (Acts 2:41). Miraculous works are performed by the disciples (chap. 3), but the Sanhedrin attempts unsuccessfully to silence them.

In response to the opposition, the church prays, and with the filling of the Spirit, continues to grow (chap. 4). Difficulties and persecutions are experienced (chap. 5); nevertheless, the church becomes so large that it organizes the first group of deacons to care for the many widows (chap. 6). Persecution becomes violent when one of the deacons, Stephen, is stoned to death.

The witness in Judea and Samaria (8:1—12:25). Consenting to the death of Stephen is a young Pharisee named Saul (8:1). So great is Saul's animosity towards the church that he becomes the key figure in its persecution. At this time, many leave Jerusalem, extending the gospel into Samaria and Ethiopia (8:2–40). Saul obtains extradition papers from the high priest in Jerusalem and sets off for Damascus with the intention of arresting any followers of Jesus. As he journeys down the road, Jesus appears to him, temporarily blinding him and leading to a dramatic conversion. Upon regaining his sight, he champions the cause he had formerly tried to destroy (9:1–30).

Further inroads into the Gentile world are made when Peter, by reason of a vision, preaches the gospel to the household of a Roman centurion named Cornelius (chap. 10). When word of this reaches the church in Jerusalem, some criticize Peter, not believing that God would save Gentiles who had not first become Jews through ritual circumcision (11:1–4). Peter's explanation momentarily causes all objections to cease (11:5–18). At this time, Saul comes to Antioch with Barnabas. Shortly after, James, the brother of John, is beheaded, and Peter is arrested by King Herod. Miraculously, Peter escapes (12:1–19).

The witness to the Roman world (13:1—28:31). Obeying the command of the Holy Spirit, Saul and Barnabas depart from Antioch on their first missionary journey which takes them to the island of Crete and from there to Galatia (chaps. 13—14). On this trip, Saul begins to go by his Roman name, Paul (13:9). John Mark accompanies them but turns back before the journey is completed (13:13).

After the successful conclusion of that trip, Paul and Barnabas go to Jerusalem to participate in the first general council of the church. The subject of whether Gentiles had to be circumcised and embrace the Mosaic Law before being saved has returned despite Peter's earlier experience. The conclusion of the council is that one does not have to become a Jew prior to becoming a Christian (15:1–35).

When Paul and Barnabas plan their second missionary journey, they disagree over whether John Mark, Barnabas's cousin (Col. 4:10), should accompany them, leading to the decision to go their separate ways (15:36–41). Paul completes his second missionary journey with Silas and meets Timothy who joins the band (15:40—16:5). On this trip, they take the gospel to Europe, going to the country of Macedonia and the cities of Philippi and Thessalonica. From there they journey to the major cities of Greece—Athens and Corinth. They conclude the second missionary journey by returning to Antioch. Later, Paul and his companions launch a third missionary journey. They come to Ephesus where converts destroy their occult books (19:19). A prosperous two-year ministry arouses enough jealousy among the idol makers to cause a riot (chap. 19).

After traveling throughout Macedonia and Greece, Paul returns briefly to say good-bye to his Ephesian friends, then presses on to Jerusalem (20:1—21:26). However, Jews in Jerusalem recognize Paul and attack him. This leads to his arrest by the Roman authorities (21:27—22:29). When it becomes dangerous for Paul to remain in Jerusalem, he is sent to the provincial capital of Caesarea where he languishes in prison for two years (23:12—24:27). It is evident that justice will not be found in Caesarea, so Paul appeals to Caesar (25:1—12). After a near-fatal journey by sea (27:1—28:10), Paul arrives in Rome where he is placed under house arrest but is allowed to continue preaching to visitors for two years (28:30–31).

Theological Highlights

Concerning the Holy Spirit. The Holy Spirit is shown to be the power behind Christian witness (1:8). He baptizes believers (i.e., enters their lives to dwell; see 10:45). Thereafter, he fills believers, giving them boldness and effectiveness in their witness (4:31).

Concerning the church. The offices in the church expand to two in Acts 6 with the addition of deacons. It is also shown to be a body formed on the basis of repentance (a key component of faith) rather than by the works of the Law (11:18; 15:8–11).

Key Verse

Acts 4:12: "Nor is there salvation in any other; for there is no other name under heaven given among men by which we must be saved."

Key Chapters

Chapter 2: the beginning of the church.

Chapter 9: the conversion of Saul (Paul).

Message of Acts

From its beginning, the Book of Acts shows that the church is to be missionary-minded. The mandate of Christ that the gospel be carried to the ends of the earth has never been repealed. At the end of the twentieth century, there remain more than a thousand language groups in the world without copies of the Scripture available in their native tongues or churches in their culture. So the work of proclaiming the good news vigorously begun in the time of Acts is to continue to the return of Christ.

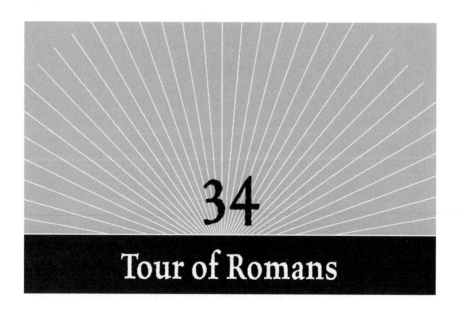

Tour of Romans

Preview of Romans

Romans has been called the "gateway to the Bible" because of its expression of doctrine. It is recognized as Paul's greatest work. It is also the longest of the letters or epistles of the apostles. In Romans Paul sets forth the doctrines of justification, sanctification, and election.

Introduction to Romans

Author. Paul, the former Pharisee whose conversion is described in Acts 9. The first thirteen letters of the New Testament are by him (with some holding that he also wrote Hebrews). The letters that he wrote are presented in the order of their length rather than in the order of their composition. They are named after their recipients (in contrast to the General Epistles, which are named after their authors). Leading ideas found in Paul's letters include the following:

- Man is sinful and stands under the wrath of God.
- God is gracious and willing to forgive sins.

- Through the redemption available in Jesus, we can be set free from sin.
- The grace of redemption is received by faith in Jesus.
- God is the Father of those who believe in Jesus.
- Those who experience redemption in Jesus may expect transformation into his likeness by the Holy Spirit.
- The church is the body of Christ in this world.
- Christ will come again in glory and power.

Date of writing. Romans was written on or near A.D. 57, towards the end of Paul's third missionary journey (15:25; Acts 20:2). The mentioning of Cenchrea (16:1), a harbor near Corinth, suggests that Paul was in the latter city when the letter was written. He also mentions Erastus, the director of public works (16:23) whose name has been found on a paving stone in Corinth.

Theme. Righteousness by faith (1:16–17). Righteousness has to do with being "right" with God. Paul views this righteousness as a free gift from God (3:24; 5:15–16; 6:23) that is received through faith (1:17; 3:26). The gift of righteousness from God is credited to the account of those who believe (4:2–5, 22–24). A word that frequently is used in Romans is *justification* and its verb, *justify*. This judicial term refers to someone being declared not guilty before the bar of justice. Justification confers a righteous standing before God.

Purpose. Paul anticipated a visit to Rome (15:23–24), and the apparent purpose of this letter was to prepare the way for his coming. Perhaps, too, he wanted to set forth his mature understanding of the Christian faith.

Textual Problems. Some early manuscripts of Romans omit chapters 15 and 16. However, the personal nature of these verses may explain their omission, or these manuscripts could follow a damaged copy.

History and archaeology. Rome was the greatest city-state of all time. Its rise to power was meteoric. In the course of sixty years

(264–202 B.C.), it went from being a city of no consequence to the greatest power the world has known. In the Punic Wars, Rome defeated Carthage, its greatest rival, leaving it the undisputed master of the Mediterranean. Over the next two centuries, Rome extended its power to the east, entering Jerusalem in 63 B.C. Originally a republic, Rome became a monarchy in 45 B.C. under Julius Caesar. The advantage to Christianity was a unified world in which the spread of the gospel was much easier. The mentioning of visitors from Rome on the day of Pentecost (Acts 2:10) suggests that the gospel reached Rome very early in the Christian era.

Geography. At its greatest outreach, the Roman Empire extended from the British Isles to Babylon and included all of North Africa. See map 11, page 191.

Outline of Romans

    I. Prologue and theme (1:1–17)
   II. The guilt of Gentiles and Jews (1:18—3:20)
 III. The gift of righteousness in Jesus Christ (3:21—5:21)
 IV. The effect of righteousness upon conduct (6:1—8:39)
  V. The error of Israel in pursuing righteousness by the Law (chaps. 9:1—11:36)
 VI. The practical behavior of righteous people (12:1—15:13)
VII. Conclusion (15:14—16:27)

Overview of Romans

Prologue and theme (1:1–17). Paul introduces himself as a bond-servant of Christ. Never having been to Rome, he mentions his desire to go there to preach the gospel, which is the power of God for salvation. The gospel has this power because it reveals a righteousness that is by faith (the theme of the letter). This righteousness is for everyone.

The guilt of Gentiles and Jews (1:18—3:20). The need for righteousness conferred by God, rather than earned by people, is seen in their desperately sinful conditions (1:18–32). Sin is not just a problem for idolatrous Gentiles but also for Jews who despite their possession of the Law, act in ways contrary to the Law (2:1—3:8). The conclusion is that all are under sin and that no one—whether by the Law of Moses or the law of conscience—will be declared righteous in God's sight on the basis of the Law (3:19–20).

The gift of righteousness in Jesus Christ (3:21—5:21). Rather than being by Law, righteousness is available from God through justification by faith in Jesus (3:21–31).[56] This was how Abraham, the father of Israel, found righteousness (4:1–8). Furthermore, he was declared to be righteous by faith prior to the institution of circumcision. This practice was intended to be a sign and seal of the righteousness that is by faith (4:9–15). What was true for Abraham is true for all humankind: God credits righteousness on the basis of faith in him who raised the Lord Jesus from the dead (4:16–25).

The happy consequence of justification by faith is peace with God (5:1). Believers may endure suffering, knowing they will be saved from God's wrath (5:2–11). Justification by faith results in the removal of the condemnation that falls upon all Adam's descendants (5:12–21).

The effect of righteousness upon conduct (6:1—8:39). To the objection that such grace encourages further sinning, Paul replies that faith unites individuals with Christ in his death to sin and life to God. This means that in our union with Christ, the penalty of sin has been paid and a relationship with God established. Consequently, we believers must consider ourselves dead to (i.e., done with) our old ways of sinful living. Instead, we are is to regard ourselves alive to (i.e., living to please) God. We should therefore present our bodies as instruments of righteousness (6:1–11).[57] To the further objection that people will only abuse grace since it removes the penalty of the Law, Paul replies those who give themselves to sin become the slaves of sin, resulting in a living death (6:15–21). The benefit of grace is that it leads to holiness by setting us free from sin (6:22).

Marriage illustrates the relationship between a person and the Law and a believer and Christ. No one can be married to two people at once;

likewise, no one can simultaneously be under the authority of the Law and the authority of Christ. By dying to the Law, the believer is free to follow Christ and serve in the Spirit (7:1–6).

The Law itself is holy and good (7:12). However, rather than providing power to live righteously, the Law reveals the extent of our sinfulness. Even moral persons who sincerely desire to obey the Law and to do what is right will find they lack the power to consistently do so.[58] The only hope for such persons is found in Jesus Christ (7:7–25) who delivers us from the Law's condemnation and sin's bondage. (Chapter 8 explains the deliverance from the bondage to sin.)

Those who are in Christ experience the liberating power of the Spirit. By giving attention to the prompting of the Spirit rather than the prompting of the lower nature, we can experience life and peace while pleasing God (8:1–8). The Spirit lives within all who belong to Christ, animating their spirits and assuring them of a future resurrection of their bodies (8:9–11). For this reason, we believers are obliged to live in obedience to the Spirit who assures us that we are God's children (8:12–17).

We people of the Spirit may anticipate a glorious future, even as we now have the comfort of knowing that the Spirit prays for us (8:18–27). Because we can never be separated from the love of God, we are more than conquerors (8:28–39).

The error of Israel in pursuing righteousness by the Law (9:1—11:36). What has happened to Israel, God's chosen people to whom he gave the Law and the temple and through whom Christ came? Historically, it must be admitted that physical descent from Abraham did not in itself ensure that one belonged to Israel. Rather, membership in Israel was according to God's promise and election (9:1–18). God is within his rights to show mercy to whomever he chooses. This includes showing mercy to Gentiles who respond by faith but not to those Jews who pursue righteousness by works (9:22–33).

Despite the zeal of the Jews, they rejected the gift of righteousness by rejecting Christ (10:1–4). If they will believe, they will be given righteousness by faith (10:5–13). It is not as though they had not heard, for the prophets spoke of these things (10:14–21). God has not rejected

Israel. Temporarily, a portion of Israel has been hardened. Eventually, all Israel will be saved, for the gifts and call of God are irrevocable (11:1–36).

The practical behavior of righteous people (12:1—15:13). The gift of new life in Christ should lead to new ways of living. Sacrifice (12:1–2), humility (12:3–8), and love (12:9–21) are all part of such living. So, too, is obedience to rulers (13:1–7). Whatever requirements are in the Law, love will fulfill them (13:8–14). In matters of conscience, we Christians must show tolerance for one another (14:1—15:8).

Conclusion (15:14—16:27). After offering his prayer for the Roman Christians (15:13), Paul concludes with personal remarks and greetings (15:14—16:24). A beautiful benediction closes the letter (16:25–27).

Theological Highlights

Concerning God. In the person of Christ, God assumed human form. Such is the significance of 9:5, "Christ came, who is over all." This is one of the strongest declarations of the deity of Christ to be found in the writings of Paul.

Concerning salvation. Salvation is shown to be a gift from God rather than the reward of good behavior (3:24; 5:15–17; 6:23). Good behavior is to be expected from those who have experienced salvation but as a result rather than a cause (chap. 6). Salvation (meaning "deliverance") is specifically shown to be deliverance from the wrath of God (1:18–32), death (5:21), the power of sin (6:1–14), and the Law (7:1–6). These are all consequences of the gift of righteousness.

The gift of God is through Jesus Christ (6:23). Four terms are used to describe the various aspects of the death of Christ leading to salvation.

- Justification (3:24, 26; 4:25). This is the judicial act of God whereby he declares someone not guilty. It is the opposite of condemnation. The death of Christ justifies those who believe in Him.

- Propitiation (3:25). This term refers to the satisfaction of God's wrath. J. I. Packer wisely explains, "God's wrath in the Bible is never the capricious, self-indulgent, irritable, morally ignoble thing that human anger so often is. It is, instead, a right and necessary reaction to objective moral evil."[59] In his death, Jesus satisfied the demands of divine justice against the sins of humankind (5:9).
- Redemption (3:24; 8:23). This refers to a payment made to obtain a slave's freedom. The death of Jesus made a payment that sets believers free from condemnation and death.
- Reconciliation (5:10–11). This term refers to the restoration of a relationship. The relationship of man to God was broken in the fall of the first Adam. It is restored by the death of the second Adam, Jesus Christ (5:12–21).

Concerning the Holy Spirit. The Holy Spirit indwells every Christian (8:9). He produces righteous desires (8:5) that we must follow in order to have life and peace (8:6). Further, he intercedes for us in order to help us with our weaknesses (8:26).

Key Verse

Romans 6:23: "For the wages of sin is death, but the gift of God is eternal life in Christ Jesus our Lord."

Key Chapter

Chapter 3: the doctrine of justification.

Message of Romans

The eternal question is, How can a person be right with God? Romans gives the most complete answer found in the New Testament. Consequently, it remains the source of much Christian theology.

I had conceived a burning desire to understand what Paul meant in his Letter to the Romans, but thus far there had stood in my way, not the cold blood around my heart, but that one word which is in chapter one: "The justice of God is revealed in it." I hated that word, "justice of God," which, by the use and custom of all my teachers, I had been taught to understand philosophically as referring to formal or active justice, as they call it, i.e., that justice by which God is just and by which he punishes sinners and the unjust.

But I, blameless monk that I was, felt that before God I was a sinner with an extremely troubled conscience. I couldn't be sure that God was appeased by my satisfaction. I did not love, no, rather I hated the just God who punishes sinners. In silence, if I did not blaspheme, then certainly I grumbled vehemently and got angry at God. I said, "Isn't it enough that we miserable sinners, lost for all eternity because of original sin, are oppressed by every kind of calamity through the Ten Commandments? Why does God heap sorrow upon sorrow through the Gospel and through the Gospel threaten us with his justice and his wrath?" This was how I was raging with wild and disturbed conscience. I constantly badgered St. Paul about that spot in Romans 1 and anxiously wanted to know what he meant.

I meditated night and day on those words until at last, by the mercy of God, I paid attention to their context: "The justice of God is revealed in it, as it is written: 'The just person lives by faith.'" I began to understand that in this verse the justice of God is that by which the just person lives by a gift of God, that is by faith. I began to understand that this verse means that the justice of God is revealed through the Gospel, but it is a passive justice, i.e. that by which the merciful God justifies us by faith, as it is written: "The just person lives by faith." All at once I felt that I had been born again and entered into paradise itself through open gates. Immediately I saw the whole of Scripture in a different light....

I exalted this sweetest word of mine, "the justice of God," with as much love as before I had hated it with hate. This phrase of Paul was for me the very gate of paradise.

—Martin Luther, "Preface to the Complete Edition of
Luther's Latin Works" (1545), translation
by Bro. Andrew Thornton, OSB,
© Stain Anselm Abbey, Project Wittenberg,
Concordia Theological Seminary.

35

Tour of First and Second Corinthians

Preview of First and Second Corinthians

If churches were children, then the church at Corinth was Paul's "problem child." Multiple problems beset this congregation, and distrust and misunderstanding cloud their relationship with Paul. Patiently, yet firmly, he deals with the problems and misunderstandings and in the process gives us rich insights to many matters of faith and practice.

Introduction to First and Second Corinthians

Author. The apostle Paul. His first contact with Corinth is recorded in Acts 18. He wrote these letters from Ephesus (1 Cor. 16:8).

Date of writing. A.D. 56, near the beginning of Paul's ministry in Ephesus (Acts 19:10).

Theme. In the first letter, the theme is *the church without love*. The multiple problems existing in the church can be traced back to a deficiency of love. In the thirteenth chapter, love forms a contrast to the behaviors and problems of the Corinthians, as shown by the chart below.

Character of Love and Behavior of the Corinthians

Love is ...	The Corinthians were ...
Patient and kind	Quarreling (1:11)
Not jealous	Jealous (3:3)
Not boastful or proud	Arrogant (4:18)
Not unbecoming	Acting improperly (7:36)
Not self-seeking	Seeking their own good (10:24)
Not provoked	Suing each other (6:1)
Not delighted with evil	Tolerating incest (5:1)
Able to endure all things	Unable to endure weaker brothers (chaps. 8—10)

In the second letter to the Corintians, the theme is *the character of Paul*. This was under attack by adversaries at Corinth (1:15–19, 23; 2:17; 4:1–2; 10:1—12:21). They questioned both his veracity and his credentials as an apostle.

Purpose. Paul wrote his first letter with the intention of addressing problems in the church, which had been reported to him (1:11), and answering questions raised by church members (7:1). In the second letter, Paul clearly wrote to vindicate himself and to prepare the Corinthians for a forthcoming visit (13:1).

Problems. Statements in both letters raise the possibility that Paul wrote other letters to the Corinthians that are no longer in existence. First Corinthians 5:9 reads, "I wrote to you in my epistle not to keep company with sexually immoral people." Thus, it appears that a letter preceded First Corinthians. Likewise, Second Corinthians 7:8 says, "For even if I made you sorry with my letter, I do not regret it." This "sorrowful letter" (also mentioned in Second Corinthians 2:3–4) is thought by some to be a letter that fell between First and Second Corinthians. Thus, there were possibly two, three, or four letters to Corinth. But when evaluating First Corinthians 5:9, we must remember that it was the custom to speak of what one was writing in the past tense (since it would be past when the reader received the letter). So while we say, "I am writing," a Greek of the first century might say "I wrote." If this is the case, then First Corinthians 5:9 refers only to First Corinthians. As far as the "sorrowful letter" is concerned, it is hard to conceive of a letter more sorrowful than First Corinthians with its rebukes and reprimands.

An interpretive problem exists in First Corinthians 15:29, which mentions baptism for the dead. While it is possible that the Corinthians were engaging in the otherwise unknown practice of proxy baptism, it seems unlikely. A better explanation is that this should read baptism "because of" the dead, meaning baptism performed because of the persuasive testimony of some deceased (possibly martyred) Christians.

History and archaeology. Corinth, a city of some five hundred thousand people, was notorious even among the pagans for its immorality. The phrase "to act as a Corinthian" meant "to behave immorally." A temple to Aphrodite sat atop the highest part of the city in which one thousand prostitutes practiced their trade. Calling someone "a Corinthian" was pejorative. Because the city straddled the isthmus of Greece, it was a stopping place for sailors. It was possible for seamen to have their boats hauled across the isthmus, sparing them a difficult and longer voyage around the Peloponnesus.

Among the many ruins found in Corinth is the *bema* or "judgment seat" from which judges rendered decisions or awarded prizes in the Corinthian games. Paul used this to picture the place from which Christ would give his rewards to believers (2 Cor. 5:10).

Geography. As mentioned above, Corinth sat on the isthmus of Greece, giving it easy access to both the Aegean and Adriatic Seas. See map 11, page 191.

Outlines of First and Second Corinthians

First Corinthians

    I. Introduction (1:1–9)
   II. Responses to the report of problems (1:10—6:20)
 III. Answers to specific questions (7:1—16:9)
 IV. Conclusion (16:10–24)

Second Corinthians

    I. Introduction (1:1–7)
   II. Paul defends his character (1:8—7:16)
 III. Instructions concerning giving (8:1—9:15)
 IV. Paul defends his calling as an apostle (10:1—13:4)
  V. Conclusion (13:5–14)

Overviews of First and Second Corinthians

First Corinthians. Having received disturbing news from some brothers belonging to Chloe's household (1:11), Paul addresses the many problems plaguing the Corinthian church. These include quarrels (chaps. 1—4), toleration of incest (chap. 5), lawsuits among believers (6:1–8), and immorality in general (6:9–20). After speaking to each of these issues, the Apostle then answers specific questions brought to him (7:1). These include questions concerning marriage (chap. 7), food offered to idols (chaps. 8—11), spiritual gifts (chaps. 12—14, with a reminder in chap. 13 that love is greater than giftedness), and the resurrection of the dead (chap. 15). Briefly, he mentions a collection for the relief of the Christians in Jerusalem (16:1–4), a topic he returns to in the second letter. He then concludes with personal remarks.

Second Corinthians. After briefly mentioning his sufferings, Paul explains why he had not come to Corinth as previously promised. The reason given is that under the circumstances a visit would have caused them pain (1:23—2:4, perhaps meaning he would have had to invoke apostolic discipline in light of their many problems). He calls upon the church to forgive one individual who had caused grief to him and to the church as a whole (2:5–11), referring, it seems, to the individual excommunicated for incest (1 Cor. 5).

Beginning the defense of his ministry, Paul reminds the Corinthians that he is a minister of the new covenant (2:12—4:18; see Jer. 31:31–34 for Old Testament background and Luke 22:20 for the New Testament inauguration). Knowing the eternal glory and resurrection body that awaits him, he confidently serves the Lord despite all the dangers (5:1–8), anticipating Christ's reward (5:10). As the Lord's minister, it is his task to try and persuade men to be reconciled to God through Christ (5:11–21). As God's worker, he urges the Corinthians not to receive the grace of God in vain (6:1–2). He reminds them of his conduct among them and urges them not to join themselves to unbelievers (6:3–18). Rather, he appeals to them to open their hearts to him, since he has served them in all sincerity (7:2–16).

Returning to the collection for the saints in Jerusalem mentioned in the previous letter, he urges them to complete this task, giving joyfully, not reluctantly (8:1—9:15).

A vigorous defense follows in which Paul contrasts himself with the false apostles attempting to steal the allegiance of the Corinthians (10:1—12:21). Having done this, he then urges the Corinthians, who had been examining him, to examine themselves to see if they truly are "in the faith" (13:5). He then quickly concludes this letter.

Theological Highlights

Concerning salvation. Second Corinthians 5:18 describes the work of Christ as an act of reconciliation. Reconciliation has to do with the repair of a ruptured relationship. People broke the relationship, moving away from God, but Christ provides a way to return.

Concerning the Holy Spirit. First Corinthians 12 gives the most extensive teaching in the New Testament on the subject of spiritual gifts. These are abilities imparted by the Holy Spirit to believers whereby they may in one way or another serve Christ. "Each one" receives a gift (12:11). Further, the Holy Spirit baptizes all believers into the one body of Christ (12:13). The evidence of this baptism is a confession that "Jesus is Lord" (12:3), meaning a confession that Jesus is the Lord God.

Concerning the resurrection. First Corinthians 15 gives the most complete description of the resurrection bodies that await believers.

Key Verses

1 Corinthians 13:8: "Love never fails. But whether there are prophecies, they will fail; whether there are tongues, they will cease; whether there is knowledge, it will vanish away."

2 Corinthians 5:20–21: "Now then, we are ambassadors for Christ, as though God were pleading through us: we implore you on Christ's behalf, be reconciled to God. For He made Him who knew no sin to be sin for us, that we might become the righteousness of God in Him."

Key Chapters

1 Corinthians 13: the love chapter.

2 Corinthians 5: the ministry of reconciliation.

Message of First and Second Corinthians

With its strong emphasis on the primacy of love (1 Cor. 13), the Corinthian correspondence reminds us that the authentic Christian life is built upon this quality (see John 13:34–35). However, the love displayed in these letters is not a weak thing that tolerates all types of behavior. Rather, it vigorously promotes the good and does not hesitate to confront sin.

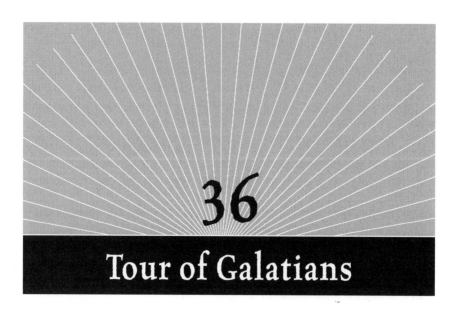

36

Tour of Galatians

Preview of Galatians

Called the "Magna Carta of Christian freedom," Galatians was Paul's white-hot denunciation of encroaching legalism in the Galatian churches. In this letter, he defends the doctrine of justification by faith. This is the teaching that believers obtain righteous standing before God as a consequence of having faith in Jesus as opposed to a strict observance of the Law of Moses. The function of the Law is that of a tutor who helps people see their need of Christ. Persons had come to Galatia teaching the immature Christians that faith in Christ was not sufficient to make them righteous before God. They needed to add the works of the Law. The Galatians were accepting this message, and it is against this corruption of the gospel that Paul is arguing in the letter.

Introduction to Galatians

Author. The apostle Paul. His first contact with the region of Galatia is recorded in Acts 13 and 14 where he and his companions traveled on the first missionary journey.

Date of writing. This is problematic. Some think Galatians was the first letter the apostle wrote and date it to A.D. 49. Others believe he wrote it later, about A.D. 55. The reasons for this are discussed below.

Theme. Gospel of Christ. Persons distorting the gospel (1:7) were disturbing the churches of Galatia. These preachers were attempting to convince the Galatian believers that it was necessary to embrace the Old Testament Law with its ritual regulations in order to achieve perfection or justification (3:3). Paul argues in a varied and vigorous fashion that justification is by faith in Christ, not by works of the Law (2:16).

Purpose. Paul wrote to refute the false teachers and to make perfectly clear that righteousness is achieved by faith in Jesus Christ alone.

Problems. The major problem surrounding this letter, affecting its dating, concerns its original recipients. The term *Galatians* could be used two ways. It could refer to ethnic Galatians, a distinct cultural group of that day, or it could refer to people living within the Roman province of Galatia (which included other ethnic groups).

A similar problem in U.S. history illustrates. Originally, Texas was part of Mexico. When American immigrants succeeded in establishing Texas as an independent nation, they found within their border people who by culture, language, and affection were Mexican. However, by reason of their location, they were Texans. What were they, Mexicans or Texans?

The southern Galatians to whom Paul preached in Acts 13 and 14 were not ethnic Galatians and might have referred to themselves by other terms. On the other hand, whether or not Paul actually ministered to the ethnic Galatians in the north of the province is questionable (though some think Acts 16:6 and 18:23 refer to such a ministry). So if one decides that he wrote to the southern Galatians, then the earlier date is preferred. However, if one believes that he addressed the northern, ethnic Galatians, then the later date must be assumed.

History and archaeology. One branch of the Gaelic people that settled Europe in the third century B.C. were invited by the king of

Bithynia in Asia Minor to serve as mercenaries in his army. The land where they settled became known as Galatia. It was enlarged upon incorporation into the Roman Empire in 25 B.C. Large numbers of Jews and Romans settled in the major towns.

Geography. The province of Galatia was located in what is today Turkey or Asia Minor. See map 11, page 191.

Outline of Galatians

   I. The denunciation of a different gospel (1:1–10)
   II. The defense of Paul's gospel (1:11—2:21)
   III. The defense of justification by faith (3:1–14)
   IV. The explanation of the Law (3:15–29)
   V. The appeal to live as God's sons (4:1–31)
   VI. The call to stand free (5:1–12)
   VII. The call to godly living (5:13–26)
   VIII. The call to do good to others (6:1–10)
   IX. Conclusion (6:11–18)

Overview of Galatians

The denunciation of a different gospel (1:1–10). Unlike the customary introductions to Paul's letters, this contains no words of commendation for the Galatians. Rather, the apostle expresses his amazement that the Galatians are embracing another "gospel" which is a distortion of the true gospel (1:6–7). So serious is this that twice he pronounces a curse upon those who preached this false gospel (1:8–9).

The defense of Paul's gospel (1:11—2:21). Paul begins a spirited defense of his authority as an apostle and the gospel that he preached, which he received by a direct revelation from Christ (1:12). The great change in his life from persecuting the church to proclaiming Christ is evidence of his call by Christ (1:11–24). Further, the apostles in Jerusalem approved of his message (2:1–10). The essence of his gospel, as he said to Cephas (Peter), is that "a man is not justified by the works of the law [i.e., religious ceremonies and rituals] but by faith in Jesus Christ" (2:16). Unlike those preaching the false gospel, Paul does not nullify God's grace by teaching that the Law can obtain righteousness (2:21).

The defense of justification by faith (3:1–14). Turning from his spiritual history, Paul asks the Galatians to reflect on how they received the Holy Spirit, by works of the Law or by hearing with faith (3:1–2)? Since they began the Christian life with faith, it was foolish to think that they could complete it by performing the works of the Law (3:3–5). Indeed, the man from whom these false teachers proudly claimed descent, Abraham, the father of Israel, serves as an example of one who obtained righteousness by faith (3:6–9, cf. Gen. 15:6). Even the Law that the false teachers tout explicitly says, "The just shall live by faith" (3:11, cf. Hab. 2:4).

The explanation of the Law (3:15–29). The Law was not given to nullify the promise of righteousness by faith made to Abraham. Rather, it was to teach men of their need for Christ.

The appeal to live as God's sons (4:1–31). Having obtained the adoption as God's sons, Paul cannot understand how the Galatians could revert to the elementary observance of the Law (4:1–11). Out of his concern for them, he begs them to disown these teachers of the Law (4:12–20). Resorting to the use of allegory (a popular teaching method among the Jews), he argues that persons who attempt to receive God's blessing by means of the Law are like Ishmael who did not receive God's blessing, whereas those who are of faith are like Isaac who received the promise (4:21–31).[60]

The call to stand free (5:1–12). Having thus stated his case, Paul appeals to the Galatians to maintain their freedom from the Law and not submit to the legal observance of circumcision in the vain hope that such submission to the Law might enhance their salvation (5:1–4). Righteousness before God is a matter of faith, and true faith will express itself in a life of love (5:5–6).

The call to godly living (5:13–26). Faith is not license to sin (5:13), for Christian love compels us to serve one another and thus fulfill the Law (5:13–14). If we are obedient to the prompting of the Holy Spirit within us, we will not do sinful deeds but bear spiritual fruit (5:16–26). This fruit (5:22–23) includes:

- Love
- Joy
- Peace
- Patience (longsuffering)
- Kindness
- Goodness
- Faithfulness
- Gentleness
- Self-control

The call to do good to others (6:1–10). Paul appeals to those who heed his message to deal gently with those who might have been carried away with this false gospel of Christ plus the Law. Those who are spiritual should help restore the fallen (6:1–5). He further urges that they support those true teachers among them (6:6–10).

Conclusion (6:1–18). Paul concludes with a final appeal to turn from the false teachers and to cause him no further trouble (6:11–18).

Theological Highlights

Concerning Scripture. In defending the message he preached, Paul asserts that it came to him by a revelation of Jesus Christ (1:12). That is, it was something that was disclosed to him by the Lord. By extension, one may speak of the apostle's writings as God's revelation to man.

Concerning Christ. Both the divine and human natures of Christ are alluded to in 4:4. On the one hand, Christ is the Son of God, but on the other, he was born of a woman. This and similar Scriptures gave birth to the confession in the Athanasian Creed that "our Lord Jesus Christ, the Son of God, is both God and man equally. ... He is God from the Being of the Father ... and He is man from the being of His mother."

Concerning the Holy Spirit. The Spirit of God enters our lives when we respond with faith to the gospel message (3:2). The Spirit then becomes the power behind godly living (5:16, 22–25).

Concerning salvation. One of the Bible's clearest and strongest affirmations of justification by faith is given in 2:16. The object of saving faith is Jesus. In contrast, the works of the Law will justify no one (cf. 2:21; 3:21).

Concerning Christian living. The Christian life is defined as a matter of faith working through love (5:6; cf. 5:14; 6:10).

Key Verse

Galatians 2:16: "Knowing that a man is not justified by the works of the law but by faith in Jesus Christ, even we have believed in Christ Jesus, that we might be justified by faith in Christ and not by the works of the law; for by the works of the law no flesh shall be justified."

Key Chapter

Chapter 3: the necessity of justification by faith.

Message of Galatians

The idea persists that salvation is a matter of "doing the right things," whether by keeping certain rules or observing particular rituals. Galatians answers that salvation is a matter of faith in Christ alone. While faith leads to godly living, such godliness is a consequence and not a cause of salvation.

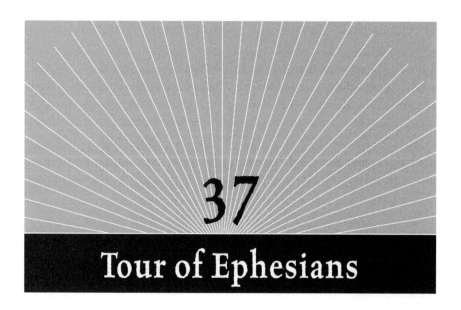

Tour of Ephesians

Preview of Ephesians

Like a cornucopia overflowing with the fruit of harvest, Ephesians over-flows with the good things God has done for us in Christ. It details our blessings, celebrates our position, and exhorts us to believe that the Lord loves us immeasurably. Then it applies these wonderful truths to our relationships in church, home, and society.

Ephesians is the first of four letters that Paul wrote while a prisoner (most likely in Rome), which are collectively known as the Prison Epistles. In addition to Ephesians, they are Philippians, Colossians, and Philemon. The close similarities between Colossians and Ephesians suggest that they were written one after the other while the same thoughts were in the mind of the apostle.

Introduction to Ephesians

Author. The apostle Paul, whose visits to Ephesus are mentioned in Acts 18, 19, and 20. This ancient view of the church[61] has been attacked by modern critics on the basis that the book has many words (eighty-six) unique to it and the style is not like that of a letter to a specific church so much as a general discourse. However, the subject determines the choice of words, and many stylistic features are characteristic of Paul (e.g., dealing with doctrine in the early portion of the letter and practical matters afterwards).

Date of writing. A.D. 60, during the Roman imprisonment described at the end of Acts.

Theme. Every spiritual blessing. Paul begins the letter with the declaration in 1:3, "Blessed be the God and Father of our Lord Jesus Christ, who has blessed us with every spiritual blessing in the heavenly places in Christ." More than any other letter of the New Testament, Ephesians describes the great spiritual wealth that belongs to all who are in Christ. Its exposition of God's plan of redemption (1:1–14) is without parallel.

Purpose. Paul's purpose in writing to the Ephesians may have been to prevent potential problems. In Acts 20:29–30 we find a warning he gave to the elders of the Ephesian church: "For I know this, that after my departure savage wolves will come in among you, not sparing the flock. Also from among yourselves men will rise up, speaking perverse things, to draw away the disciples after themselves." Another problem that may have been behind his writing was a growing coldness on the part of the Ephesians. We see later that Jesus, in his Revelation to John, had this word of rebuke for the Ephesians: "Nevertheless I have this against you, that you have left your first love" (2:4). The exhortations to love in Ephesians suggest that a deficiency in love was a persistent problem for the church.

Problems. The major problem with respect to Ephesians is the absence of the words "in Ephesus" (1:1) in some of the oldest manuscripts. A few ancient writers remark that these words were also missing from their manuscripts. This has led to the suggestion that Ephesians was a circular letter, meaning it circulated among several churches (perhaps the very letter mentioned in the last verses of Colossians as coming from Laodicea.)[62]

History and archaeology. Ephesus was the most important city in Asia, being both the provincial capital and a religious center. The most notable cult practiced there was that of Artemis whose temple was one of the seven wonders of the ancient world. All that remains of this structure are its foundation stones. Paul visited it twice and had contact with its elders a third time at Miletus nearby (Acts 18:19–21; 19:1—20:1; 20:17–38). The apostle John made Ephesus his headquarters in his later years. There is a tradition that Mary, the mother of Jesus, died in Ephesus. Because of malaria and the congestion of its harbor with silt, the city was gradually abandoned. In modern times it has been extensively excavated.

Geography. Ephesus was located on the mouth of the Cayster River between the mountains and the sea. See maps 11 and 12, page 191.

Outline of Ephesians

  I. The blessings for Christians (1:1—3:21)
 II. The behaviors of Christians (4:1—6:24)

Overview of Ephesians

The blessings for Christians (1:1—3:21). In a fashion unparalleled in his other writings, Paul sets forth the doctrine of salvation (1:1–14). He prays that the Ephesians might have a deeper understanding of these things (1:15–23). The changes made by God in Christians are nothing less than a change from death to life (2:1–10). A result of God's work is that Jews and Gentiles are united as one people in Christ (2:11–22). Paul's task as the "prisoner of God" (not Rome) is to make this mystery known (3:1–13). Therefore, he again prays that they might grasp the extent of God's love in Christ (3:14–21).

The behaviors of Christians (4:1—6:24). So great are the spiritual changes God works that they must be matched with behavioral changes that preserve the unity of the Spirit (4:1–6). The church in its members has been equipped for spiritual growth, and all Christians are responsible to do their part in helping the body of Christ mature (4:7–16). Consequently, behavior characteristic of the former way of life must be put off and new, loving behavior put on (4:17—5:21).

Not the least of the relationships to be changed by redemption is marriage (5:22–33). Likewise, relationships between parents and children and masters and servants should be God-honoring (6:1–9).

Because of the powers of darkness that believers encounter, it is imperative that they take up the armor of God and be wholehearted in prayer (6:10–20). Paul concludes with reference to a messenger that he is sending their way (Tychicus), then gives a benediction of peace (6:21–24).

Theological Highlights

Concerning God. The Book of Ephesians gives great insights into the sovereignty of God, particularly as it relates to his saving work. God conceived the plan of salvation prior to the foundation of the world (1:4).

Concerning humankind. In their natural condition, people are spiritually dead and under wrath (2:1–3). That is, they have no relationship with God that would give them eternal life. Rather, their character and conduct merit judgment by God.

Concerning salvation. Paul again stresses that salvation is a gift of God to be received by faith (2:8–9), a theme set forth at length in Romans.

Concerning the church. The church is not merely a voluntary association of people; it is a body in which members share an organic relationship through Christ and in the Spirit (2:14–22). The indwelling of the Spirit in the church makes it the new temple of God (cf. 1 Cor. 3:16).

Concerning the Holy Spirit. The command to be filled with the Spirit (5:18) shows that the normal condition of the Christian life should be one that manifests the fruit (cf. Gal. 5:22–23) and power (Acts 1:8) of the Holy Spirit. The idea of filling is that one voluntarily submits to the moral control and direction of the Spirit.

Concerning Christian marriage. Ephesians contains one of the Bible's principal passages on marriage (5:22–33). Marriage among Christians is to be grounded on sacrificial love and respect.

Key Verse

Ephesians 1:3: "Blessed be the God and Father of our Lord Jesus Christ, who has blessed us with every spiritual blessing in the heavenly places in Christ."

Key Chapter

Chapter 5: Christian relationships.

Message of Ephesians

In a time when many people speak disparagingly about doctrine and seek "relevant" teaching, Ephesians demonstrates the inseparable link between doctrine and practice. Theological truth provides the foundation and reason for Christian behavior. Therefore, the better we know doctrine, the better we should relate faith to life.

38

Tour of Philippians

Preview of Philippians

Joy and difficulty might seem to be mutually exclusive, but not so for the Philippians. This group of believers in the province of Macedonia were experiencing "a great trial of affliction" and "deep poverty" according to Second Corinthians 8:1–2, yet Paul's letter to them has been called "the epistle of joy" because of its many references to joy and rejoicing. The apostle himself was in prison facing possible death, yet joy bubbled up within him, too. This little epistle has much to teach about the joyful Christian life.

Introduction to Philippians

Author. Paul. This is another Prison Epistle.

Date of writing. Around A.D. 62, near the end of Paul's first Roman imprisonment.

Theme. Plea for unity. While the overall tone of this letter is one of joy, it makes a serious appeal. The peace and harmony of the fellowship was being disturbed by a quarrel between two women mentioned in 4:2. As early as chapter 2, Paul makes his appeal for all parties to preserve unity within the body. He pointedly asks the quarreling parties to come to an agreement in 4:2.

Purpose. The primary purpose for which Paul wrote was to protect the church from schism. Another purpose was to express his thanks to the church for help shown him by one of them, Epaphroditus, and for a monetary gift (2:25–30; 4:10–19).

Problems. A question that continues to be debated is whether or not 2:6–11 is a primitive Christian hymn that Paul incorporated. Another suggestion is that it is an early Christian confession. However, it is entirely possible that the apostle wrote it himself.

History and archaeology. The city of Philippi derives its name from Philip of Macedon, the father of Alexander the Great. In Roman times it was the site of a famous battle that helped Octavian succeed Julius Caesar. Once his power was consolidated, Octavian assumed the title Caesar Augustus and made Philippi an Italian colony (Acts 16:12). This gave it the rights and privileges of an Italian city. Philippi was where the apostle Paul first preached the gospel on what would later become European soil.

Geography. Philippi, along with Thessalonica, was part of Macedonia. See map 11, page 191.

Outline of Philippians

   I. Paul reports on his circumstances (1:1–30)
  II. Paul appeals to the example of Christ (2:1–30)
 III. Paul warns against the circumcision party (3:1–21)
 IV. Paul appeals for peace (4:1–23)

Overview of Philippians

Paul reports on his circumstances (1:1–30). While in prison awaiting trial, Paul is filled with joy because of the camaraderie shown him by the Philippians. He assures them that they are constantly in his prayers. He informs them that despite the limitations imposed by his imprisonment, the gospel continues to go out as others are emboldened by his example. So whether he lives or dies, Paul is full of joy. His one great desire is that they continue to stand firm for Christ.

Paul appeals to the example of Christ (2:1–30). The outcome of being in Christ should be Christian unity. This unity proceeds from an attitude of self-denial like that of Christ. The Savior emptied himself[63] by laying aside all the privileges of deity and became a man. He later died in obedience to the will of God. For this reason, he is exalted above all creation. Given such an example, we Christians should cultivate our likeness to Christ, refusing to complain or argue. Briefly, Paul mentions two men that exemplify the attitude for which he is calling: Timothy and Epaphroditus.

Paul warns about the circumcision party (3:1–21). Following on the heels of the apostle are men who want to convince immature Christians that it is necessary to be circumcised and embrace the Law of Moses. While this was refuted at the Jerusalem council (Acts 15), these "evil workers" continue to confuse people. All of the Christian's confidence should be in Christ and the righteousness he bestows through faith. There is power to be found in Christ, power so great that it will lead to the resurrection for which Paul longs. He urges the Philippians to follow his example and turn away from those who deny the sufficiency of the cross.

Paul's appeal for peace (4:1–23). Given the example of Christ, Paul urges Euodia and Syntyche to reach a peaceful agreement. The Christian life should be one of joy and peace (4:4–7). The peace of God belongs to those whose minds are set upon godly things (4:8). Paul then thanks the Philippians for their support and sends greetings.

Theological Highlights

Concerning Christ. Philippians 2 contains the well-known passage concerning the *kenosis* (self-emptying) of Christ. It clearly affirms that prior to the incarnation, Jesus existed in the form of God. But he "emptied" himself (2:7 ASV) and assumed the form of a servant. Thus, as Jesus was truly a servant, he was truly God. The question is whether by his self-emptying he ceased to be divine. It most likely means that he laid aside all appearances and privileges of deity, rather than his essential nature. This was done so he could die on the cross in obedience to the will of God the Father.

Concerning the afterlife. Following death, we believers go to be with Christ, experiencing a better state than what is possible in this life (1:21–23). But even this is not our final state. Someday a physical resurrection will transform our bodies into the likeness of Christ's body (3:21).

Key Verse

Philippians 4:4: "Rejoice in the Lord always. Again I say, rejoice!"

Key Chapter

Chapter 2: the example of Christ.

Message of Philippians

As long as Christians have discouraging times and disheartening disagreements, Philippians will be a relevant book. Knowing the Savior and the hope before us is the key to joy. The quarreling too often found in churches is out of harmony with the Savior whom fighting Christians profess to follow. An attitude like that of Christ is the best way to guarantee peace in the church.

The New Testament Epistles

Those by Paul, in order of composition:

Journey Epistles

- Galatians
- 1 Thessalonians
- 2 Thessalonians
- 1 Corinthians
- 2 Corinthians
- Romans

(Paul's letters are named after the recipients.)

Prison Epistles

- Ephesians
- Philippians
- Colossians

Pastoral Epistles

- Philemon
- 1 Timothy
- Titus
- 2 Timothy

Those by others:

To Jewish believers

- Hebrews
- James

(With the exception of Hebrews, the other epistles are named after the authors.)

To all believers

- 1 Peter
- 2 Peter
- 1 John
- 2 John
- 3 John
- Jude

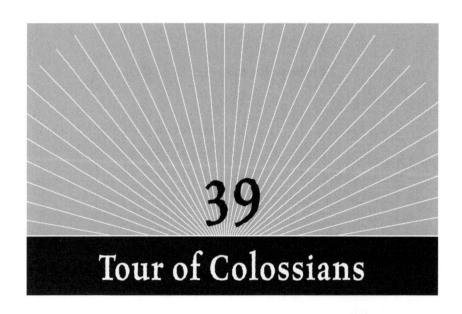

Tour of Colossians

Preview of Colossians

What makes a person "spiritual"? Do visions, fasts, or self-denial? If we combine Christian beliefs with Eastern mysticism or observe religious rituals, will we be more spiritual? Questions like these are as new as the day we live in and as old as the letter to the Colossians. Paul writes to this church where a new religious movement was heading believers in wrong directions in their quest for spirituality.

Introduction to Colossians

Author. Paul. This is the third of the Prison Epistles.

Date of writing. A.D. 60, close to the time of the composition of Ephesians.

Theme. Christ over all (1:15). Members of the church at Colossae were being subjected to a strange heresy. While little is known of this aberrant teaching, it seems to have been a blend of Greek philosophy, mysticism, and Judaism that diminished the prominence of Christ. Paul vigorously exalts Christ, proclaiming him Lord of all creation.

Purpose. Paul wrote to pull the Christians of Colossae away from this cultic teaching by assuring them that all their spiritual needs could be met in Christ, in whom they were complete (2:9–10).

Problems. The largest problem regarding this letter is the identification of the heresy at Colossae. Exactly what it was, how it related to the legalism combated in the churches of Galatians and Philippians, and how it got started so early are questions that cannot be fully answered. Another problem is the nature of 1:15–20. Some scholars think this was a pre-Pauline hymn rather than an original composition of the apostle.

History and archaeology. Prior to Roman times, Colossae lay along a major East-West trade route. But by New Testament times, the city was in decline because a newer road bypassed the city. In A.D. 60, the city was struck with a major earthquake. The failure to mention this indicates that the letter was written prior to this event.

Geography. Colossae lay about one hundred miles east of Ephesus in the Roman province of Asia. See map 11, page 191.

Outline of Colossians

   I. Paul gives thanks for the Colossians (1:1–14)
  II. The supremacy of Christ over all (1:15—2:3)
 III. The call to remain loyal to Christ (2:4–23)
 IV. The Christian way of life (3:1—4:6)
  V. Final greetings (4:7–18)

Overview of Colossians

Paul gives thanks for the Colossians (1:1–14). While Paul did not bring the Gospel to Colossae, he gives thanks upon hearing of their acceptance of the message brought to them by Epaphras. In keeping with his thankfulness, he prays for the Colossians.

The supremacy of Christ over all (1:15—2:3). Knowing that the heresy at Colossae is clouding their understanding of Christ, Paul launches into a description of Christ in cosmic terms. He is the image of God, the firstborn[64] of all creation, Creator and Sustainer of all. In him is the fullness of God. He accomplishes redemption. For him Paul suffers. The apostle's purpose is to bring these believers to a true understanding of Christ.

The call to remain loyal to Christ (2:4–23). Knowing that Christ is over all, the Colossians must be on guard against any religious ideas that would ruin the simplicity of their faith in Christ. Neither philosophy (2:8), nor circumcision (2:11–17), nor mystical experiences (2:18) can improve upon the benefits of Christ.

The Christian way of life (3:1—4:6). Christian living stems from a heavenly focus (3:1–4). Such a focus causes believers to put a stop to sinful behavior while taking up gracious and holy behavior (3:5–14). Relationships in the church and home become peaceful and just (3:15—4:1). A strong practice of prayer rounds out the Christian life.

Final greetings (4:7–18). Paul mentions many brothers assisting him in the work, including Luke the doctor (4:14). He urges them to read another letter of his (Ephesians?) coming to them from Laodicea. He then gives his farewell.

Theological Highlights

Concerning Christ. Unlike any other of Paul's letters, Colossians brings out the universal scope of Christ's redemption (1:20). However, it would be incorrect to conclude that this means that eventually everyone will be saved since that would contradict the clear teaching of the apostle elsewhere (2 Thess. 1:8–9). Rather, it indicates that the present universe in its corrupt state will someday be transformed and brought into a state of perfection.

Key Verse

Colossians 2:10: "And you are complete in Him, who is the head of all principality and power."

Key Chapter

Chapter 2: the heart of Paul's argument.

Message of Colossians

Modern Christians are offered a smorgasbord of new religions that attempt to combine Christianity with Eastern religions or New Age philosophy. Just as ancient Christians could be sure that Christ, as Paul preached him, was sufficient to meet all their spiritual needs, so we believers today can be confident that we are spiritually complete in Christ.

40

Tour of First and Second Thessalonians

Preview of First and Second Thessalonians

The rapture, the resurrection, the Antichrist, the Tribulation, the day of the Lord—we hear these events spoken of, and many of us wonder what they mean and where the Bible teaches about them. A substantial amount of teaching on these prophetic themes is found in the two letters to the Thessalonians.

Introduction to First and Second Thessalonians

Author. The apostle Paul. His ministry in Thessalonica is recorded in Acts 17:1–10. We also find that his traveling companions included men from this city (Acts 20:4; 27:2).

Date of writing. A.D. 51 (both letters). This was during Paul's stay at Corinth (Acts 18:5 compared with 1 Thess. 3:6) where his second missionary journey took him after preaching in Philippi, Thessalonica, and Athens. Those who hold the north Galatian theory[65] regard the Thessalonian epistles as the oldest of Paul's letters.

Theme.   In the first letter, the theme is *the Second Coming*. This refers to the physical return of Jesus Christ in power and glory to visibly establish the kingdom of God on earth. This letter repeatedly comments on this event. The hope that just as he has departed to heaven, so he will return to earth is widely taught in the New Testament (e.g., John 14:3; Acts 1:11; Rev. 19). Every chapter in First Thessalonians contains a reference to this blessed hope of Christians.

- 1:10, "And to wait for His Son from heaven, whom He raised from the dead, even Jesus who delivers us from the wrath to come."

- 2:19, "For what is our hope, or joy, or crown of rejoicing? Is it not even you in the presence of our Lord Jesus Christ at His coming?"

- 3:13, "So that He may establish your hearts blameless in holiness before our God and Father at the coming of our Lord Jesus Christ with all His saints."

- 4:14–17, "For if we believe that Jesus died and rose again, even so God will bring with Him those who sleep in Jesus. For this we say to you by the word of the Lord, that we who are alive and remain until the coming of the Lord will by no means precede those who are asleep. For the Lord Himself will descend from heaven with a shout, with the voice of an archangel, and with the trumpet of God. And the dead in Christ will rise first. Then we who are alive and remain shall be caught up together with them in the clouds to meet the Lord in the air. And thus we shall always be with the Lord."

- 5:23, "Now may the God of peace Himself sanctify you completely; and may your whole spirit, soul, and body be preserved blameless at the coming of our Lord Jesus Christ."

Second Thessalonians is similar to First Thessalonians in that it, too, has a prophetic theme: *the Tribulation day*. The precise term for this is the "day of the Lord." This term refers to a time of God's judgment upon the earth during the end times. It corresponds to the day of Tribulation spoken of by Christ (Matt. 24:21, 29) and in the Book of Revelation (7:14).

Purpose. In the first letter, Paul wished to encourage suffering (1:6;, 2:14; 3:3) and grieving (4:13) Christians with the hope of Christ's coming. This would give them the stamina they needed to endure their trials. In the second letter, he wished to clear up some confusion regarding the arrival of the day of the Lord (2:1–2).

Problems. Some scholars believe that the order in which First and Second Thessalonians were written has been reversed. The arguments for this are 1) First Thessalonians 5, which mentions the day of the Lord, would make more sense if Second Thessalonians, which has this as its theme, had already been written; 2) persecutions seem to be present in Second Thessalonians but passed in First Thessalonians; and 3) internal strife appears new in Second Thessalonians but not in First Thessalonians.

In answer, it can be said that 1) First Thessalonians 5 with its reference to the day of the Lord can be explained on the basis of prior instruction; 2) persecution does not seem past in First Thessalonians; 3) strife in Second Thessalonians is merely a continuation of that in First Thessalonians 5:14.

History and archaeology. Founded in 315 B.C., Thessalonica became the leading city of Macedonia when that country was made a Roman province in 148 B.C. Its prosperity lay in the fact that it was a major port and was along the Egnatian Way, the major East-West highway between Rome and the East. In Acts 17:6, Luke refers to the civic leaders as *politarchs*, an unknown title thought to be a historical inaccuracy until an inscription using this term was unearthed at Thessalonica.

Geography. Refer to map 11, page 191.

Outlines of First and Second Thessalonians

First Thessalonians
    I. Commendation of the Thessalonians (1:1–10)
   II. Reflections of a personal nature (2:1—3:13)

III. Exhortations to excellence (4:1–12)
IV. The hope of the Lord's coming (4:13—5:11)
V. Practical behavior appropriate for Christians (5:12–28)

Second Thessalonians
I. Words of encouragement (1:1–12)
II. Correction of a misunderstanding of prophecy (2:1–17)
III. Exhortations on Christian living (3:1–18)

Overviews of First and Second Thessalonians

First Thessalonians. The apostle shares his personal reflections of his visit to Thessalonica (1:1–10). The suffering he experienced prior to coming there is evidence that his motives were pure, as was the conduct he manifested towards them (2:1–12). He applauds them for the manner in which they received the Word and endured suffering (2:13–16). His concern for them led him to send Timothy back, and the report that he has brought the apostle gives him comfort (2:17—3:10). He prays that he might come to them again (3:11–13). Meanwhile, they are to live in a way that pleases God (4:1–12). Paul does not want them to grieve, as do those who have no hope (4:13). The Lord will bring the Christian dead with him on his return, translate the living,[66] and all believers will be reunited (4:14–18). Further, they know that those who are persecuting them will be overtaken by the day of the Lord, so they should be encouraged to live for Christ (5:1–11). Living for Christ involves practical behavior towards one another (5:12–22). As they so live, the Lord will sanctify and keep them (5:23–28).

Second Thessalonians: After a brief salutation, Paul commends the Thessalonians for their endurance, adding that the Lord at his coming would destroy persecutors (chap. 1). He then moves to the primary purpose of the letter and clarifies their misunderstanding that the day of the Lord has already begun. That this time of tribulation has not begun is evident because the apostasy and the man of lawlessness have not yet appeared.[67] The Holy Spirit restrains him, but he will be revealed just prior to the Second Coming (2:1–12). Believers may rejoice that God has chosen them for salvation rather than tribulation (2:13–18).[68] Paul concludes by asking for their prayers and commanding them to not tolerate members in their midst who live Christ-dishonoring lives.

Theological Highlights

Concerning Scripture. The apostle commends the Thessalonians for receiving his message as "the Word of the Lord" (1 Thess. 2:13). This was characteristic of the way in which Old Testament prophets described their messages. Thus, the communications of the apostle Paul, being written, have the force of Scripture.

Concerning the future. The Thessalonian epistles give valuable insights as to how the present world order will come to an end. Five great events will occur:

- The return of Christ with the believing dead (1 Thess. 4:14)
- The resurrection of the bodies of believers (1 Thess. 4:14–16)
- The rapture of the living saints (1 Thess. 4:17)
- The reunion of believers (1 Thess. 4:17)
- The retribution of the wicked in the Tribulation (1 Thess. 5:1–11; 2 Thess. 1:6–10).

Key Verses

1 Thessalonians 4:16–17: "For the Lord Himself will descend from heaven with a shout, with the voice of an archangel, and with the trumpet of God. And the dead in Christ will rise first. Then we who are alive and remain shall be caught up together with them in the clouds to meet the Lord in the air. And thus we shall always be with the Lord."

2 Thessalonians 1:7–10: "And to give you who are troubled rest with us when the Lord Jesus is revealed from heaven with His mighty angels, in flaming fire taking vengeance on those who do not know God, and on those who do not obey the gospel of our Lord Jesus Christ. These shall be punished with everlasting destruction from the presence of the

Lord and from the glory of His power, when He comes, in that Day, to be glorified in His saints and to be admired among all those who believe, because our testimony among you was believed."

Key Chapters

1 Thessalonians 4: the Rapture.

2 Thessalonians 2: the Antichrist.

Message of First and Second Thessalonians

The person who said, "I'm interested in the future because I'm going to spend the rest of my life there," would love these letters. Together they clarify many aspects of God's prophetic plan for the world. Knowing how matters will end enables us as Christians to live more wisely in the world today.

The Pretribulational Rapture

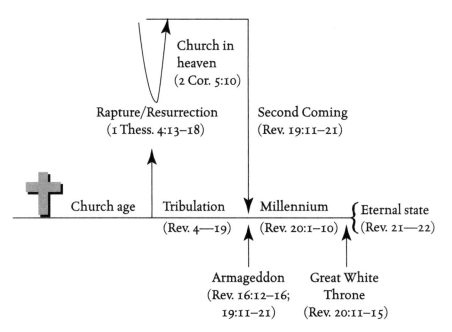

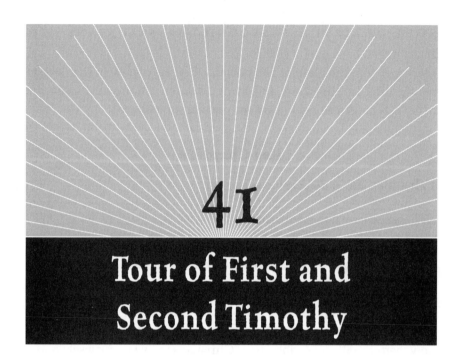

41

Tour of First and Second Timothy

Preview of First and Second Timothy

In the early days of Christianity, there were no schools for training pastors and other Christian leaders. Gifted men were trained by older men, much like Jesus trained the Twelve. Among the men Paul trained were Timothy and Titus to whom he wrote his last three letters. They are called the "Pastoral Epistles" because in them Paul gave them directions for the conduct of their pastoral ministries. The order in which these letters were written was First Timothy, then Titus, and last of all, Second Timothy. Sometime between the writing of Titus and Second Timothy, Paul was arrested for the second time. He wrote Second Timothy while awaiting execution (2 Tim. 4:6–18).

Introduction to First and Second Timothy

Author. The apostle Paul.

Dates of writing. A.D. 63 and 67. Following the Roman imprisonment described at the end of Acts, Paul enjoyed about five years of freedom prior to being rearrested and executed.

Theme. *Teaching pastoral conduct* is the theme of First Timothy. In Second Timothy, written when the death of Paul was imminent, the theme is *transferring ministry responsibility*. Paul charges Timothy to carry on the work of the gospel.

Purpose. In the first letter, Paul wrote to help Timothy know how to combat false teachers who were threatening the church at Ephesus (1:3; cf. Acts 20:29–30). In the second letter, his purpose was to motivate Timothy to continue the ministry after the apostle's death.

Problems. Because of an alleged difference in style, vocabulary, and doctrinal emphases, critical scholars question whether Paul actually wrote these letters. However, all objections raised against Paul's authorship can be reasonably answered. The uniform view of antiquity was that Paul authored both letters.

History and archaeology. Ephesus, a major port city, was filled with vice and corruption. This would challenge a young pastor like Timothy. His mentor, Paul, according to Clement of Rome (who wrote about A.D. 95), was put to death by Nero about A.D. 67.

Outlines of First and Second Timothy

First Timothy
I. Opposing the dangers of false doctrine (1:1–20)
II. Giving directions for worship (2:1–15)
III. Description of godly leaders (3:1–16)
IV. Defense against false teachers (4:1–16)
V. Duties toward the elderly (5:1–25)
VI. Dealing with wealth (6:1–21)

Second Timothy
I. Appreciation for Timothy (1:1–18)
II. Appeal for Timothy to be strong (2:1–26)
III. Advice about the last days (3:1–17)
IV. Admonition to preach the gospel (4:1–22)

Overviews of First and Second Timothy

First Timothy. The first letter to Timothy begins with a charge to combat false teachers (1:1–11). So that sound doctrine will be taught, God has called both Paul and Timothy to service (1:12–20). Those who profess sound doctrine should adorn that doctrine with acceptable worship (chap. 2). Likewise, the preservation of doctrine demands that godly men have leadership in the church (chap. 3). Dangers lie ahead for those who contend for the faith, for in latter times many will embrace deception (4:1–5). Therefore, the good minister of Christ will nourish God's people with sound doctrine while maintaining a good example (4:6–16). Elderly people should receive special respect and care in the church (5:1–16), and leaders of the church should likewise receive honorable treatment (5:17–25). Slaves should honor their masters (6:1–5), and the wealthy should pursue contentment and not put their hope in earthly riches (6:6–21).

Second Timothy. The last letter written by Paul begins with a tender expression of appreciation for Timothy (1:1–5). He then encourages Timothy to rekindle his gift and stand for the gospel (1:6–18). Paul urges Timothy to be strong, to endure suffering like a soldier, to compete like an athlete, and to work hard like a farmer (2:1–7). Young Timothy must remain faithful to Christ and accept the responsibility of teaching others (2:8–19). Such faithfulness includes living a godly and gentle life (2:20–26). Although difficult times are ahead, he must not deviate from the things taught in Scripture (chap. 3). Difficult or not, he must preach the gospel and fulfill his ministry (4:1–5). Paul notes that his days are drawing to a close and urges Timothy to come for a final visit (4:6–22).

Theological Highlights

Concerning Scripture. Second Timothy 3:16–17 contains one of the most important passages in the Bible concerning Scripture. Paul says it is inspired, using a word he coins that literally means "God-breathed." The value of Scripture is fourfold, leading to the equipping of believers for every good work.

Concerning church leadership. First Timothy 3 indicates that there are two primary offices in the church, those of overseer (or bishop) and deacon. In Titus, the first of these terms is used interchangeably with elder. The latter office may be open to women according to some interpretations of First Timothy 3:11.

Key Verses

1 Timothy 3:14–15: "These things I write to you, though I hope to come to you shortly; but if I am delayed, I write so that you may know how you ought to conduct yourself in the house of God, which is the church of the living God, the pillar and ground of the truth."

2 Timothy 4:1–2: "I charge you therefore before God and the Lord Jesus Christ, who will judge the living and the dead at His appearing and His kingdom: Preach the word! Be ready in season and out of season. Convince, rebuke, exhort, with all longsuffering and teaching."

Key Chapters

1 Timothy 3: the qualifications of church leaders

2 Timothy 2: the conduct of a faithful minister

Message of First and Second Timothy

These two letters continue to offer practical wisdom to those called to lead local churches. The principles of leadership found here are perpetually relevant.

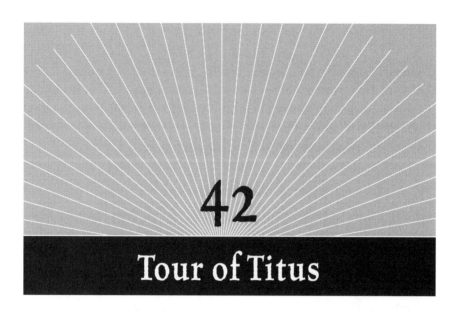

42

Tour of Titus

Preview of Titus

Like Timothy, Titus had been dispatched by Paul to give pastoral leadership to a troubled church. It emphasizes leadership, as does First Timothy.

Introduction to Titus

Author. The apostle Paul. This is the third of his so-called Pastoral Epistles, giving advice and guidance to a young pastor.

Date of writing. A.D. 66. Paul was probably released from his first Roman imprisonment (described in Acts) around A.D. 62. He then traveled about freely, writing First Timothy and Titus. He seems to have been arrested suddenly in Troas (2 Tim. 4:13) and sent back to Rome from which he wrote Second Timothy. Nero put Paul to death in A.D. 67.

Theme. Truth silences error. Paul sent Titus to the island of Crete (1:5) to silence deceitful men who apparently had done great damage to the church (1:10–11). Titus was to carry out his assignment by appointing elders in each church (1:5) who were able to teach sound doctrine (1:9), and by Titus himself engaging in sound teaching (2:1).

Purpose. Paul wrote to Titus to teach him how to deal with the dissension and deceptions within the church at Crete, particularly to tell him the caliber of men needed as church leaders.

History and archaeology. Cretans were despised in the ancient world, their low reputation being proverbial (see the quotation of Epimenides in 1:12). "To Cretanize" was slang for "to lie." Certainly, Titus had a demanding task ahead of him. He is unusual in that he was a Gentile (Gal. 2:3). Most leaders of the early church were Jews.

Geography. Crete is one of the large islands in the Mediterranean Sea. It enjoyed fertile lands and prosperity. See map 11, page 191.

Outline of Titus

I. Appointing Christian leaders (1:1–16)
II. Teaching Christian behavior (2:1—3:11)
III. Brief instructions and greetings (3:12–15)

Overview of Titus

Appointing Christian leaders (1:1–16). Paul has sent Titus to Crete to deal with the problem of misguided teachers upsetting churches. To do this, he must appoint elders who can teach true doctrine and thereby silence those teaching falsehood.

Teaching Christian behavior (2:1—3:11). Titus should carefully teach the Christians how to behave. This includes instructions for older men and women, as well as younger. The reason for this is that God's grace, which has saved us, also teaches us to live godly lives

(2:11–13). In mentioning how Christians should live, Paul says that we are to wait for the "blessed hope" and "appearing" of Christ (2:13), indicating that the coming of Christ has no necessary intervening events. It could come at any moment. The Christian's well-mannered conduct extends to society at large, beginning with governing authorities but excluding no one (3:1–7). Any so-called believers who are troublemakers are to be shunned (3:8–11).

Brief instructions and greetings (3:12–15). Paul concludes by giving Titus brief instructions about helping other missionaries, then he sends a greeting.

Theological Highlights

Concerning God. God cannot lie (1:2). He is truthful in all he promises, including eternal life to those who believe.

Concerning Christ. He is both God and Savior (2:13). This is one of the strongest assertions of Christ's deity to be found in Paul's letters.

Concerning the Second Coming. The command of 2:13 to look for the coming of Christ supports the concept of imminence, the idea that no necessary intervening events must occur before the Second Coming.

Concerning salvation. Salvation is a matter of God's grace and mercy (2:11; 3:5). In saving us, the Holy Spirit does a work of spiritual cleansing and renewal that involves regeneration (being "born again"). Salvation does not condone living in sin, but leads believers to live godly lives (2:12). Those who are saved should live in expectation of the return of Christ at any moment (2:13).

Key Verse

Titus 1:5: "For this reason I left you in Crete, that you should set in order the things that are lacking, and appoint elders in every city as I commanded you."

Key Chapter

Chapter 1: the qualifications of church leaders.

Message of Titus

Titus reminds us that the Christian life must be lived with vigilance. Both the possibility of infiltration by false teachers and of the Lord's sudden return should arouse us to be devoted to the Master.

Tour of Philemon

Preview of Philemon

No one enjoys being in the middle of a disagreement between friends, yet that was the situation that prompted Paul to write this short letter. It is the last of the Prison Epistles (see preview of Ephesians) and one of Paul's most personal letters.

Introduction to Philemon

Author. The apostle Paul. The reason Philemon is placed last among Paul's epistles is because they are arranged according to length, from longest to shortest, rather than by date.

Date of writing. A.D. 61, during the imprisonment described at the end of Acts.

Theme. People are equal. This brief letter to Paul's "beloved friend" (1:1), Philemon, concerns a runaway slave named Onesimus. Every large Roman household had slaves, including that of Philemon. It was a capital offense for a slave to run away. To compound matters further, Onesimus had stolen from Philemon (v. 18). Somehow, he journeyed to Rome and found Paul. The apostle led him to faith (and freedom) in Christ. But, not to presume on the good graces of Philemon, Paul sends Onesimus back with the insistence that Philemon receive him, not as a slave but as a beloved brother (v. 16). Tradition says that Onesimus went on to become the bishop of Ephesus. In this brief letter, Paul puts the ax to the practice of slavery among Christians, for in Christ, all are brothers and sisters.

Purpose. Paul wrote to ease the reentry of Onesimus into the household of Philemon. But the occasion also gave him the opportunity to set forth his views on slavery. The influence of this letter has been out of proportion to its length.

History and archaeology. William Barclay writes concerning the Roman institution of slavery,

> It has been computed that in the Roman Empire there were 60,000,000 slaves. In Paul's day a kind of terrible idleness had fallen on the citizens of Rome. Rome was the mistress of the world, and therefore it was beneath the dignity of a Roman citizen to work. Practically all the work was done by slaves. . . . Basically the life of the slave was grim and terrible. In law he was not a person but a thing. Aristotle lays it down that there can never be friendship between master and slave, for they have nothing in common; "for a slave is a living tool, just as a tool is an inanimate slave." . . . If the slave ran away, at best he was branded on the forehead with the letter F for fugitivus, which means runaway, at worst he was killed. The terror of the slave was that he was absolutely at the caprice of his master. . . . A Roman writer lays it down: "Whatever a master does to a slave, undeservedly, in anger, willingly, unwillingly, in forgetfulness, after careful thought, knowingly, unknowingly, is judgment, justice and law."[69]

It was against this cruelty that Paul protested.

Geography. On the basis of the reference to Archippus here (v. 2) and in Colossians 4:17, as well as to Onesimus (v. 10 and Col. 4:9), it is assumed that Philemon was a resident of Colossae and allowed the church of that city to meet in his home. See map 11, page 191.

Outline of Philemon

  I. Thanksgiving for Philemon (vv. 1–7)
  II. Appeal for Onesimus (vv. 8–25)

Overview of Philemon

After greeting Philemon, his wife Apphia, and (son?) Archippus, Paul expresses his heartfelt appreciation for Philemon, a man of love and faith (vv. 1–7). Knowing the sort of man he is, Paul appeals to him to receive Onesimus, his runaway slave who has become a Christian. Onesimus is no longer "just" a slave but a brother in Christ and worthy of the same acceptance that Philemon would show Paul (vv. 8–17). Paul offers to repay any losses Philemon might have incurred when Onesimus ran away (v. 18). He expresses his confidence that Philemon will do even more than he asks and extends the greetings of others to him.

Theological Highlights

Concerning man. This brief letter upholds the essential equality of all people. Christians cannot maintain the social distinctions common in the world (cf. Gal. 3:28).

Key Verse

Verse 16: stating that Onesimus could no longer be regarded as a slave but as a brother in the Lord.

Message of Philemon

The book of Philemon teaches by a specific example the truth voices in Galations 3:28: "There is neither Jew nor Greek, there is neither slave nor free, there is neither male nor female; for you are all one in Christ Jesus."

Tour of Hebrews

Preview of Hebrews

Persecution has been common throughout Christian history, as Hebrews testifies. Jewish believers in Jesus were under attack by their fellow countrymen. As a result, some wavered in their commitment to Christ. This epistle urges them to stand fast, since Jesus is God's last word to man.

Introduction to Hebrews

Author. This is the first of the General Epistles (which are sometimes called the Catholic or Universal Epistles). There are eight in all. With the exception of Hebrews, these eight are named after their authors, whereas Paul's letters are named after their recipients. The author of the Book of Hebrews is unknown. However, many suggestions have been made. Tertullian (c. A.D. 155–222) ascribed the work to Barnabas. However, a contemporary, Clement of Alexandria, was of the opinion that Paul wrote it. Later, Origin (c. A.D. 185–254) noted two other opinions, that

247

either Clement of Rome or Luke wrote the book. Origin concluded, "God only knows for certain."

Date of writing. A.D. 68. Many references to Jewish sacrifices and priesthood are in this book. The absence of any reference to the destruction of the temple and priesthood suggests that the sacrificial system was still operative when the book was written. Since the forces of Rome destroyed the temple in A.D. 70, a date somewhat earlier is plausible.[70]

Theme. Heaven's last word. "God, who at various times and in various ways spoke in time past to the fathers by the prophets, has in these last days spoken to us by His Son" (1:1). So begins the epistle, indicating its theme. The burden of the writer is to demonstrate the finality and superiority of Christ. He does this through a series of contrasts in which Christ is shown to be higher than angels, Moses, and priests.

Purpose. This epistle was written to strengthen the endurance of persecuted Christians (10:32–39). If the dating of the book is correct, then these would likely have been Hebrew Christians being persecuted by Jews during the rebellion against Rome.

Problems. Authorship aside, there is some question as to whether Hebrews was originally a letter or a sermon. Unlike other letters of the New Testament, it has no salutation. This has led to speculation that it was originally the text of a preacher's remarks made to a church.

History and archaeology. In A.D. 66 Jewish freedom fighters succeeded in ousting the Romans from Palestine. The rebels enjoyed a brief period of liberty before the Romans under Titus crushed the rebellion and burned Jerusalem. In that span of two or three years, they turned their fury against the followers of Jesus. Excavations in Jerusalem and elsewhere in Palestine reveal the terrible destructiveness of this war.

Outline of Hebrews

   I.   Christ is superior to angels (1:1—2:18)
   II.   Christ is superior to Moses (3:1—4:13)

III. Christ is superior to any other priest (4:14—10:18)
IV. Christ is worthy of our faithful endurance (10:19—13:25)

Overview of Hebrews

Christ is superior to angels (1:1—2:18). In Jesus, God has spoken in these last days, and through Jesus all things are upheld. Consequently, he is much better than the angels are (1:1–4). Both in his person (1:1–14) and his position as the Savior of mankind (2:1–18), he is superior to the angels.

Christ is superior to Moses (3:1—4:13). Moses was faithful to God as a servant in God's house. But Jesus is the Son in the Father's house (3:1–6). Unlike the Israelites who tested God in the wilderness, we should be careful to obey him by holding fast to our confession of faith in Jesus. Then we will enjoy his rest (3:7—4:13).

Christ is superior to any other priest (4:14—10:18). Though Christ did not come from the tribe of Levi, he is a better priest in that he sympathizes with us in our moral weakness but is without sin of his own (4:15). He was appointed by God to this priesthood and has entered the tabernacle of heaven where he ministers on our behalf. His priesthood is like that of Melchizedek (cf. Gen. 14:17–20 and Psalm 110:4), who was not from Levi but to whom Abraham paid a tithe (6:20—7:28). As the high priest of heaven, Jesus has become the mediator of a better covenant (8:1–6). The prophets spoke of a new covenant that would make an end of sin (8:7–13). Christ has inaugurated this covenant with his own blood (chap. 9). The Law and its sacrifices cannot deal with sin or else they would not have to be offered repeatedly (10:1–4). But Jesus by his death has once for all sanctified those who have faith in him (10:5–18). "By that will we have been sanctified through the offering of the body of Jesus Christ once for all" (10:10).

Christ is worthy of our faithful endurance (10:19—13:25). Having this superior salvation in Christ, we must not turn away from him but endure (10:19–39). Before us are the examples of the faithful men and women of the Old Testament who endured great hardships (chap. 11). Given their examples, we should patiently run the race before us, accepting hardship as God's discipline (12:1–13). We Christians must be gracious toward all people out of reverence for God (12:14–29). Especially must we love one another and keep ourselves untainted by wrongdoing (13:1–19).

The book concludes with a benediction and expressions of grace (13:20–25).

Theological Highlights

Concerning Christ. Hebrews presents Christ in his three offices of prophet (1:1–2), priest (4:14—10:18), and king (1:3; 7:1–3). More than any other book, it shows him to be the fulfillment of the symbolism of the Old Testament sacrifices and worship. The book also asserts the dual nature of Christ, giving emphasis to his deity (1:3, 8) and his humanity (2:9, 17).

Concerning salvation. Salvation is accomplished through the once-for-all offering of Christ's body (10:10, 12, 14). The way to heaven is by the blood of Jesus (i.e., by faith in the sufficiency of his death, 10:19). Only those with faith please God and inherit righteousness (11:6–7).

Key Verses

Hebrews 1:1–2: "God, who at various times and in various ways spoke in time past to the fathers by the prophets, has in these last days spoken to us by His Son, whom He has appointed heir of all things, through whom also He made the worlds."

Hebrews 12:25: "See that you do not refuse Him who speaks. For if they did not escape who refused Him who spoke on earth, much more shall we not escape if we turn away from Him who speaks from heaven."

Key Chapters

Chapter 10: the exhortation to hold fast to Christ.

Chapter 12: the call to persevere in suffering.

Message of Hebrews

Not unlike Colossians, Hebrews gives a strong reminder to Christians today that we cannot improve upon the salvation that is ours in Christ. Rituals and ceremonies such as those in the Old Testament have no saving benefit. He is all we need.

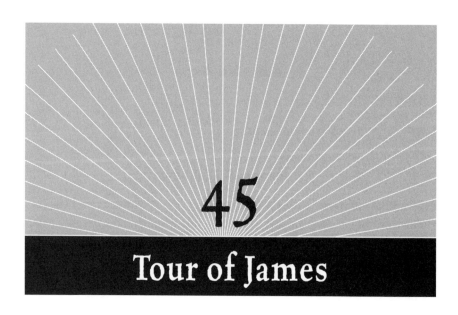

45

Tour of James

Preview of James

The Christian life is like running the high hurdles in that we must overcome certain obstacles to achieve victory. The Book of James examines six of these hurdles or tests of faith that were common both then and now. Overcoming them is necessary for our sanctification or perfection (1:4).

Introduction to James

Author. James, the half brother of Jesus (Mark 6:3). He is not to be confused with James, the brother of John, who was martyred under Herod Antipas (Acts 12:2). Following his resurrection, Jesus appeared to him (1 Cor. 15:7), which led to his conversion. As we see in Acts 15, he became a leader of the church in Jerusalem. Critical scholars dispute James' authorship on the basis that the Greek used is too good. However, the large Gentile population residing in Galilee suggests that

James could very well have been fluent in Greek. Tradition tells us that he had knees like a camel's because he prayed so much.

Date of writing. The question of the date of writing is closely bound to the place of writing. If written in Palestine, the date would have to be prior to A.D. 70, the time when Roman forces destroyed the country. Evidence for this is found in the reference to farm laborers in 5:4. Only in Palestine were hired laborers used in farming. Elsewhere, slaves worked the fields. The use of the word *synagogue* for *church* in 2:2 also suggests an early date. Furthermore, historical sources indicate James died in A.D. 61. So perhaps the book was written about A.D. 50.

Theme. James wrote to Jewish believers outside of Palestine concerning the trials they were experiencing (1:1–2). In the letter, he presents six ways in which faith is tested. So the theme may be stated as Jewish Christians tested.

Purpose. James desired to give ethical instruction to people of faith. He seems to draw heavily on the Sermon on the Mount, with about fifteen allusions to it.

Problems. Few books of the Bible have raised more problems than James. Debates rage over its authorship, date, recipients, and unity.

History and archaeology. The Jewish historian Josephus writes that James was stoned at the instigation of the high priest Ananus in A.D. 61. Recently, an ossuary (box for bones) was found in Jerusalem inscribed, "James son of Joseph, brother of Jesus." This is the only archaeological reference to Jesus or members of his family.

Outline of James

   I. The purpose of testing (1:1–18)
  II. The test of obedience to God's Word (1:19–27)
 III. The test of partiality (2:1–13)
 IV. The test of one's works (2:14–26)

Overview of James

The purpose of testing (1:1–18). Believers should joyfully accept the tests that come their way since such tests produce endurance. Those who persevere under trials receive the crown of life. But no one should think that God tempts us, for temptation arises from within our own characters.

The test of obedience to God's Word (1:19–27). Believers must prove themselves by being doers of God's Word, not merely hearers. The practice of God's Word leads to merciful deeds and pure conduct.

The test of partiality (2:1–13). Showing favoritism to the rich violates God's Law, which teaches us to love our neighbors, whatever their station in life, as we love ourselves. Therefore, genuine faith will love the poor and the rich equally.

The test of one's works (2:14–26). Genuine faith is working faith. It does not merely say the words, but it does the deeds. Mere acknowledgment of spiritual truth does not save, as evidenced by the fact that demons acknowledge truth. Rather, true faith is dynamic, as seen in the lives of Abraham (vv. 23–24) and Rahab (Josh. 2).[71]

The test of the tongue (3:1–12). Faith not only governs a person's deeds but also his speech. The unbridled tongue creates immense problems.

The test of ambitions (3:13—5:6). Selfish ambitions lead to strife. Such quarrels arise from inordinate desires for the things of the world. Believers may turn to God for the grace to overcome selfishness, but it requires single-minded devotion to him. Often, ambitious people are presumptuous, not realizing that God holds their futures. Furthermore, people who long to be rich often treat the poor unjustly.

The test of patience and prayer (5:7–20). Those undergoing various tests of faith should be patient and prayerful. Meanwhile, they should help others stay on the path of truth.

Theological Highlights

Concerning salvation. James clarifies the matter of saving faith. By his insistence that faith works, he shows that saving faith is transforming faith. It is not merely assent to the correct doctrines; it is obedience to the living God.

Key Verse

James 1:22: "But be doers of the word, and not hearers only, deceiving yourselves."

Key Chapter

Chapter 1: the purpose of testing.

Message of James

In a day when statisticians tell us that there is no difference between the behavior of professing Christians and non-Christians, the message of James is greatly needed. It warns that the "churchianity" of many is not the Christianity of the Bible. What we are is the truest test of what we believe.

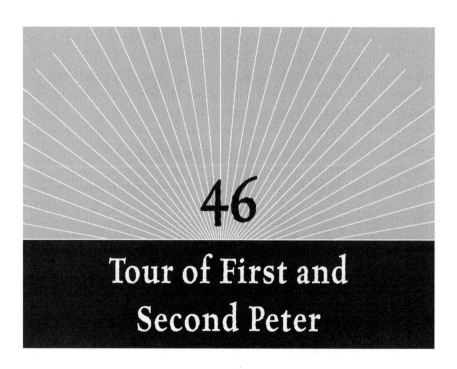

46

Tour of First and Second Peter

Preview of First and Second Peter

An old chorus says, "This world is not my home; I'm just a-passin' through." Our passage is made difficult by opposition from the world and deception in the church. Peter's two brief letters encourage us to remain steadfast to the end.

Introduction to First and Second Peter

Author. The apostle Peter. A uniform church tradition from earliest times says the apostle by this name wrote First Peter. While the great majority of early Christians accepted the genuineness of Second Peter, a few questioned it. This hesitation on the part of some may be because it had a more limited circulation, was not quoted by writers prior to the third century, and had to overcome suspicions raised by other books known to be falsely attributed to Peter.[72] Against this is the positive claim of the book to be by Peter (2 Pet. 1:1), the personal account of the transfiguration (1:16–18), and its high moral tone.

In the nineteenth century, it became customary among critics of the Bible to deny that Peter wrote either book. In both instances, the style of writing is a major reason. The style of Greek in First Peter is said to be too good for a fisherman from Galilee. On the other hand, the style of Second Peter is too different from First Peter to be by Peter. The answer to this objection is found in the fact that Silvanus helped with the writing of First Peter (5:12) but not with Second Peter. He may have been what is called an *amanuensis*, a professional letter writer. Modern critics advance other arguments, but none are conclusive or unanswerable.

Dates of writing. The references to persecution scattered through the first book of Peter suggest that it was written at a time of mounting hostility to Christians. Since Nero was actively persecuting Christians in Rome from A.D. 64–68, it is plausible that officials in the provinces mentioned (1:1) were doing likewise. So First Peter may be dated around A.D. 64. Second Peter was written when the apostle's death (A.D. 67) was imminent (1:14), so a date of A.D. 67 may be assumed.

Themes. *Persecution for Christ* is the subject of First Peter (1:6; 2:12, 20–21; 4:1, 12–14). Second Peter sounds a warning: *pretenders present danger.* Chapter 2 is devoted to alerting Christians to the dangers posed by false teachers.

Purpose. First Peter was written to encourage suffering believers. Second Peter warns of false teachers.

Problems. A significant problem with respect to Second Peter is the similarity of chapter 2 to the Book of Jude. Three possibilities exist: Both biblical writers relied on a third document; Peter copied Jude; or Jude copied Peter. A discussion of these alternatives is reserved for the study of Jude.

History and archaeology. The Roman governor of Bithynia, Pliny the Younger, c. A.D. 112, wrote to the Emperor Trajan about the spread of Christianity throughout the region to which First Peter was sent. His remarks indicate that Christianity had been present long enough to grow to considerable size.

Geography.

The geographical references in First Peter 1:1 are to provinces located in what is now Asia Minor. They are noted on map 11, page 191.

Outlines of First and Second Peter

First Peter:
  I. The Christian's salvation (1:1–12)
  II. The Christian's sanctification (1:13—2:12)
  III. The Christian's submissiveness (to government, masters, husbands, and others) (2:13—3:12)
  IV. The Christian's suffering (3:13—5:14)

Second Peter:
  I. Developing as Christians (1:1–21)
  II. Denouncing false teachers (2:1–22)
  III. Difficulties of the last days (3:1–18)

Overviews of First and Second Peter

First Peter. A magnificent statement of the Trinity opens the first letter of Peter (1:2). He follows with praise for the mercy of God and affirmation of his power to keep us through trials (1:5–9). The prophets of old (1:12) foresaw the salvation God has given us. Because our Savior is a holy God, we ourselves must live lives of holiness, reverence, and love (1:13–25). Christians constitute the temple, priesthood, and nation of God (2:1–10). Therefore, we ought to keep our behavior excellent (2:11–25). Marriage between Christians should manifest respect and understanding (3:1–7). Within the church there should be harmony and kindness (3:8–12). If called to suffer for Christ, we should accept it as Christ himself accepted suffering, being careful not to sin (3:13—4:19). The elders of the church are to gladly shepherd God's flock, providing good examples for all to follow (5:1–4). Humility and spiritual vigilance should characterize all (5:5–9). Peter concludes with an assurance of the coming glory and greetings (5:10–14).

Second Peter. Addressed to those with a faith like his, Peter affirms that God has given us all that is needed for spiritual growth (1:3–11). In light of his impending death, Peter wishes to remind us of Christian beliefs. Far from being "tales," he witnessed the reality of Christ. Further, prophecy testifies to Christ (1:12–21). He warns that false teachers will enter the church and gives a lengthy description of them (2:1–22). Another difficulty to be encountered by Christians is the scoffing of those who mistakenly think that Christ's delayed return means that Christianity is not true, when in fact it means God is merciful (3:1–9). However, the day of the Lord (i.e., the day of judgment) will come, so believers ought to live above sin and be on guard against unprincipled men (3:14–18).

Theological Highlights

Concerning God. A clear reference to the Trinity is found in 1 Peter 1:2. While no passage in the New Testament attempts to prove the Trinity, it is a conclusion drawn from evidence such as this.

Concerning Scripture. Second Peter 1:20–21 makes the declaration that Scripture is not a matter of human invention but of divine guidance. Peter uses a word for the moving of the Spirit upon the writers of Scripture that is used elsewhere for the driving of a ship by a storm (Acts 27:17). This signifies that the force of the Spirit upon the writers of the Bible was as irresistible as the winds that blow a sailing vessel across the sea.

Concerning salvation. Peter supports the concept of Christ's substitutionary atonement in First Peter 2:24 and 3:18. Substitutionary atonement means that Christ died in the place of the sinners, carrying the penalty of the sins they committed.

Concerning the church. Leadership in the church is given to men called elders (1 Peter 5:1–4). Another term used interchangeably for this is overseers (see Titus 1:5, 7).

Key Verses

1 Peter 3:18: "For Christ also suffered once for sins, the just for the unjust, that He might bring us to God, being put to death in the flesh but made alive by the Spirit."

2 Peter 1:3–4: "As His divine power has given to us all things that pertain to life and godliness, through the knowledge of Him who called us by glory and virtue, by which have been given to us exceedingly great and precious promises, that through these you may be partakers of the divine nature, having escaped the corruption that is in the world through lust."

Key Chapters

1 Peter 1: the Christian's new life.

2 Peter 2: false teachers and their destruction.

Messages of First and Second Peter

The message of First Peter continues to encourage believers to be strong in places like these. The twentieth century has seen more martyrdom of Christians than any other century in history. While American Christians have largely been insulated from persecution, it has fallen with fury on believers behind the former Iron Curtain, in China, Iran, the Sudan, and throughout the Islamic world.

Second Peter's call to vigilance is also still needed. With the advent of higher criticism[73] of the Bible, the twentieth century has seen more falsehood in the church than in any other. The demise of Christianity in Europe and its weakened condition in America can be traced to the destructive effect of the critical school of thought.

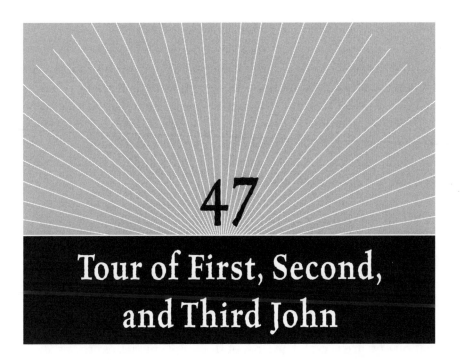

Tour of First, Second, and Third John

Preview of First, Second, and Third John

Tradition says that John the apostle lived to be an old man, spending his latter years in Ephesus where he exercised pastoral care over the churches in the province of Asia. According to legend, in Christian gatherings he would stretch out his hands and say, "Children, love one another." We see this pastoral heart reflected in three short letters that bear his name.

Introduction to John's Epistles

Author. The letters themselves are anonymous, but it has been traditionally understood that the author was the apostle John. Altogether, the apostle wrote five books of the New Testament—these three, the fourth Gospel, and Revelation. First John is the best attested of the three letters with a uniform tradition behind it. Second and Third John, being smaller works, are not as well attested, but no serious doubts ever existed as to their genuineness. Because an early writer (Papias) refers to the author as "John the elder" rather than "John the apostle," some have argued that the writer was an otherwise unknown church leader. However, this seems to be based upon a misunderstanding of Papias. The many similarities between these writings and the fourth Gospel argue forcefully for a common author.

Date of writing. Probably near the end of the apostle's life, around A.D. 90.

Themes. First John invites its readers to *join in fellowship* with the Father and the Son (1:3). The letter gives many tests of fellowship or relationship with God. Second John addresses the problem of heresy, telling its readers to *judge false teachers*. The heresy denied the incarnation of Christ (v. 7). The final of the three epistles expresses *joy in hospitality* shown by Gaius to itinerant Christian workers. The early church employed a system of traveling preachers that relied on the help of believing people much like the early Methodist circuit riders did on the American frontier.

Purposes. Both First and Second John arose out of a problem with heresy (1 John 2:18–23; 2 John 7–9). The essential error of this heresy was that it denied the incarnation of Christ (i.e., that he was the preexistent Son of God who became a man).

Problems. What was the heresy John wrote against? This could have been one of two things. One view is that John battled the teaching of a man named Cerinthus who taught that Jesus was only a man who had the Holy Spirit descend on him at his baptism and leave him at the cross. The other view is that John was addressing an early form of Docetism that taught that Jesus did not have a material body but only appeared to have one.[74] In either case, these heresies denied the incarnation and thus the deity of Christ was denied. Third John was written to encourage Gaius to continue helping Christian workers, particularly Demetrius (v. 12).

History and archaeology. Tradition holds that John moved to Ephesus in his later years. From there he exercised jurisdiction over the churches of Asia. The Emperor Domitian exiled him to the island of Patmos where he wrote the Book of Revelation and, presumably, died.

Outlines of First, Second, and Third John

First John:
  I. The joy of fellowship with the Father and the Son (1:1–4)
  II. Principles of fellowship (1:5—2:14)
  III. Threats to fellowship (2:15–29)
  IV. Tests of fellowship (3:1—4:21)
  V. Assurances of fellowship (5:1–21)

Second John
  I. Commendation of the church (vv. 1–4)
  II. Command to love one another (vv. 5–6)
  III. Caution concerning deceivers (vv. 7–13)

Third John
  I.   The hospitality of Gaius commended (vv. 1–8)
  II. The inhospitality of Diotrephes condemned (vv. 9–11)
  III. Demetrius introduced (vv. 12–14)

Overviews of John's epistles

First John. Lacking the salutation common to epistles, First John reads more like a discourse. It begins with a proclamation of its theme, fellowship with the Father and the Son (1:1–4). John had experienced this fellowship himself (1:2). The God with whom we may have fellowship is holy, and those who would fellowship with him must themselves walk in the light (i.e., in obedience to him, 1:5–7). Several conditions for continued fellowship with God are given (1:8—2:14). Both love for this world (2:15–17) and involvement with those who deny Christ (2:18–29) will destroy fellowship with God. Several characteristics of those who enjoy fellowship with God follow (3:1—5:21).

These include purity of life (3:3; 5:2), love for other believers (3:11; 4:7, 11), and confession that Jesus Christ has come in the flesh (4:2). By these we can know that we have eternal life (5:13).

Second John. Addressed to "the chosen lady" and her "children,"[75] this letter continues the warnings against heresy mentioned in 1 John 2:18–23. After commending the walk of the children (v. 4) and reminding them to love one another (v. 5), John warns them to beware of deceivers (v. 7).

Third John. The most personal of the letters of John, this is addressed to a Christian man named Gaius who was walking in the truth (v. 3) and helping traveling preachers who came his way (vv. 5–8). Such help was not coming from Diotrephes (vv. 9–10). But John urges Gaius to continue to show hospitality, especially to Demetrius (v. 12), who probably delivered this letter.

Theological Highlights

Concerning Christ. John emphasizes the incarnation of Christ (1 John 4:2; 2 John 7–9). By so doing, he upholds the true humanity of Christ as well as his deity.

Concerning salvation. One of the clearest statements in the Bible regarding the assurance of salvation is found in First John 5:13. Christians can know by their lives and confession that they do indeed possess eternal life.

Key Verses

1 John 1:9: "If we confess our sins, He is faithful and just to forgive us our sins and to cleanse us from all unrighteousness."

2 John 7: "For many deceivers have gone out into the world who do not confess Jesus Christ as coming in the flesh. This is a deceiver and an antichrist."

3 John 5–6: "Beloved, you do faithfully whatever you do for the brethren and for strangers, who have borne witness of your love before the church. If you send them forward on their journey in a manner worthy of God, you will do well."

Key Chapter

1 John 2: Love the brethren, not the world, and confess that Jesus is the Christ.

Message of John's letters

The letters of John remind us of the primacy of love, a theme first sounded in his Gospel (13:34–35). They further warn us that any attempt to define Jesus as something less than God in the flesh is heresy. Jesus must not be regarded as a good man nor even as an angel but as the Son of God who was made man that he might be a sufficient Savior. John further reminds us of the Christian responsibility to support preachers and missionaries so that the truth might go out into the world (3 John 6–8).

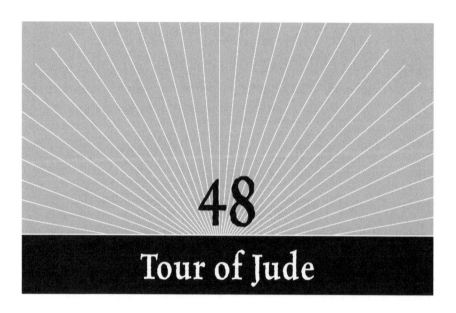

Tour of Jude

Preview of Jude

Some things are so important that they bear repeating. Jude reissues the warning about false teachers in the church that was found in Second Peter 2.

Introduction to Jude

Author. Jude, a half brother of Jesus (Matt. 13:55; Mark 6:3).

Date of writing. The date of the letter is closely tied to its relationship with Second Peter as discussed below. If written after Second Peter, a date of about A.D. 68 seems likely.

Theme. Judgment on apostates (v. 4). Certain people who denied Christ and turned grace into licentiousness had entered the fellowship of Christians. Presumably, these people denied the uniqueness or saving power of Jesus and understood the concept of grace as meaning "anything goes."

Purpose. Jude wanted to show that such heterodox teachers were condemned and to warn Christians from joining in their evil.

Problems. The similarities between Jude and Second Peter 2 are so strong that some dependence between the two must exist. While it is possible that both drew on a common source, it is more likely that one possessed a copy of the other's writing and made use of it. Opinion is divided, but it seems more likely that Second Peter was written first and that when Jude received a copy of it, he was moved to reiterate its message to his audience (v. 3).

Another problem encountered in Jude is its allusions to the apocryphal books known as the Assumption of Moses and First Enoch (vv. 9, 14–15).[76] The Jews, Christ, and the apostles did not recognize these books as part of the Bible. Did Jude? Interpreters have handled this in a variety of ways. Some have said Jude recognizes a kernel of truth in these writings; others say he is simply using them the way a modern preacher would use illustrative material; still others conclude that he considers them to be Scripture. Assuming that Jude's views were not different from those of his contemporaries, the first or second possibilities are more likely.

Outline of Jude

I. The need to contend for the faith (vv. 1–4)
II. The description of the apostates (vv. 5–16)
III. The exhortation to believers (vv. 17–23)
IV. The benediction (vv. 24–25)

Overview of Jude

Having originally intended to write about salvation, Jude is moved to ask the believers to contend for the faith. Evil people, denying Christ and perverting grace, have crept into the church. But God will judge these evil doers, just as he judged the people who sinned in the wilderness, the angels who joined in Satan's rebellion, and the sinners of Sodom and Gomorrah. It is characteristic of such people to reject authority. They will perish like Korah (Num. 16). Meanwhile, they are a danger to all. Enoch had such in view when he predicted the Lord's coming in wrath. Believers should keep themselves far from such people. Jude ends with a benediction.

Theological Highlights

Concerning salvation. In his benediction, Jude affirms the power of God to keep believers until they stand in his presence, thus affirming the permanence of salvation.

Key Verse

Jude 3: "... contend earnestly for the faith which was once for all delivered to the saints."

Message of Jude

Jude warns us to be vigilant and not seduced by false teachers among us, especially those who turn grace into an excuse for sin.

49

Tour of Revelation

Preview of Revelation

As all doctrine finds its headwaters in Genesis, so all doctrine reaches a climax in Revelation. John the apostle pulls back the veil on the future, revealing the glorious end God has in sight for Christ and his church. In the difficult times of life, Revelation keeps hope alive by showing that ultimately Christ, not evil, will triumph.

Introduction to Revelation

Author. The apostle John (1:4). This is the fifth of five books to come from the apostle's pen, the others being the Gospel of John, and the three Epistles of John.

Date of writing. Traditionally thought to be near the end of the apostle's life when he was exiled to the penal colony of Patmos, perhaps as late as A.D. 96.

Theme. John's burden in this book is to describe the return of Christ (1:7; 19:11–21; 22:12, 20).

Purpose. John was given this revelation to assure Christians of the ultimate triumph of Christ. At the time, the Emperor Domitian was demanding that he be worshiped as "Lord and God." Refusal to do so was considered seditious. So many Christians suffered greatly. The Book of Revelation gave them hope.

Problems. While interpreters agree on the theme, they disagree as to their understanding of the contents of the book. Four main schools of interpretation have grown up around Revelation.

- The *preterist* ("bygone") view understands the book to be about the first century persecutions under Domitian, jumping across the centuries to the ultimate triumph of Christ.
- The *symbolic* view interprets the book as an idealized presentation of the struggle between good and evil that will continue until the Second Coming.
- The *historical* view believes the book is a presentation of church history from the first century to the Second Coming.
- The *futurist* view sees chapters 4–19 of the book as a predictive prophecy of events that will unfold during the end times, climaxing with the return of Christ. This seems to have been the earliest view of the book.[77]

History and archaeology. As noted under the discussion of John's epistles, he spent his later years in Ephesus from which he exercised apostolic jurisdiction over the churches of Asia. Under the persecutions of Domitian, he was exiled to an island called Patmos from which he wrote the Book of Revelation, employing what to modern readers is a strange literary form.

Beginning with the prophets Isaiah, Ezekiel, and Daniel, a literary form known as apocalyptic grew up. During the Intertestamental Period, nonbiblical books in apocalyptic form were written. In the New

Cities in Revelation 2 and 3

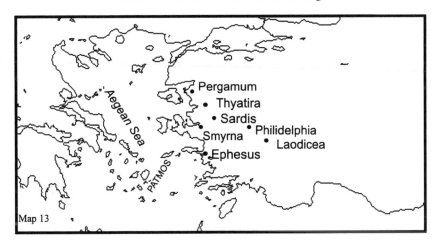

Map 13

Testament, Revelation belongs to this genre. Characteristic of apocalyptic literature is symbolism. Empires are pictured as beasts, judgment as fire, nations as women, and so forth. The intent of such symbolism was to make complex truths comprehensible to anyone ("a picture is worth a thousand words"). Another characteristic of apocalyptic literature is its triumphalism: It sees history moving towards a predetermined end in which evil will be defeated and God enthroned.

Geography. As mentioned above, John wrote Revelation while confined to the penal colony at Patmos, an island in the Mediterranean Sea. It lay between Greece and the seven cities of Asia addressed in chapters 2 and 3.

Outline of Revelation

    I.   Prologue (1:1–8)
   II.   The vision of Christ in majesty (1:9–20)
 III.   The messages to the seven churches (2:1—3:22)
 IV.   The events of the Tribulation and millennium (4:1—20:15)
  V.   The kingdom of heaven (21:1—22:5)
 VI.   Epilogue (22:6–21)

Overview of Revelation

Prologue (1:1–8). John received a revelation (i.e., an unveiling of the future) from Jesus Christ. It concerns the Lord's coming (1:7).

"The things which you have seen" (1:9–20). Chapter 1:19 suggests that the contents of this book can be divided into three major portions: The things John had seen, the things that are, and the things which will take place. The things John had seen would refer to the overwhelming vision of Christ in his majesty found in 1:9–20. Christ is seen in his power, by which he will subjugate all foes.

"The things which are" (2:1—3:22). Messages to seven contemporary churches follow. Christ commends the strengths and reproves the failings of each. He promises them rewards if they heed his word.

Condemnations and Reproofs
of Churches in Revelation 2 and 3

Church	Commendation	Reproof
Ephesus	Sound doctrine	Lacks love
Smyrna	Enduring persecution	None
Pergamos	Holding fast	Doctrine of Balaam
Thyatira	Works	Tolerating Jezebel
Sardis	A few unsoiled	Dead works
Philadelphia	Not denied Christ	None
Laodicea	None	Lukewarm

"The things which will take place" (4:1—22:5). The scene moves from earth to heaven where John sees Christ take a scroll from the Father's hand representing the title deed to the earth (chaps. 4—5). As Christ begins to break the seals on the scroll, judgments begin to pelt the earth (6:1–17). The action pauses long enough to assure the reader that there will be redeemed people during that time (chap. 7). Then another series of judgments take place as angels sound trumpets (chaps. 8—9).

John is not yet finished prophesying as God gives him a scroll to consume, representing further revelation (chap. 10). John then describes prominent characters who will be present on the earth during the time of tribulation (chaps. 11—13). In prelude for the coming climax, a series of warnings are issued from heaven to earth (chap. 14). Then, with the patience of heaven exhausted (chap. 15), the final series of judgments commence. They are portrayed as huge bowls of wrath being poured upon the earth (chap. 16). This leads to the destruction of Babylon, symbolic of godless civilization (chaps. 17—18). Thereafter, Christ returns in power and glory with his bride, the church (chap. 19). Chapter 20 briefly mentions that Christ will reign for a thousand years (a millennium) and then describes the great white throne judgment of the unsaved dead. With all evildoers removed, God ushers in the New Jerusalem, the heavenly kingdom, in a cosmic marriage of heaven and earth (21:1—22:5).

Epilogue (22:6–21). John closes with a promise and a prayer— Christ's promise that he is coming soon, and the prayer that it will be so.

Applying the Book of Revelation

Problem: How Can a Futuristic Book Be Applied to Contemporary Audiences?

1. By finding an implication. Answer the question, If thus and such is true, so what? *Example:* In 10:6 the Lord says a time will come in which there will no longer be a delay. Fortunately, we live in the time of delay. (So what?) Take advantage of it, and turn to Christ.

2. By applying an underlying principle. *Example:* After the millennium, Satan will be released to deceive the nations (20:7–8). Principle: Satan's primary work is deception. Application: He deceives today by promoting the ideas that the blood of Christ cannot save, the Bible is not true, or that all religions are ways to God.

3. By making a comparison. *Example:* A false prophet appears in 13:11–18. He is like ministers who are lovely people but who deny Christ.

4. By making a contrast. *Example:* Martyrs will be willing to lay down their lives for Christ (12:11). How different they are from those Christians who are unwilling to even give of time and money to the Lord.

5. By counterbalancing one truth against another. *Example:* The great white throne judgment of 20:11–15 shows us that God will judge all who reject Christ. However, Calvary shows us that God will show mercy to all who put their faith in Christ.

6. By finding an example to follow. *Example:* In chapter 5, the inhabitants of heaven worship Christ by acknowledging his right to reign over earth. When we worship, we ought to acknowledge Christ's right to reign over our lives.

7. By noting a tendency in society that conforms to something in the text. *Example:* People will not repent of their "sorceries," according to 9:21. The Greek word for "sorceries" is *pharmakia* from which we get "pharmacy." It refers to the use of drugs in contacting the spirit world. Today's explosion of drugs might harbinger the end-time return of sorcery.

Theological Highlights

Concerning the future. The Book of Revelation is the source of much eschatology (the doctrine of last things). From it we gain insights into the coming Tribulation (elsewhere called the "Day of the Lord"). It describes the second coming of Christ. In sobering terms, it portrays the final judgment of the unsaved at the great white throne where all the facts (represented by books) will be brought to light. Even more sobering is the description of the final state of the unsaved as "a lake of fire"—a graphic portrayal of the unending wrath of God. But for believers there is the joyful prospect of heaven where "God will wipe away every tear from their eyes; there shall be no more death, nor sorrow, nor crying. There shall be no more pain, for the former things have passed away" (21:4).

Key Verse

Revelation 1:7: "Behold, He is coming with clouds, and every eye will see Him, even they who pierced Him. And all the tribes of the earth will mourn because of Him. Even so, Amen."

Key Chapter

Chapter 19: the second coming of Christ.

Message of Revelation

Revelation appeals to man's deepest longings—for good to triumph over evil, for the downtrodden to be lifted up, for pain and suffering to end, for a world without the necessity of toil and drudgery. As long as people have such longings, Revelation will be relevant, for it kindles hope in the hearts of believers.

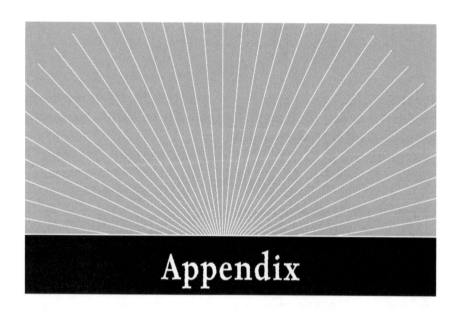

Appendix

How to Get Started in Bible Study

It is far better to study the Bible itself than to study others' thoughts about the Bible. The reflection on the thoughts of others concerning the Bible can never satisfy the way reflection on the thoughts of the Bible itself can do. Yet most people shy away from personal reading and study of the Bible. Either it seems daunting or dry. Below is a simple method of Bible study that can make personal reading of Scripture more rewarding. It is known as the SPECK analysis and simply involves asking five simple questions about any passage.

S = Is there a *sin* for me to avoid?
P = Is there a *promise* for me to claim?
E = Is there an *example* for me to follow?
C = Is there a *command* for me to obey?
K = How can this passage increase my *knowledge* of God or Christ?

- By using these five questions, any person can read the Bible with profit.

- Remember: God is not impressed with how much we know about the Bible but with how teachable we are when we read the Bible.

    "But on this one will I look: On him who is poor and of a contrite spirit, and who trembles at My word" (Isa. 66:2).

- You can read through the entire Bible in a year by reading three chapters a day and five on Sunday. Why not make that your goal for the year ahead?

Notes

1. Samuel Chadwick, quoted in *Samuel Chadwick* by Norman G. Dunning (London: Hodder and Stoughton, 1933), 18.

2. J. Sidlow Baxter, *Explore the Book* (Grand Rapids: Zondervan Publishing House, 1960), 23.

3. Herbert Lockyer, *All the Books and Chapters of the Bible* (Grand Rapids: Zondervan Publishing House, 1966), 9.

4. Howard F. Vos, "Flood (Genesis)" in *The International Standard Bible Encyclopedia*, II (Grand Rapids: Wm. B. Eerdmans Publishing Company, 1982), 319.

5. J. Sidlow Baxter, *Explore the Book* (Grand Rapids: Zondervan Publishing House, 1960), 75.

6. Passover is so named because God "passed over" the homes of the Hebrews during the tenth plague. Unleavened Bread commemorates the haste of the departure of Israel from Egypt.

7. *Manna* is Hebrew for "What is it?" They ate this miraculous bread from heaven for all the years they wandered through the wilderness.

8. The Mosaic covenant differs from the Abrahamic in that the latter puts God under obligation to Israel, but the former puts Israel under obligation

to God. The Mosaic covenant did not nullify the promises to Abraham (Galatians 3:17).

9. Merrill F. Unger, *Unger's Bible Handbook* (Chicago: Moody Press, 1967), 107.

10. Unclean and defiling items included corpses, skin diseases, eating dead animals, semen and periodic bleeding, certain birds of prey or disease-carrying animals, and bodily deformities. The common thread seems to be that these items were associated with or affected by the Fall of man.

11. The Sabbath, the Feast of the Passover, the Feast of Unleavened Bread, the Feast of Firstfruits, the Feast of Pentecost, the Feast of Trumpets, the Day of Atonement, and the Feast of Tabernacles were the major religious days or festivals of the Old Testament.

12. B. G. Wood, "Prophecy of Balaam Found in Jordan," *Bible and Spade* 6 (1977), 121-124. An extra-biblical reference to Balaam, son of Beor, has been discovered.

13. Henrietta C. Mears, *What the Bible is All About* (Ventura CA: Regal Books, revised ed., 1983), 73-74.

14. Arthur E. Cundall, *Judges and Ruth, The Tyndale Old Testament Commentaries* (Downers Grove: Intervarsity Press, 1968), 11.

15. Do not fail to notice the irony of what follows. In mimicking the nations, they fell prey to the nations.

16. In ancient Israel, the custom was for the closest male relative to marry a widow. This provided for the widow, thus "redeeming" her from poverty and want. The children of the second marriage would inherit the property of the deceased husband and carry his name (see Deut. 25:5–10).

17. The Philistines were far superior to the Israelites in metallurgy (1 Sam. 13:19).

18. Following his repentance, David wrote two of the most loved psalms, 32 and 51. Both deal with the subject of sin and forgiveness.

19. Polygamy was tolerated but not taught in the Old Testament. The model of monogamy was given in Adam and Eve. Moses warned Israel to not multiply wives (Deut. 17:17). Numerous Old Testament stories report the strife occasioned within polygamous families.

20. Elijah means "The Lord is God." His very name challenged the status quo.

21. G. Campbell Morgan, A *Bible Survey: Genesis to Revelation* (Chattanooga: AMG Publishers), n.d.

22. The seventy years were predicted in Jeremiah 25:11–12.

23. The cupbearer in the court of the king was his closest confidante and most trusted official. It carried the weight that the chief-of-staff has at the White House.

24. Haman must have demanded some type of obeisance that Mordecai found idolatrous. Haman realized that his problem was not just with one Jew, but with all Jews whose religion strictly forbade the worship of any other than the LORD (Exod. 20:3).

25. *Purim* comes from the Persian word for "lots." Haman had cast lots to determine the best time to kill the Jews. By naming their festival Purim, the Jews employed irony, declaring that it is God, not pagan powers, that determines what will happen to his people.

26. The author is indebted to Michael G. Wechsler who published these insights. Michael G. Wechsler, "Shadow and Fulfillment in the Book of Esther," *Bibliotheca Sacra* 615 (July 1997), 277.

27. Scribes were summoned on the thirteenth day of the first month (Nisan) according to 3:12. Its publication and Esther's fast probably began the next day.

28. Answers: synthetic, emblematic, synonymous, antithetic, climatic.

29. 3:1—42:6 are written as poetry. Only chapters 1–2 and 42:7–17 are in prose.

30. From John Calvin, *The Book of Psalms*, "The Author's Preface," James Anderson, translator, 1845 (Christian Classics Ethereal Library) http://www.ccel.org/c/calvin/comment3/comm_vol08/htm.vi.htm.

31. Quoted by J. Sidlow Baxter, *Explore the Book* (Grand Rapids: Zondervan Publishing House, 1960), 130.

32. Henry Ward Beecher. Source unknown.

33. The Hebrew term for *woe* occurs in 28:1; 29:1, 15; 30:1; 31:1; and 33:1.

34. A lament is a formal expression of sorrow and grief.

35. The New *Testament* means the New *Covenant. Testament* is just an older word for *covenant*. Thus, Jeremiah's prediction forms the basis of the Christian faith.

36. The date of Daniel is one of the most disputed subjects of Old Testament scholarship. Critical scholars, dismissing predictive prophecy, date the book to around 167 B.C., based on the remarkably accurate predictions in chapter 11:1–35 of events up to that date. The portion of prophecy in Daniel

11:36 and following, which pertains to the end of time, is simply considered the writer's guesses. However, the discovery of the Book of Daniel at Qumran among the Dead Sea Scrolls militates against such a late date. The scroll at Qumran may be as old as 100 B.C. It is unlikely that Daniel would have achieved canonical status in 67 years.

37. The dramatic signs are found in 4:1–3, 4–8, 9–17; 5:1–4; 12:1–16, 17–19; 21:1–17, 18–20; 24:15–24.

38. While there have been many more than four great world empires since the time of Daniel, these are given special attention because each in turn subjugated the Jewish people and the land promised to them.

39. Norman Geisler, A *Popular Survey of the Old Testament* (Grand Rapids: Baker Book House, 1977), 235.

40. Ostraca are broken bits of pottery used for writing, much as people today use memo pads.

41. Many interpreters equate Joel's vision of the slaughter at Jehoshaphat with the Battle of Armageddon in Revelation.

42. 1 Kings 12:25–33 tells how the first king of the Northern Kingdom, Jereboam I, established two sanctuaries with idols like golden calves,at Dan and Bethel. These were intended to rival the temple of the Lord in Jerusalem.

43. Recall that the Northern Kingdom had revolted against the house of David. See how this prophecy is used in Acts 15:16—17 to show that people of all nations will be included in Christ's kingdom.

44. The story of the fish sounds "fishy" to many. Hebrew had no distinct word for *whale*, so it might have been a whale that swallowed him. A. J. Wilson in the *Princeton Theological Review* 25 (1941) as cited by W. C. Williams in the *International Standard Bible Encyclopedia*, II (Grand Rapids: Wm. B. Eerdmans Publishing Company, 1982, 1115) contained the story of a whaler, one James Bartley who was swallowed by a whale that overturned his whaling boat. He was found alive the next day when the crew began rendering the carcass of the whale, not knowing what had happened to him. Other similar accounts have been reported elsewhere.

45. Note how Paul uses Nahum 1:15 in Romans 10:15.

46. Bruce Wilkinson and Kenneth Boa, *Talk Thru the Bible* (Nashville: Thomas Nelson Publishers, 1983), 301.

47. The uniform view of antiquity was that the apostle Matthew wrote the first Gospel. Papias, Origen, and others so stated. The heading "According to

Matthew" is found on the oldest manuscript evidence. This strong tradition was not challenged until the nineteenth century.

48. Papias, Irenaeus, Clement of Alexandria, Origin, and Jerome credit Mark with authorship.

49. Among the witnesses are the Muratorian Canon, the anti-Marcionite Prologue to Luke, Irenaeus, Clement of Alexandria, Origen, and Tertullian.

50. It has been suggested that the genealogy of Matthew traces Jesus' legal descent through Joseph and Luke his physical descent through Mary.

51. Irenaeus (130–200 A.D.) was bishop of Lyons. As a boy he is said to have sat under the teaching of Polycarp, a disciple of the apostle John himself.

52. Despite the strong evidence in favor of authorship of the fourth Gospel by the apostle John, modern critical scholars prefer to say that the author is unknown.

53. The doctrine of the Trinity states that there is one God eternally subsisting in three persons. This is not polytheism (three separate Gods) nor modalism (one God assuming three separate roles). A triangle illustrates: one object with three distinct sides or one egg with shell, white, and yoke.

54. Bruce Manning Metzger, *The New Testament: Its Background, Growth, and Content*, second ed. (Nashville: Abingdon Press, 1983), 177.

55. "Be baptized": The nature of baptism has been a matter of debate. In New Testament times, it seems to have been understood as an act by which someone symbolically identified with Jesus. The word *baptizo* means "immerse." There was another word for "sprinkle," *rantizo*. The latter is never used in the New Testament with respect to baptism.

56. *Justification*—one of the most important terms used in the New Testament—refers to the judicial act of God whereby a person is declared "just" or "righteous." A popular way of defining justification says that it is being made "just as if I'd never sinned."

57. Death to sin is not a mystical event that takes away the desire to sin. It is our justification from sin's penalty. The old self that was crucified refers to our old, pre-Christian way of life, not the sin nature. Transformation occurs through remembering the kindness of God towards us and the godly lives to which he calls us.

58. The identity of the "I" in this passage is the key to interpretation. It cannot refer to Paul's experience as a Christian; otherwise, that would contradict chapter 6. It may refer to Paul's struggles with sin while living as a Pharisee. It

quite likely is Paul speaking on behalf of everyone who tries to attain perfect righteousness through self-effort rather than upon reliance on the Spirit.

59. J. I. Packer, *Knowing God* (Downers Grove, IL: Intervarsity Press, 1973), 136.

60. The story of Ishmael and Isaac is told in Genesis 16—21. While God had promised a child to Abraham and Sarah, they became impatient and tried to help God fulfill his promise by having a child (Ishmael) through a surrogate mother (Hagar). God did not bless this fleshly effort. Later, according to God's promise, Isaac was born. God continued his promised blessings of Abraham through Isaac. Tensions in the home became so great that eventually Ishmael and Hagar had to go. In the same fashion, Paul is arguing that those who try to help God save them by striving for a ritual righteousness are not going to be blessed. Blessing is obtained by trusting in the promise of God.

61. Some stating this view are Ignatius, Polycarp, Irenaeus, Clement of Alexandria, Tertullian, Marcion, Clement of Rome, and Hippolytus.

62. In Marcion's listing of the books of the New Testament, c. A.D. 140, he calls Ephesians "Laodicians."

63. The verb *kenoo* in 2:7 is variously translated "emptied," "made himself nothing," "made himself of no reputation," and the like. Scholars have long debated its exact significance when applied to Christ. The most likely meaning is that in the incarnation Christ voluntarily divested himself of the privileges of deity.

64. "Firstborn" does not mean "first-created." It refers to the person who has rights of inheritance. As the firstborn of God, Christ is the inheritor of all creation.

65. The north Galatian theory is the view that Paul wrote to people living in north Galatia rather than south Galatia. Such a view necessitates a later date for Galatians.

66. The translation of the living is called the *rapture* from the Latin word for "catch up."

67. This and other statements in Scripture lead to the conclusion that there will be a widespread turning away from God (but not necessarily religion) in the last days. At that time, a great impostor, the Antichrist, will appear and lead the world in its final transgression.

68. The salvation spoken of here may be in the form of a removal of Christians from the earth prior to the events of the Tribulation. This view is termed the Pretribulational Rapture.

69. William Barclay, *The Letters to the Galatians and Ephesians*, rev. ed. (Philadelphia: Westminster Press, 1976), 179–180.

70. Many scholars date the book after the fall of Jerusalem. They point out that the references to the sacrificial system mention the tabernacle rather than the temple. However, if the temple had been already destroyed, it seems this would have been mentioned, as it would have strengthened the author's argument.

71. The supposed differences between Paul and James as to faith and works are differences of definition. James uses *faith* to mean assent, Paul to mean trust. Paul clearly expected believers to do good works (Eph. 2:10).

72. Works falsely claimed to be by Peter include The Gospel According to Peter and The Apocalypse of Peter.

73. *Higher criticism* is the term applied to the scholarly study of the Bible as practiced in most academic settings. It proceeds from the assumption that the Bible is a natural, not supernatural, book. Therefore, it rejects all miraculous elements of the Bible such a prophecy. It also discounts early church tradition as a reliable source of knowledge on matters of authorship.

74. The name *Docetism* comes from the Greek verb *dokein*, which means "to seem" or "to appear."

75. "The chosen lady" and her children might either be a local church and its members or some prominent Christian woman and her family.

76. *Apocrypha* means "hidden." Perhaps they were so-called because they purport to reveal "hidden truths."

77. Irenaeus obviously had Revelation in mind when he wrote, "But when this Antichrist shall have devastated all things in this world, he will reign for three years and six months, and sit in the temple at Jerusalem; and then the Lord will come from heaven in the clouds, in the glory of the Father, sending this man and those who followed him into the lake of fire. . . ." as quoted from Ireanaeus, *Against Heresies*, 5, chapter XXX, par. 4 in the *Anti-Nicene Fathers*, Vol. 1 (Christian Ethereal Library) http://www.ccel.org/fathers2/ANF-01/anf01-63.htm#P9283_2709558.